Free Spirit

Free Spirit

Illustrated Memoirs and Related Tales

Kester Brown

Published by Brolga Publishing Pty Ltd
ABN 46 063 962 443
PO Box 12544
A'Beckett St
Melbourne, VIC, 8006
Australia
email: markzocchi@brolgapublishing.com.au

National Library of Australia
Cataloguing-in-Publication data

Brown, Kester, 1935– .
Free spirit : memoirs and related tales.
Bibliography.
ISBN 1 920785 53 1

1. Brown, Kester, 1935– .
2. Anesthesiologists – Australia – Biography.
I. Title.

617.96092

Printed in China
Cover Design by Trish Hart – www.trishhart.com
Typeset by Diana Evans

DEDICATION

This book is dedicated to Janet and our family –
Catherine, Maryann, Fraser, Kester and Ken –
Who have shared many of the experiences,

AND

Duncan Forrester
who introduced me, when I was a student, to many enjoyable experiences in the Highlands and Islands of Scotland.

And also to commemorate three friends, with whom I travelled on several of these journeys, who died many years ago on mountains – **Richard Carles** on Mt Kenya; **Ken Stockall** (pilot) and **Henry Busse** (photographer) crashed near the Nahanni.

Legend for Cover Photographs

1 Victoria Falls
2 Painting in the Antarctic
3 Canoeing on Frame Lake, Yellowknife, Canada
4 Bird friends – Dove and Java finch
5 Grass of Parnassus, northern Canada
6 Dew drops on a eucalyptus leaf
7 15th century Adilaj stepwell, India
8 Photographing Banksia
9 Evening light on scallops
10 Winter on the Tay, Scotland

Back cover:

Aurora Borealis – northern Canada (Henry Busse)

ACKNOWLEDGEMENTS

Many people help in the production of a book. Encouragement to write my memoirs came from people to whom I regaled my stories, sometimes on long flights on planes or at work. I have had an interesting life and so I am grateful to those who encouraged me to share some of it with you.

Writing is an absorbing occupation. I appreciate immensely the support of my wife, Janet, while I have worked on the books.

Several people who have given me advice have been thanked in the first volume, my medical memoirs – *Catalyst.* Many of these gave constructive criticism and advice on how to present these memoirs. In the end it seemed logical to write two books. Some read chapters and guided me on structure, relevance and in some cases accuracy of information. These included John Roberts, Flora and Graham Fisk, Anne Bryan, Jenny Scott, Jane McConnell, Wendy Sutherland and some of my family, one of whom thought I remembered too much!

My colleague, Ian McKenzie, now Director of Anaesthesia at the Royal Childrens Hospital, Melbourne, wrote the Foreword.

My brother, Monty, provided some information and corrected details in the early chapters and provided me with several photographs from his family archives.(1.3, 1.4, 1.5, 1.6, 1.7, 2.2, 2.3, 24.2).

Many photographs came from my father's collection. They create an important window into the past. (1.1, 1.9, 2.5, 2.6, 2.7, 3.1, 3.3, 3.6, 4.1, 4.4, 4.5, 4.6, 4.7, 5.6, 6.1, 7.1, 7.2, 7.3, 7.4, 7.5, 9.1, 28.1)

Oxford University Press gave me permission to include the photograph of Jim Corbett with the man eating leopard. (3.5) "Them Days", a quarterly historical magazine published in Goose Bay, Labrador gave permission to use the photograph of Tony Paddon. (13.2) and was the source of some historical comments about Labrador. Photographs of several people were derived from school and university team photographs. Grenfell (13.1) was taken from his autobiography published about 1921.

Janet, my wife, was the source of photographs 12.6, 16.1, 18.2, 18.3 and18.1. My daughter, Catherine, provided C19.6.

Sue Jervis, who painted my portrait, gave me permission to include it.

Léonie Mathieson kindly allowed me to refer to her grandfather's journals from the early colonial days in Kenya. Isobel Macmaster helped with corrections of some Scottish place names.

Robert Reitmeir and Bert Di Paolo, from the Royal Childrens Hospital Educational Resource Centre, scanned the photographs and organized them into order.

Mark Zocchi of Brolga Publishing oversaw the production. Diana Evans edited and undertook the layout and Trish Hart designed the cover. I appreciate all their contributions.

Contents

Part 1. Kenya

Part 2. Scotland

Part 3. Summer in Labrador

Part 4. Colour Pictures

PART 5. CANADA

PART 6. AUSTRALIA AND BEYOND

FOREWORD

It is fashionable now to refer to a "small world", shrunk by advances in transportation and communication. There is something disconcerting about hearing that someone has "done" some country or tourist trail. The description of such journeys usually reveals more about the traveler than the destination.

Starting when the world was a "big place", when people travelled by land and sea rather than air, Kester Brown has criss-crossed the globe in all phases of his extraordinary life. These were not the journey of a dilettante. They were journeys with a purpose. From his childhood home in Kenya to the family roots in Scotland, from Scotland to the wilds of northern Canada, from Canada to Australia he made myriad forays to every corner of the globe from these bases. Once established as a paediatric anaesthetist, his journeys were to teach and to help, motivated by a desire "to make a difference".

The travels of Kester Brown are usually even more about people than places. The places are remarkable but it was the people that provided the purpose. Whether connecting family and friends, educating himself and others, helping those in a remote outpost or linking and training like minded people to serve their local communities better, no journey was wasted.

Kester Brown's parallel biography of his professional career is appropriately named "Catalyst". That career shows how people management at a micro level can produce, not only a work place where talents can blossom, but also a world wide web of people linked with a common purpose. This "world wide web" was happening long before the "internet". The growth in the seeds Kester has sown around the globe has produced an exponential explosion in the quality of paediatric anaesthesia around the world. The process is self propagating due to the adoption, decades before it was fashionable, of a "train the trainer" approach.

Those who have read Catalyst might wonder what the origins of such a career are. The answer is "between the lines" in this book. This well illustrated volume is full of entertaining stories about fascinating people and places. For me, the real thrill of this journey is the opportunity to see, like a time lapse movie, the way in which the acorn grows into the oak.

Ian McKenzie,
Melbourne, 2005.

PREFACE

I was walking through Victoria Station in London to catch a train one afternoon when I came upon a man struggling under the burden of two large suitcases, without wheels, and a full set of golf clubs. He was having difficulty balancing the clubs and lifting a suitcase with the same arm. I offered to help him as I was only carrying a small overnight bag. He accepted with alacrity and his life became much easier when he only had the clubs and one case to carry. It happened that we were going on the same train – the three twenty five to Brighton. We entered the same compartment, one of those which opened directly on to the platform, and sat down opposite each other. He was a rather heavy man, average height and I estimated he was in his forties.

After a period of silence during which he caught his breath he suddenly said, "You must have wondered what was in the suitcase to make it so heavy." I hadn't given the matter any thought as I was young and strong then. He proceeded to tell me that it contained a large metal pineapple, a finial, to adorn the top of a metal gate post. He had seen it during his visit to Scotland and could not resist buying it for his friend Spike Milligan. That put an interesting perspective on my companion. I knew that Spike Milligan was one of the Goons but I did not recognise his friend who was now my companion. Anyway this suggested that he had a sense of humour, or maybe a sense of the ridiculous! Maybe he was associated with the Goons but I did not follow them. Then silence.

I must have conversed a little with him for he suddenly said "You have an interesting accent". Many people have said that to me but he was one of only two who have worked it out correctly. My companion worked out that there was some Scottish in it, some Canadian and something from Africa – not quite South Africa – maybe East Africa. He was correct.

He then said, "I am interested in accents. You see I am an actor and have to imitate many of them." Should I know who this man is, I wondered? I wasn't very good at recognizing actors because I did not go to plays in London, only occasionally went to the cinema and television was still a novelty. I had no idea who he was and I was probably too embarrassed, or could have been if he was famous, to ask him his name or maybe it just didn't matter to me at the time as I didn't expect to meet him again.

So these are the tales of someone who was born and brought up in Kenya of Scottish parents, attended university at St. Andrews in Scotland, emigrated to Canada where my Scottish "a's" were enhanced and finally moved to Australia. The latter had a slight effect on the accent over 38 years but the earlier vowel sounds were not changed.

In Australia "a" becomes oi or i – for example, he came to the hospital to-die, not today.

In New Zealand the vowel transposition differs again. I is sounded -e- so that six sounds like se-ex. The classic example of the problem this can cause is when a New Zealander tells you the telephone number of an obstetric hospital in Melbourne – 666046 – sex, sex, sex, oh for sex!

These memoirs tell you about the places where I have lived for significant periods of my life, about my experiences, some of them amusing, some hair-raising, in these and many other countries where I have travelled or worked. My story draws you in to many wider experiences of life. It is made more intriguing by many other amazing stories which I have often told – coincidental meetings and connections between people; walking out the front door of our house into a temperature 75°C lower; visiting the first hut built in Antarctica; standing on the highest point in Africa, the top of Mt Kilimanjaro; being the repository of a legend and many other tales. It will also tell about interesting people I have met and related stories about people and events. The world has changed during my life-time and some of the trips and many of the experiences I recount are things of the past, some over 50 years ago. Relatively few people will remember colonial Kenya before independence in 1963. Dams have obliterated roads on which I travelled and settlements, such as Hebron in Labrador, closed down. Many of the photographs are over forty years old, some showing people dressed in clothing no longer used. I believe they are all worth recording for their interest and as a historical record.

I studied medicine and expected to spend my life as a country general practitioner, but in the end I only did this for a year and a half in northern Canada and then went to the Vancouver General Hospital for more training. Eventually I became a paediatric anaesthetist at the Royal Childrens Hospital in Melbourne, Australia and became heavily involved in teaching and training anaesthetists worldwide. My professional life had many interesting aspects which are recorded fully in my previously published medical memoirs – *CATALYST – Memoirs of a world anaesthetist* – and will only be mentioned briefly in this volume.

I have recounted stories from my life to hundreds of people. One day in 1988, flying home from New Zealand, the lady sitting next to me, having heard a few of my tales, said "You should write a book. I have written my autobiography." I obtained a copy of *Bread and Roses*, an intriguing tale of the life of Sonia Davies. In many ways she was a lady ahead of her times. Later, when I was travelling home from Bangkok I found myself sitting next to a young lawyer, Genevieve, originally from Mudgee, now living in Sydney. She told me about her trip beginning in Singapore, to places in Malaysia and on into Thailand. I told her some of my stories. After three hours, during which the time flew, they announced that we were now ready for departure. We had not noticed that we had not left Bangkok. Sometime later she sent me a card and said that I ought to write a book. So the idea started to germinate and several years later, when I semi-retired, I began to write. I found I remembered so much that I had enough for two books. After much deliberation I decided to write my medical memoirs separately.

Join me on my wanderings, enjoy the stories and the interesting collection of pictures. They are not the tales of a hero or adventurer but those of someone who has had a very interesting life through rapidly changing times.

Kester Brown,
Melbourne. 2005

Part 1

Early Days and Kenya

Chapter 1

Family Background

My parents were both Scots. We can trace our family back six generations on both sides to the late 1700s but family trees are only names unless one knows something of the people. Sometimes an occupation is listed on a family tree. Photographs may survive three or four generations back but they only show us what the person looked like and little really about their personality. Nevertheless, some of these photographs are included. They are interesting because they were taken in the early days of photography and they show something of the fashions of the time.

Occasionally a letter remains which can be revealing. One set remains from relatives on my mother's side who went to the goldfields in Ballarat in 1853, several generations back. One brother wrote his mother asking her to send him a wife as all the girls in Ballarat in 1856 were wild Irish girls!

A letter to my father from his uncle in London during World War II tells him about his cousin and the wonderful youth club work he had been doing, transforming young hooligans into a well behaved group that became so responsible that were able to carry on their own youth club after the cousin was killed in the Blitz of London. It also said he was a great reader, who thought over what he read and would not accept things unless he could reason them out. I could identify with this as I constantly tell my trainees not to accept they are told or read without considering whether it is reasonable.

1.1. The author's paternal grandfather, Thomas J.Y. Brown (1868-1946).

My paternal great grandfather was a quarry-master and builder – his initials, WMB, are carved on a building in the High Street in Stirling, an ancient burgh which at one time was Scotland's capital. It was near here that William Wallace and King Robert Bruce defeated the invading English at the Battles of Stirling Bridge (1296) and Bannockburn (1314).

My grandfather became a solicitor and

also was town Clerk of the small town of Alva, near Stirling, for half a century. From him I derived the first of my names, Thomas. His will allotted me his gold pocket watch for carrying his name. I was to receive it when I turned 21 but that was inconvenient as I was a student then and we didn't wear gold pocket watches. When eventually I went to claim it, the watch had disappeared. Maybe my inheritance from the name was to carry an element of doubt – not believing all I was told. Genetically my grandfather may have contributed to my interest in painting as he did watercolours.

1.2. Paternal grandmother, Jessie Brown.

My grandmother's parents died young leaving her to bring up her younger siblings. Her interest in photography, developed before the turn of the last century, has passed on through my father to my brother and me. She lived until she was 94 and was still making jam at the age of 92.

1.3. Maternal grandfather – John Macmaster – shinty player in 1888.

Her daughter, Jean, also a solicitor, lived with her. They lived comfortably at 4 Park Avenue in Stirling.

My mother (C1.1) came from Strathpeffer (C5.3.) which is 40 km beyond Inverness. It is, in contrast, a village which developed into a spa in the late nineteenth century. It has many fine Victorian houses and hotels and the shops are centred around an attractive little square. (C5.4) It is beautifully situated in a valley with Ben Wyvis to the north and a long hill running from Knock Farrell at one end to the Cats Back at the other on the south side. Above the village

1.4. John Macmaster (1870-1946) in 1940.

1.5. The author's mother's maternal grandmother – Betsy MacDonald (Fraser) (1835-99)

1.6. The author's mother's maternal grandfather – John Fraser (1830-1904).

1.7. The author's mother's paternal grandmother – Janet Anderson (Macmaster). (d. 1901)

there is an interesting golf course. (C5.5)

My grandmother, Catherine Fraser, whose names have been passed on to many of her descendants, lived in a valley over Ben Wyvis. We have photographs of three of my mother's grandparents, but I know little about them.

My grandmother died in 1958 when I was a student. She was a great favorite of mine. I still remember the last time she came to the gate to wave me goodbye. I think she knew it was farewell as she died two months later.

My father, William Monteith Brown, always known by his second name, was born in Stirling on 21st October 1900. He was top student and gold medalist at school and graduated from Glasgow University as a doctor in 1923. Like many young people he enjoyed a bit of adventure. He cycled through Belgium and Holland and climbed the castle rock in Stirling with his brother, much to the surprise of the people inside when they appeared over the ramparts! He decided to go to Africa as a

1.8. Tumutumu Hospital

medical missionary in 1925 after his pre registration hospital jobs.

1.9. Tumutumu Hospital Staff including Dr Brown and Peggy Fergusson, the matron, about 1950.

My father was a remarkable man. He had tremendous enthusiasm for his wide range of interests and he took a great interest in the people he met. He ran a 120 bed hospital single handed for most of his thirty seven years in the mission in Kenya, with only one or two Scottish nurses and local Kikuyu nurses and dressers whom they had trained. He operated, oversaw anaesthetics, looked after all sorts of sick adults and children and was a wonderful obstetrician. He did six months training in ophthalmology during his leave in 1929 and thereafter did cataract extractions, some of his patients coming from as far as the coast, 650km away. He also oversaw six out-dispensaries around the district, run by dressers whom he had trained, the furthest being 60km away. He visited them nearly every month. He had many other interests. He designed and built parts of the hospital and most of the church at Tumutumu, maybe a trait inherited from his grandfather and passed on to his sons. He had many interests including astronomy, architecture, music (he played the piano and tried to learn the violin and cello when he was over fifty), history, carpentery and car mechanics. To him "it was never too late to learn". He even changed his service action at tennis when he was fifty. Above all he was an outgoing, kind, compassionate and generous man and a great example to us children.

He was known throughout the land and many years later I met people who remembered him – one was a member of the Kenya Olympic committee who I met on a plane flying from South Africa – he had been a patient of my father's on three occasions when he was a boy. My brother met an ophthalmologist who told him that our father was still remembered in Kenya for his cataract work- 35 years after he had died. He was a greater inspiration to me than I realized when I was young – I followed in his footsteps and became a doctor.

My mother was rather more reserved but had a dry sense of humour, which I did not always understand when I was young. Maybe I acquired some of it as sometimes people are not sure when I am joking. She was an effective disciplinarian but a very loving mother who taught me many things which will be referred to later. She was keen on sport and made a point of teaching us to be good losers. She was an enthusiastic fisher (a trait my brother inherited), incredibly observant (she frequently found four leafed clovers)and a keen gardener. She also shared many of my father's interests. She was always punctual – my father wasn't! That gene I inherited from her.

They both set out to work for the Church of Scotland mission in Kenya in 1925, my father at Kikuyu and my mother at Tumutumu. Coincidentally they travelled on the same ship. My father could not have believed his luck when he found a lovely, reserved and somewhat wistful lass from the Highlands going to a similar destination. They were married two years later on 1st March 1927.

My father died in Kenya in 1968 but my mother lived until 1991. It was a poignant coincidence that she left Kenya after 58 years, on the very day I watched the film *Out of Africa*, which ended with Karen Blixen leaving Kenya after living there for16 years.

So much happened during my parents' lifetimes. Cars had only just been invented. Electricity was still novel when they were born and we didn't have it at home until 1949. Even then the lights went up and down during the evening if they were cutting logs at the sawmill on the end of our line. Before that we used Dietz and Tilley mantle lamps with paraffin. Railways and canals existed but transport still depended significantly on the horse and carriage. Children thought nothing of walking a few kilometres to school – my mother did at least 3km each way. During their lifetimes radio, telephones, moving pictures (movies) and, half a century later, television came into being. Music was played on gramophones which had to be wound up manually – no tapes or CDs in those days.

Cavalry was still important in war until tanks and aeroplanes made their debut in World War I. My father died in 1968 so he didn't live to see man landing on the Moon in July 1969 but he was very excited by the first Russian Sputnik making it into space in 1957. I remember going to Eastleigh airport in Nairobi to see the first modern four engined aeroplane to land there in 1948. A four engined biplane had landed at the old Nairobi airport in 1934.

Much of the world was still relatively unknown to the Western world when my parents were born. The first Europeans to stay in Kenya were only arriving then. It is not surprising that my parents both had a great interest in exploration, particularly of the Antarctic, because, when they were children, Scott, Shackleton and Amundsen were making their heroic attempts to reach the South Pole and Peary, the North Pole. And there were still great mountains to be climbed.

These interests of theirs had considerable influence later in my life leading me to visit the high latitudes, beyond 70° N and S, and enjoy mountains although I was never a real mountaineer.

Chapter 2

Early Years In Kenya Colony

Kenya! What does that conjure up in your mind? Probably animals, game parks and viewing wildlife. Or maybe a country which has produced many great long distance runners.

It was a wonderful country in which to grow up when I was young. It had nearly everything – all variety of climates and vegetation from sea level to over 5000 m, deserts in the north, wide open plains, rich hilly country in the middle and beautiful beaches and coral reefs at the coast. It is divided down the middle by the Great Rift Valley. Even around Mt. Kenya, rising grandly in the middle of the country to its peaks and glaciers which were more extensive when I was young, the land varies depending on whether it is in the rain shadow on the north west or on the wetter eastern side. Being on the Equator, the seasons are wet and dry rather than summer and winter. April and November are supposed to be the rainy seasons and July and August are cold and misty in parts of the Highlands such as where we lived between the mountains above 1700m.

Kenya has a phenomenal variety of wildlife and plants. It is said that one can see a hundred varieties of birds in a day if one is with a knowledgeable ornithologist.These might include iridescent purple or green sunbirds, larger, delicately coloured rollers, starlings of several varieties, hornbills (C20.7), a great variety of birds of prey including possibly the ever searching vultures circling in the sky or scavenging over a carcass, or the regal looking crested crane. On the Rift Valley lakes thousands of pink flamingoes might be seen (C19.7), or African jacanas or lily-trotters, with their long toes adapted to provide increased buoyancy on the leaves of waterlilies. Unfortunately the animals have decreased considerably with the increasing population encroaching on their habitat. Poaching has also taken a toll, particularly of the elephants for their ivory and rhinos for their horns, which are said to have aphrodisiac properties and were used in Chinese folk medicines. Fortunately, the National Park System was established before independence, enabling the preservation of this valuable asset, which people from all over the world have come to enjoy.What a thrill to see the large elephants blowing dust on themselves as they wander through

2.1. Impala

the bush as a family. They are not always popular as they can be destructive, even uprooting trees. The sight of a stately giraffe peering over the trees, or some of the big cats, leopard or cheetah, which can run at 110 kph, is exhilarating. The antelope, from the giant eland to the tiny dikdik or duiker are beautiful to behold. The impala with its beautiful horns is one of my favorites. It featured on our school badge with the three Prince of Wales feathers and the motto, "To the Uttermost."

We should be grateful to Mervyn Cowie who became the first director of National Parks. The story goes that he badgered the government without success to set up the Parks to preserve the game. Eventually he wrote a letter to the newspaper suggesting that a day should be selected for a massive shoot where everyone with rifles would go out and shoot as many animals as they could to get rid of them. The response was rapid – one of horror and disbelief. There was a huge outcry. National Parks were established soon afterwards

Kenya is populated by many tribes, each with its own language, tribal dress and customs. Joy Adamson, well known for bringing up the lion cubs which became famous through the book and film "Born Free", was commissioned to paint many of the people in their tribal costumes in the late 1940s. This was just in time, shortly before they disappeared in the winds of post war political change and development. Most of these paintings can be seen in the Nairobi Museum. This is worth visiting as it also traces much of the Leakey's work on early man, it has a good collection of natural history and another fine collection of paintings by Joy Baillie (later Adamson) of East African wildflowers.

After centuries of marauding by Arab slavers under the Sultans of Oman, who resided in Zanzibar the British announced a blockade of the East African coast to stop the slave trade. The political position became complicated by Germans occupying the mainland of what became Tanganyika. The Sultan chose to seek British support, which was not granted, so he worked through the British presence, the Imperial British East Africa Company. It pulled out and the British took over control of the coast – the British East African Protectorate – in July 1895.

On the 30th May 1896 the first rails were laid at Mombasa for a railway to Lake Victoria in the interior. It was to give Britain supremacy of the hinterland, and eventually, Uganda. The slave trade had ended. There were many difficulties in building the railway. Malaria ravaged the men in some low country areas and the man-eating lions around Tsavo generated fear when some men were taken.

British colonisation lasted a mere 68 years, less than my parents' lifetimes, but coincidental with them. When they arrived the population was sparse as there had been virulent small pox epidemics. As the railway pushed past Nairobi into the Highlands and the Rift Valley towards Lake Victoria, the world's second largest inland sheet of water, some attractive farmland appeared with few inhabitants, some of whom were nomadic Maasai. It is little wonder that adventurous British people were encouraged to migrate and set up life in such a wonderful, promising land.

Missionaries came. Some from Scotland settled at Kibwezi, nearer the coast where mosquitoes took their toll by transmitting diseases such as malaria. The missionaries died and their successors moved further inland to a higher, healthier, location at Kikuyu in 1898. Mosquitoes rarely lived over 1600m. Ten years later another mission station was established at Tumutumu where my parents spent most of their working lives. It is about 140km north of Nairobi looking out on Mt. Kenya about 65km away.

Marion Stevenson worked at Kikuyu and was asked to go to Tumutumu when it was established. It was decided that she should not go by road through the malaria infested Fort Hall district but take the train to Naivasha in the Rift Valley and then cross the Aberdare Range which reached over 3000m. It involved walking 100 km during the rains which meant some of the rivers were flooded, making it more difficult to ford them. She must have had "guts". Her biography describes many of the hardships that she endured. It also describes how the people came to see and hear the white, Kikuyu speaking, woman who had come amongst them.

There are some beautiful descriptions of old Africa in her biography – *A Saint in Kenya*. For example, "One can picture the scene on an evening when the setting sun bathes the land in a strange, ethereal beauty that is Africa's own. Impalpable mists of gold and amethyst and rose enhance all colour and mould and lengthen shadows into the deep softness of velvet... In the still air minute sounds can be heard – the distant tinkle of goat bells of homing flocks".

A clear African night, away from towns and settlements, is something majestic when the stars are shining brightly, the insects are making their music, which can sometimes be resounding, and the moths, sometimes large and magnificently decorated , flutter around the lights, all contribute to a feeling of great activity, but also tranquility.

Tumutumu was established by Ruffelle Barlow in 1908. He wrote the Kikuyu grammar and as an old man was an interpreter at Jomo Kenyatta's trial when he was accused of leading the MauMau. In the early days Barlow cycled the 140 miles from Nairobi to Tumutumu which was a great feat at the time when roads were primitive and bicycles had no gears. The road would have had plenty of hills, the last being a climb of 600m in about 20km.

2.2. Ruffelle Barlow.

Nairobi, the eventual capital , was first established in 1899 as a depot on the Uganda Railway. Some of it was swampy land then that had to be drained. By 1950 it was a beautiful city with parks and gardens laid out by a man named Greensmith. I doubt if those who established it would have had any idea that a century later it would have become one of Africa's major cities with a population of around 10 million.

My brother, Monty, writes historical books about Kenya. Twice I have been able to help him with research. The first time I put him in touch with an Italian surgeon who gave me his address before returning home after working with us for a year. He helped him to obtain information about a famous adventurer from Parma, Vittorio Bottego, who explored the Lake Rudolf (Turkana) area of north west Kenya.

The second occasion was when he wrote asking for information about two Australians who went to the Boer War (1899-1902) and subsequently moved to Kenya. They were involved in outfitting several major safaris in Kenya which Monty was writing about. He gave me their names, year of birth and state. My first reaction was "What a crazy request. These fellows went to the Boer War nearly 100 years ago!" I then thought that the War Memorial Museum in Canberra might be able to help. They couldn't. Then I thought that Victor Newland might be related to Malcolm Newland, an elderly anaesthetist in Adelaide who had been President of the Australian Society of Anaesthetists about 1971. Victor Newland was his uncle and eventually he tracked down Victor's grand-daughter, Léonie Matheson, who had his journals from Africa. I contacted her and she invited me to dinner. We had a most interesting evening during which she produced these documents. His journal had been typed and some additional comments from contemporaries had been added. She kindly allowed me to copy these.

It was fascinating to read Victor (Marra) Newland's account of the Boer War and his time in Kenya. He was born at Marra Station on the Darling River in New South Wales which explained why Monty had been given that as his state rather than South Australia. So what had seemed a ridiculous request by Monty had become a fascinating journey of discovery. The papers also included a letter from Major Robert Foran who retired to Nanyuki where my father ultimately practiced. He was there when we visited in 1963.

One of Newland's contingent to the Boer War was Breaker Morant who became the subject of a film in the 1980s. He was a rather unruly but good-hearted man who was excellent with horses. He was executed after a controversial court martial instigated by General Kitchener. The question remains – was justice done or, more likely, was he a political scapegoat? Sometimes the British treated their colonial troops as dispensable.

After the war Newland and his friend Tarlton proceeded by sea to Mombasa. They planned to farm but ended up with a safari outfitting business which also did transport contracting, and Newland became an auctioneer and estate agent. He auctioned blocks in Government Road, one of the main streets in Nairobi, for £10 in 1904 and sold them for £3000 in 1907. Newland and Tarlton, N&T as they were known, outfitted the early major hunting safaris from Nairobi including those for many eminent clients such as Theodore Roosevelt in 1909.

Nairobi town council was established in 1900 and Newland became a member in 1905. In 1910 he became a member of the three-year-old Kenya Legislative Council. In 1911 he went for a trip to Britain and was shipwrecked off Tangier on the return trip. The ship ran aground in a big storm about 300 m from shore. A French frigate came to their help. The ladies and children were taken off during the day but some of the men had a nerve racking night and were taken off the next morning. Obviously the ship didn't sink overnight. Three people were lost.

Foran also mentions how Newland shot a man-eating lion that came into the camp and was dragging one of his men off. The man survived after Newland dealt with his wounds.

In 1922 the government changed the currency from rupees to pounds, shillings and cents and in the process devalued the currency by one third. It proved to be an economic disaster to many people. Newland decided to return to Australia in 1923 due to a decline in business after the War and ill health. He became a stockbroker and, later, a member of the South Australian Parliament.

2.3. The author's father on his Matchless motorbike in the 1920s.

By 1925, when my parents arrived, Nairobi was the established capital and main city of the young Kenya colony. No one could have realized that nearly half its time as a colony had already passed. The roads were not paved. Model T Fords were on the roads as well as ox carts which conveyed many of the loads. My father had a motor bike which was well adapted to riding on rough roads.

My parents had to learn Kikuyu as that was the tribe they were working amongst. It is still the most widely spoken native language after Swahili which, with English, are the official languages in Kenya. I learnt some as a child as I lived amongst the Kikuyu. It is always amusing to see the response I get when I speak it as it is very uncommon for Europeans to speak Kikuyu. Most Europeans spoke "kitchen Swahili", a simplified form of the language. The Kikuyu language has some interesting features. There are single and plural greetings and the farewell differs depending on whether one is staying or leaving – *tigwa na wega* if addressing someone who is staying and *thie na horo* when the person is leaving. Imagine the surprise of two Kikuyus in London Airport when I offered to help them because I recognized the language which they were speaking.

It is interesting that the people, particularly in the cities, have become so integrated since independence two generations ago, on 12th December 1963, that many barely use their language or recognize their tribal connections which were so strong when people stayed in their tribal areas in years gone by.

Even in my childhood most roads were unsealed dirt or gravel with many bends. In the dry weather they became corrugated and needed to be graded from time to time. In the wet weather they could be slippery and difficult to traverse, especially if it was through country with sticky black cotton soil, where one could easily become stuck. The main roads were usually surfaced with broken stones to reduce these problems. Different driving technique and some ingenuity were needed to overcome these problems. If one did get stuck there were various methods, such as putting sticks under the wheels to give them more traction while the vehicle was pushed out. Otherwise the spinning wheels might just dig deeper and deeper ruts in which to stick.

The first major sealed road was built by Italian prisoners of war between Nairobi and Nakuru in 1944. We thought it was wonderful. How we take so much, such as sealed roads, for granted these days. This road required the building of a difficult decent down the Rift Valley escarpment. The Italians built a little chapel at the bottom to commemorate the accomplishment.

2.4. The Italian Chapel at the foot of the Escarpment.

There are still some unsealed roads and many of those that were sealed have declined so that they now have potholes making travel slower and less enjoyable.

The railway had reached Uganda. A branch line opened from Nairobi to Nyeri, reaching Nanyuki in 1931. We travelled to school on it from the nearest station, Karatina, 6km from Tumutumu. Aline Buxton gave a quaint description of this railway line in 1927. "The Thika – Nyeri railway, a single line running in apparently all directions in search of a good gradient, up narrow valleys, out over perilous embankments, or on a straight track cut out of a steep hillside." (dug by men in those days before the advent of heavy equipment) It was a good description of the tortuous journey we later took to school. There were many stations and stops where people were always selling food such as bananas, oranges and other staples.

Nyeri district, which is in the Kikuyu country, was first partly settled by George Maxwell and two others in 1906. Tumutumu is 20km east in the Kikuyu reserve area which was not to be settled by Europeans, apart from the occasional mission station. These usually provided a school, a church and sometimes a hospital. My father took over running Tumutumu hospital in 1931 and remained there most of the time until he retired in 1962. For many years he was also superintendent of the mission. He designed and built several buildings at the hospital and upgraded much of the church from a corrugated iron building.

2.5. Tumutumu church – stone renovations designed by Dr Brown and built under his supervision.

Tumutumu had both boys and girls schools, with boarding facilities for outlying students, as well as a 120 bed hospital which also had a leper colony for 20 patients.

2.6. Munuhe, my mothers gardener wearing a blanket in typical style of the time – 1940-50s.

In the early years the people often wore skins over their shoulder. But by the time I was a child these had been largely replaced by a blanket with a pair of shorts underneath. Later, after the war, many men acquired a great coat to wear with their shorts and shirt. Gradually European influences came in so that these forms of dress have not been seen for many years.

I was born at Tumutumu, in our house looking out to Mt. Kenya 65 km away, on 9th December 1935.

2.7. The first photograph of the author with his mother

CHAPTER 3

EARLY REMINISCENCES

It is amazing how we learn so much in our early years and yet have no conscious memory of all that we learnt – sitting, crawling, standing, walking, talking and all the other basic functions. We are told that the first seven years are vital in developing our character but we do not usually remember anything consciously until 3 to 4 years of age although two of my children remember much earlier.

My first memory was on my fourth birthday at which time we were in Scotland on leave. My father usually had a year in Scotland after 4 years in Kenya. My grandfather had taken me to Inverness where he had bought me a small toy horse and cart – I remember playing with it on the train going home.

My next memory was three months later, in March 1940, seeing my first film, "Snow White and the Seven Dwarfs", in Marseille on our way back to Kenya. This must have been a remarkable journey as we crossed France during a lull in the fighting after the outbreak of World War II. It must have been a worrying time for my parents but I had no idea about war at that time. We completed the journey to Mombasa on a French ship, Bernardin de St Pierre (named after a noted French novelist), and returned to our beautiful home at Tumutumu. The photograph shows that I obviously enjoyed riding my tricycle on the deck.

3.1. Riding my tricycle on the French ship, 1940

Our closest association with the war was troops travelling up the road to the Northern Frontier to stop an Italian invasion from Abyssinia (Ethiopia) which they had occupied. I have the vivid memory of my father being called out in the middle of the night to an accident where a South African army truck had missed a sharp bend on to a bridge and went over into the river. He returned with the sad news that all six soldiers had been killed.

There were prisoner of war camps, and an army hospital at Nyeri Station (Kiganjo) 30km away. A famous book, "No Picnic on Mt.

Kenya", was written by one of three Italian prisoners who were keen mountaineers. They escaped from a camp at the foot of the mountain with the sole purpose of climbing the mountain. They saved food and the only guide they had was a picture of the mountain from a tinned food label. The book describes their attempt and how they struggled up the valley on the west side, often having to traverse the river and clamber over boulders. It was tough going through fairly thick forest and undergrowth but they made it on to the moorlands at about 3000m and to the foot of the peaks. These required mountaineering skill to climb. Unfortunately they ran short of rations and had to curtail their attempt part way up the peaks. It was sad for them because they could have succeeded if they had known that it is easier and quicker to go up the ridges where there are often well worn animal tracks – their supplies would then have lasted. They then returned to camp and gave themselves up!

3.2. R.S.Baden Powell

3.3 Baden Powell's funeral – South African Army Band and guns firing salute.

I attended Lord Robert Baden Powell's funeral in January 1941, in Nyeri. He was world famous, being the founder of the Boy Scout movement but he was also a family friend. My brother and sister used to visit with him when they were less than ten while my parents attended to their business in Nyeri. They remember him as a painter and for the little doodled sketches he did for them. Baden Powell also fought in the Boer War and commanded the beleaguered garrison which defended Mafeking. He had retired to a private cottage at the Outspan Hotel in Nyeri, 24km from where we lived.

His funeral was a great occasion with the South African Army band playing and field guns firing a final salute. It is hard to know whether I actually remember the occasion or whether re-enforcement from photographs makes me think I do. I have also read my brother's

3.4. Baden Powell's grave in Nyeri cemetery.

vivid account of the occasion. The Nyeri cemetery is well situated on top of a ridge looking over to Mt. Kenya. His grave remains in good condition, with a marble headstone with a circle and a dot in the middle – the Boy Scouts sign for "Gone home".

Robert Baden Powell went to Norway in 1896 to search for his friend Fridjof Nansen, the great Norwegian explorer, who had left three years before on his specially built ship, the Fram, to attempt to float with the Arctic ice pack over the North Pole. Without radio and other means of communication he had not been heard of for three years. Coincidentally, Baden Powell arrived in northern Norway at the same time as Nansen arrived back having left the Fram and reached 86°N. He took Nansen to Tromso where, incredibly, they met the Fram when it arrived back only a week later, after three years traversing the Arctic ice. It is amazing to think of undertaking such a trip when there was no way of communicating with the outside world during their absence.

This expedition was one of the great feats of Polar exploration. Nansen was the first person to cross Greenland on foot. He figured that currents flowed across the North Pole from Siberia to Greenland because they found driftwood in Greenland where there are no trees, and debris in west Greenland from a US Naval ship called the *Jeanette* which had been crushed in the ice north of Bering Strait. His specially built ship, the *Fram* (now in the Oslo Maritime Museum), could withstand huge ice pressures. He put it into the ice over Northern Siberia and let it flow with the current. After 18 months it reached 84 degrees north and was not going to cross the North Pole. He decided to take Johansen with two sledges, two kayaks and dogs and head north. They reached 86 degrees, the furthest north at that time, before turning back because of bad ice conditions and time was running out. Their tale is an incredible adventure of hardiness and some luck, both good and bad. For instance, at one point on their way back they tied their kayaks to an ice-flow while they climbed an ice hummock to gain a better view of the water leads. His kayak broke loose and floated away. He dived in after it and after a struggle reached it. With a superhuman effort he managed to climb aboard. How did he survive the cold Arctic water? Prolonged acclimatization and maybe he derived some insulation from the grease on their polar bear skin clothes which they had made when their clothes wore out.

One remarkable item they took on the Fram was a windmill to generate electricity for the cabins during the long winter nights – a remarkable concept so soon after Edison's invention of the electric light bulb in 1879.

I had not heard of the *Jeanette* before I read Nansen's journals. By strange coincidence I found a book called *Hell on Ice* by Edward Ellsberg in the same second hand bookshop where I bought Nansen's original edition Journals. It is not the only book with that name. It was the story of the *Jeanette*'s fateful expedition re-created from the United States Senate and Navy enquiries which took place. The ship was crushed in the Arctic ice and many of those on board were ultimately drowned or starved. They dragged their three boats across the ice until they reached open water. One then sank in a storm, another reached a deserted island where all but two starved. They went for help and found the third group, who all survived, at a settlement on another island.

Jim Corbett, who was a famous hunter from India, retired to Baden Powell's cottage after India partitioned from Pakistan in 1948, and became independent. Many of the Europeans moved to Kenya. Jim Corbett, who was born in India in 1875 and had worked on the Indian Railways all his life, was one of these. He had become a household name in India because of his famous exploits successfully hunting man-eating tigers and leopard. His books, Man-eaters of Kumaon, Temple Tigers and More Man-eaters of Kumaon and the Man-eating Leopard of Rudraprayag, describe these. They killed hundreds of people. It is not surprising that he was a hero in the region. He is still remembered by many Indians 50 years after he died.

These were exciting books and were widely used in schools. Man-eaters of Kumaon was translated into 23 languages – I saw them all when I went to see him in 1951 – he inscribed my copy "To you and all my other boy friends, Jim Corbett". What a treasure to have. One particular episode stands out. He was hunting this tiger which had killed many people in the area. (Tigers usually only kill humans when they are injured and cannot catch animals to kill.) He had a boil on his neck and he was feverish and not well. He was following the animal round in a circle but he knew that the animal was following him round in the same circle. The tension rose as time passed. Eventually he climbed a tree to wait. His boil was throbbing more and more but he had to concentrate because his life depended on it. He nearly passed out. Then the boil burst – what relief – shortly afterwards he won the intense battle of wits with his adversary and shot it.

On the other hand the man-eating leopard of Rudraprayag developed a taste for human flesh in 1918 when many people died in the world influenza pandemic. The people were dying in such numbers (one million in India) that those still living were not able to cremate them all, as was their custom, and so dispatched them down the slopes towards the river to be dealt with later. The leopard found and ate them and developed a liking for human flesh. When the epidemic passed its supply ran out so it had to resort to killing live humans to satisfy its appetite. And so it ravaged an area of 500 square miles around Rudraprayag, killing at least 129 people during the next eight years. Jim Corbett spent weeks trying to kill it, frequently just missing the opportunity. His jungle lore was such that on one occasion he was able to call the animal to within 200m before it was distracted by another leopard (female) responding to the call. In fact several times he found footprints that showed that the leopard had been following him! Eventually he succeeded but not until another ten people had been killed since he had started hunting it. The books are wonderful reading.

3.5. Jim Corbett and the man-eating leopard of Rudraprayag after its conquest (with permission—OUP)

Subsequently, in February 1952, he accompanied the then Princess Elizabeth to the game lodge in the tree near Nyeri – Treetops – to tell her about the game. By the time she left she had become Queen, as the news of King George VI's death arrived while she was there. Jim Corbett is still commemorated in India with a National Park named after him. He was a wonderful, gentle man and a hero to many of the simple tribesmen in the hills where he eliminated the man-eaters.

Our home at Tumutumu (C1.3) had a wonderful view to Mt Kenya, which was sometimes visible (C1.4), but often shrouded in cloud. It depended on the weather and time of year. It was most frequently seen in the early morning or in the evening when the cloud would gradually lift, at first giving tantalizing glimpses, and then, suddenly, the whole grand vista would be on show – the main peaks, Batian and Nelion with their glaciers, Point Lenana on the right at the top of the Lewis Glacier and Point Piggott and Arthur's Seat to the left.

3.6. Playhouse and sandpit in our garden with Monty and Catherine

We had a large garden with an excavated flat lawn area where I played games of soccer or hockey against myself or anyone who was available to play with. Then there was a sloping garden with flower beds, and to the right, another section hedged off as a vegetable garden. Another part contained our playhouse made of dried banana leaves – *mugoto-* hung on horizontal bars on the frame of the house, a construction commonly used at the time by the Kikuyu. There was also a covered sandpit and a little concrete pond where we could sail our toy boats. At one time I turned the play house into a museum – among the items of interest were an elephant's femur (thigh bone), a block of asbestos and other rocks, a collection of shells collected on

3.7 View from our house with the tennis court, and Mt Kenya in the distance

Lake Victoria and butterflies, of which I was an enthusiastic collector when I was ten.

Beyond the garden was the mission tennis court where I learnt to play when I was about twelve. Before that, golf was the craze, having started at 9 years of age, when living next to a golf course in Nairobi, hitting the ball a few yards with the handle of a club which had lost its head. I even made an 18 hole golf course round the mission which was on 35 acres of land. Golf balls were very scarce. Once I lost one of my two balls in long grass – a disaster. I summoned my mother to help me look for it. She walked straight to it – I do not know whether it was her belief that she would find it or just her incredible powers of observation. She frequently found four leaf clovers which most people never see.

Behind our house there was a wood of gum (eucalyptus) trees and a section of blackwoods, originally Australian trees. This went up to a thorny kiapple hedge along the border of the mission where it changed to the native bush on the side of Tumutumu hill behind us. I had a wonderful playground in this wood with little tracks between the trees to ride my bicycle, going here and there to places with names from Wind in the Willows such as Toad Hall and others with geographical names like Lima. Toad Hall was a three storey tree house with one floor for each of us children. Roman Road was straight, following the water pipeline. There was even a bridge over a rubbish hole on one of the roads. What an idyllic playground for a child.

Sometimes in the evening my mother would take me up to the wood in the hope that some animal would appear – she taught me to sit very still and quietly and wait. Sometimes there would be a rustle of leaves and a beautiful bushbuck would come into view. It was here that my mother taught me the importance of keeping quiet if one wanted to see animals. It is the reason that I walk with a quiet step. I hate hearing noisy voices when out in the wilds – the owners scare the animals away.

We had other animals. Bats sometimes inhabited our roof and flew out like a flight leaving for an air raid – whoosh in one mass. Chameleons are the creatures which can modify their colour so that they are camouflaged against different backgrounds (C4.3). They can also vary the shape of their bodies, decreasing their thickness to allow height to increase. Their feet have two fingers on each side to grip branches. Their movement is often ponderous swaying back and forward and then with a little lunge they advance. Their eyes roll independently and they can look backwards with one eye and in another direction with the other. They have long tongues which shoot out like a dart, catch their prey, usually an insect, and retract as quickly, and the tasty morsel is gone. The Kikuyu regarded these fascinating creatures as evil and for this reason they were sometimes used during the Emergency to make people speak and provide information when it was not forthcoming. Rats were not only a nuisance but sometimes they were destructive. They would even gnaw holes through boards to gain access. I remember the great excitement when we caught two large ones in a cheese loaded rat trap in one night. The trap went off with a great bang. We reset it and not long afterwards there was another bang. There was an occasion when one was found dead in the garden. It was removed and destroyed with great care because there had been cases of plague in the district and rats were carriers.

Once, someone brought us an owl. We tied it on a long sting to a large loquat tree in the garden. There is an expression 'as wise as an owl". This one was and it did not take long to chew through the string and escape!

I learnt to ride a bicycle when I was five. This particular bike had solid rubber tyres which had the advantage that punctures did not occur. It also only had front brakes, which was a disadvantage, as I found out one day going down hill – I ended up flying over the handle bars into a cypress hedge!

On Sunday afternoons we often went for walks. Tumutumu hill was large and flat topped and stood out over the surrounding countryside. It was a beautiful part of the country with scattered villages – the houses made mainly of mud walls supported by frames of black wattle tree stems. The roofs were sometimes framed with straight sisal poles covered with either dried grass or folded dried banana leaves (mugoto) or, later, with tin or corrugated iron. Around the villages there were mainly vegetable

3.8 A Kikuyu girl carrying a baby – children and typical huts behind.

gardens – maize (corn), beans and bananas were common. Some huts had a few flowers growing beside them.

The people also used to have some cattle and goats. (C20.6) They were often supervised by the old men or by children. Some of the animals had bells round their necks. They tended to be lower pitched that those one often hears in countries like Switzerland. A man's wealth was measured in his stock and the men had to buy their wives by payment in animals. In the cold weather the children often carried a fire in a metal container to keep them warm as many did not have extra warm clothes. They could also use them to cook some food, such as potatoes. (C47.5) Women carried loads on their backs supported by a band over their forehead. These might be logs for firewood or produce from the garden which they might carry to market. (C20.2) They carried babies and small children in a similar way. Some of the other tribes carried their loads on their heads and so had very strong neck muscles and good balance. Their posture was much more erect.

3.9 Kikuyu woman carrying a typical load of firewood and maize.

Tribes also varied in their basic diet depending significantly on whether they were settled or nomadic. For instance, the Maasai were nomadic herders and hence ate mainly a meat, blood and milk diet. The Kikuyu was a settled agricultural tribe whose diet included maize, maize meal (posho), bananas, sweat potatoes and little meat. Many in our area took produce to the large market at Karatina.

When the population exploded after independence (increasing at 4% a year) the country became more intensely cultivated and inhabited and stock seemed to decrease as there was less grazing. In recent years there seem to be more herds of, particularly, goats which cause denudation and eventually, in dry times, more erosion. Overstocking, especially in the north, contributed to the advancing desert.

The mission was at the foot on the northern side of Tumutumu hill. Our walks were around the hill if we were having a long walk, or to visit Kikuyu friends in some of the nearby villages or up the hill behind our house to the "hot stone" which was a large flat stone that was warmed in the sun during the day so it was hot when we went in the later afternoon.

We had helpers in the house and garden. Munuhe was a wonderful old man who had been my mother's garden man since her early days at Tumutumu. We usually had one or two girls working in the house. Munuhe's daughter, Priscilla, was one of these (C1.2). She helped my mother for many years starting when I was at school and cared for her as she grew older. These people were not just servants – they were an integral part of our family existence. After my mother left Kenya Priscilla worked for many years at the Nanyuki Cottage Hospital. When I saw her shortly before she retired in her 70s she gave me a chicken and some potatoes to ensure I was well fed while staying with my brother! A medical student from Melbourne, who did his elective term at Tumutumu Hospital, as a number of them did, met another of the girls who had looked after me when I was a small child.

For a while our neighbours' son, Hector Dickson, was at home and we played together. I must have been a peace lover as I just went home if any disagreements occurred. He went to school before I did so I was on my own during the term time. I learnt to make my own play. I suppose that is why I have always been able to occupy myself and be content with my own company: no TV and, for a long time, not even a radio.

I had an enchanted childhood living in this beautiful, peaceful place. We did not have many toys as it was during World War II but I had small building blocks made of wood or cement and a few Dinky cars, animals and people. I remember the excitement when the war was over and these things gradually returned to the shops. I recall being allowed to buy one Dinky when we went to Nairobi – a little MG or a motor bike. Modern children tend to have too many toys which can clutter the home and create work for whoever has to tidy them up!

My mother taught me until I was nine. She was a good teacher and taught me the ethic of hard work, which has helped me through my life. Even when I was at school she used to make me work on my weak subjects during the holidays.

Chapter 4

Primary Schools and Holidays

I had just turned nine when I was sent to boarding school in Nairobi. I didn't enjoy it but it must have been much worse for those who were sent when they were only six or seven.

My first day at Nairobi Primary School was unusual. I was put in standard (Grade) 2 but by morning break I had concluded that the work was too easy and I informed my teacher. I was advanced to standard 4A but after a term I returned to standard 3 which was appropriate for my age. I didn't like my teacher, Ma Watson, in standard 4 although I think she tried to be nice to me. I was sent next door to 4B for Maths and had a lovely teacher, Mrs. Petrie, who I remember well because she drove a tiny Fiat beetle and she took us on nature study outings which we enjoyed. My best friend in standard 4 was Jim Allen who was also young for the class and whose mother later taught me in standard 3.

I had two terms of rather miserable existence, only relieved because I occasionally saw my older sister, Catherine, who was at the neighbouring Kenya Girls High School. Mrs. Allen suggested that I board with them which was a great relief. That was where I started golf because they lived beside the Railway golf course – I played in their garden beside it with the handle of a broken club. Mrs. Allen became a lifelong friend – she was an Australian who came from the hill country near Korrumburra in Victoria. Her husband, who was in charge of the Prisons, was also an Australian. Jim was brilliant and went on to Oxford and became a historian. The last time I saw him was when he visited us in Vancouver in 1964. He became an authority on East African and Arab history and established the museum in Lamu on the Kenyan Coast. He died young.

I rebelled against continuing at that school so I was sent to board with the Archers who were well known for taking about six or seven country children. Monty and Catherine had stayed with them when they were in Primary school. Mr. Archer was a well known architect in Nairobi who was followed in the profession by two of his sons. One, my friend Jim, became one of Kenya's leaders in the field. Many years later my son, Fraser, worked with him for 6 months. The Archers had a large garden, a big house and two outside rooms for extra accommodation. Mrs. Archer was a solid, good hearted woman but kept us in order. I remember her making me do eye exercises because I needed glasses. I never understood how these might resolve my fairly marked myopia.

I had a successful year in grade 4 at Parklands Primary School, topping my class (the only time) and captaining the under 11 hockey team. I failed miserably at singing and was taken out of the choir for the school concert but was allowed to perform some country dance – at the Theatre Royal in Nairobi – it sounds impressive but it wasn't really. I attended Cubs, against my will, never took the preliminary test to formally become a Cub but acquired badges for other tests which I passed. It was just one aspect of my unorthodox life.

Several of that class of only fifteen, taught by Mrs. Powley, did well. One, Michael Somen, became a lawyer, another, Derek Woolfall, a transport systems engineer in USA and another, Terry Dalley, taught art at Wimbledon Art College in London. He has been a lifelong friend. I remember the day when one of the class, Ian Cormack, arrived with the first ballpoint pen we had ever seen. We were mesmerized. It had cost 50 shillings- equivalent to five terms pocket money!

Forty years later I was invited to dinner in Tasmania by a young anaesthetist whose father had been at school with my brother. Another lady was present. Late in the evening I made a rare reference to Parklands school and found out that she had been Carol Tighe in the class below me. It is strange how conversation can unravel unexpected connections.

Our family holidays were unusual. We didn't go to the coast as so many others did to enjoy swimming in the warm Indian Ocean, sail and socialize. Probably my father's meagre mission salary was one reason but the coast was over 600 km away and my parents had this great love of mountains.

Kenya is split down the middle by the Great Rift Valley which runs south from the River Jordan, through the Red Sea, Ethiopia, down to Lake Malawi with a westwards branch containing Lake Tanganyika, the second deepest lake in the world after Lake Baikal in Russia. On the east side of the Rift Valley, north west of Nairobi is the Kinangop plateau, a strip of land where my brother in law's family had settled and where he and my sister had farmed briefly before the resettlement scheme took over all the farms in the district after Kenya's independence. It was at about 2600m and thus had a cool climate with cold nights. To the east the land rises to the Aberdare Mountains, a range that reaches about 4000 m at Satima in the north and Kinangop in the south. It is surrounded by forest which gives way around 2700 m to bamboo and then about 3,000 m to moorland country with tussock grass and heath. There are several rivers on the moors which tumble over great waterfalls into gorges that lead them down to lower country, mostly into Kikuyu land on the east. It was by one of these rivers, the Magura, that we used to camp, on the moorland at about 3000m. Getting there was a great expedition for a little boy.

We drove to a friend's cottage at Kiandongoro, which was on a pyrethrum plantation. The dried flowers used to be used for insecticide. It was on the lower slopes of the Aberdares, above the provincial township of Nyeri. Here we stayed the night. In the morning porters arrived to carry our tents, food etc. up through the forest to our campsite. The first time we went they brought donkeys that proved to be difficult and uncooperative. The walk was first through magnificent rain forest with beautiful trees, including camphor and podocarpus, dense bush and often entangled with vines. There was plenty of birdsong and sometimes monkeys, including the splendid black and white colobus, would be seen scampering in the branches. Rarely a zorilla (C4.5) would scuttle through the bushes. It is a small black and white creature that reminded me of a skunk in size and appearance but doesn't emit the foul defensive smell. Elephant and buffalo droppings were also to be seen from time to time – a reminder to keep a watchful eye, although I don't know what would have happened if we had actually met one.

After about 10km we reached the bamboo forest. In this wet, cool environment these grew in large clumps to what seemed great heights when I was small. The forest track, probably originally created by animals, wended its way between these. The tall trees (about 10m) would lean across the track to gain support from those on the other side forming what appeared like a nave of a very long meandering cathedral – a beautiful, graceful sight. The path, however, was often not smooth – donkeys were often used for transportation by the locals when crossing the mountain and their hooves made ruts across the track – unfortunately, a donkeys footstep is shorter than a humans so that the steps were an awkward length for adults although not so bad for little fellows as I was then. My first trip was when I was seven. The porters had a bad time with donkeys and were delayed. We had to stop and wait for them. Then the rain came and in Africa that means it poured. We only had the shelter of the trees so we spent a miserable couple of hours during which our mother kept us occupied playing "I spy" and such games! Our food was following with the donkeys. Eventually we started back to meet them and soon someone arrived with the picnic basket. We were very hungry by the time it finally caught up with us. After a while the porters arrived. We did not have time before dark to reach our destination over the next ridge so we camped a little above one of those tranquil little streams that run through the forest bounded by mossy banks with small wild flowers. The bamboos were smaller here and next morning we soon left them as we crossed a ridge and came out on the rolling moorland country. And there, across the valley, was our destination. Heavy rains over many years had eroded a deep gully where the track went for the first few hundred metres. We crossed a bridge over the Magura River and left the track to find a campsite on a rise above the river, amongst the heath. This grows into big, clumped bushes about two to three metres high in that area.

Our tent was pitched to look out across the moors of tussock grass. On the horizon was a forest covered, rounded hill called Mbogo-ini – Buffalo hill. (C3.5) We had walked about 15km and climbed 1000m – quite a feat for a small boy.

4.1. My mother with some porters at our camp on the moors with Mbogo-ini behind.

Not far from the camp was a steep slope to the river which was about four metres across. A large rock protruded out over it, narrowing its width so that we could build a bridge of bamboo poles over it. There was a small channel under the rock which emerged through a little fountain just below. This always intrigued me and on one occasion a budding engineer school friend of my brothers made a little waterwheel which was driven by it – fascinating! After a short rapid the river opened out into a large, very shallow pool with some flat rocks around it which even had canals through them. Can you imagine the joy of such a place for a small boy with little boat? I spent many happy hours there. To add to the beauty there were little yellow flowers with lush green leaves growing on the ground as well as mosses round the waters edge. Heath bushes adorned with "old man's beard" grew beside the river. A number of wild flowers grew on the moors including everlastings (helichrysum) and thistles – one variety grows flat on the ground.

My mother and brother were keen fishers. We walked to the Gikururu river, about 3-4 km away to fish just below an attractive waterfall. It was particularly intriguing to us because it fell over an overhanging rock which enabled one to walk under the waterfall.

I was too small to fish at first but I finally tried, in a tranquil pool on a bend in the Gura about a kilometre from camp. I caught a trout but it was a disaster. In my incredible excitement I wanted to land this fish. I didn't know the niceties of playing the fish in and using a net. No! It was whammo – jerk the rod straight over my head – I caught the fish but my mother's good rod snapped in half. What a successful disaster!! I never developed enthusiasm for fishing but did fish in various parts of the world many years later – in Labrador, Norway and at the coast in Kenya where I caught a sailfish.

We walked to one of the three big falls on the Gura River and its tributaries (C3.4), about 2km down from where we were camped. From the top we could see another big waterfall – maybe dropping 160m before cascading to the bottom of the valley – wonderful sights not seen by many in those days.

4.2. From the top of Kururu Falls looking towards the Gura Falls.

One evening we followed the track higher up on to the moorlands. It was the track which had been used since the early days to reach Naivasha on the other side of the Aberdares. At this altitude one begins to feel the effects of reduced oxygen – one breathes faster and becomes puffed more easily.

When I was just nine we made our biggest expedition to climb Mt. Kinangop. (4.3) That trip was remarkable in three ways. First we found a crashed plane that had been missing for six weeks. It was flying in from Juba in Sudan and had radioed Nairobi that it would arrive in 20 minutes. It never did. It hit the mountain side near the top on a gradual slope upwards scattering pieces over 200m. It must have been cloudy. The people were obviously not all killed outright but were

4.3. A train on the Nanyuki line chugging up through the Kikuyu reserve.
The Aberdares are in the distance with Mt Kinangop , the highest point, being about 4000 m.

injured, so that they couldn't get help. Some left notes and documents carefully laid out indicating that they must have had a slow demise, possibly from exposure and cold. It was a particularly tragic for the wife of one of those who died – her father had recently passed away and her husband was on his way to Nairobi to see her and their new baby. How cruel life can be to some people. I was not allowed to go close but my brother's description is still vivid in my mind. The 'plane had been found only the day before by someone who saw something shining on the mountain from his farm miles below.

The top of Kinangop has a small peak. It was easy to climb the first part to a flat area but then there was a very precipitous section for the last few metres which my mother felt was too dangerous for her nine-year-old son. Maybe this engendered a fear of hanging on rock faces which I have always had. It was disappointing, in retrospect, not to have reached the very top. That would have been an achievement, especially at that age.

The third memory was becoming lost on the way down. We missed the track somewhere. Our so-called guide did not really know the way. These were generally animal trails anyway. There we were sitting in the forest, waiting, big trees and fairly dense bush around us, while the men with us went to look for the track. It was late afternoon, the sun was low, we knew that the forest was inhabited by animals such as buffalo – they left their trademarks on the tracks and we were certainly becoming a bit concerned. In addition the temperature drops below freezing at night at that altitude so the outlook wasn't good. I don't know what we would have done, apart from make a fire, if we had to spend the night there. We were becoming more and more concerned as the sun dropped lower towards the horizon. Then, suddenly, there were joyful yells that they had found the way. What a relief. That trip was a great experience and undoubtedly enhanced my devotion to mountains.

As I mentioned, it froze on clear nights, so any water left in bowls would be ice when we woke up in the morning. In contrast, we had to be careful to protect against the hot, burning sun in the daytime because the atmosphere is thinner at that altitude. No 15+ or 30+ sunscreens in those days but my mother had some sort of cream that she lathered on to protect me, as well as protective clothing. Attitudes to sun have changed. When my parents came to Kenya they had to wear special sun protection – cork helmets and even red spine protectors on their backs to prevent sunstroke – it is hard to imagine that nowadays, although children in Australia have to wear hats to school and these often have a neck protector.

Later this area became part of the Aberdare National Park and several roads were built through it connecting Nyeri with Naivasha. Years later, in 1979, my brother took me up the road to where I used to play on the Gura. A shelter had been built nearby for a visit by the Queen. It was a nostalgic visit seeing the moors, the tussock grass, the familiar flowers again and, although it was relatively unspoilt, it wasn't quite the same.

Another twenty five years on we made another nostalgic trip. This time we stayed in a cabin for two nights just across the river from our old camp. Apart from the road and the cabins, little had changed. We had old photographs from 50-60 years ago and could define patches where the heath had grown. Some trees on Mbogo-ini were still there. We surmised that they are now well over a century old.

We traveled around the park and visited several waterfalls tumbling into their gorges. Two, the Kururu and Gura Falls tumbled about 300m in a series of steps, the greatest single drop being about 150m. (C3.4) It was wonderful to re-live those bygone days and see the magnificent country again, almost unchanged.

Uganda holiday

In 1944 my father was due for leave back to Scotland but it was impractical to go because of the War. Travel by sea was dangerous because of submarine attacks – a nurse, who had worked with my father, was on a troopship that went down with all hands in the Indian Ocean following a Japanese submarine attack.

4.4 Our family in 1944 sitting beside the memorial tablet commemorating Speke's discovery of the source of the Nile in 1862.

Two months leave had to be taken locally. I was eight. So

we all went off to Uganda for a month. It was exciting as we hadn't been west of the Rift Valley before. We travelled through Londiani, Kakamega, Kisumu, a port on Lake Victoria, and into Uganda. We spent a night at Jinja on Lake Victoria. Here I saw my first hippopotami, but even more interesting to a boy who was already a student of African exploration, was to sit on the tablet which commemorated Speke's discovery of the source of the Nile in 1862. Speke must have been an incredibly tough character as he was attacked in Ethiopia before that trip and suffered 11 spear wounds including two in his thighs before he escaped. It is hard to imagine how he didn't succumb to infection.

From there we went on to Kampala, where we spent Easter weekend with friends at Mulago Hospital, before proceeding to a little holiday place at Nabogabo, on the shore of a lake attached through a swamp to Lake Victoria. On the way we were crossing one of many swamps – the road was cambered but was wet and slippery. Suddenly we were skidding towards the water filled ditch. Fortunately my father controlled the skid and we stayed on the road. It would have been a potentially unpleasant end if we had rolled into the water!

4.5 The cottages at Nabogabo with a dug out canoe on the beach.

At Nabogabo there were three attached cottages close to the lakeside – an idyllic place. It was there that I learnt to swim – living so far from the sea and lakes meant that we hadn't much opportunity to learn. We also had the chance to paddle in canoes dug out from tree trunks – simple craft but a common means of transport in many primitive parts of the world. They were still in common use then.

There was also wildlife – little monkeys who brazenly entered the houses and stole bananas off the table and then sat on the verandah, peeled and ate them. And frogs that made an incredible noise at night. I remember telling one of our neighbours that "my father and brother had gone out and slaughtered them and slaughtered them" – they must have been extremely irritating. It was easy to remember when we were there because one day when writing a letter the date was 4.4.44.

Our neighbours in the cottages were Mrs Cannon, a Scot, and the McKnight family – one of them, George, was at school with me. I met him again in Kenya 50 years later. The Cannons had a rubber plantation west of Kampala which we visited on our way home. I was given a sheet of rubber which I treasured and put in my playhouse museum. Mrs Cannon became a great family friend, later visiting us at Tumutumu. She gave me her son's kilt – a beautiful tartan of McDonnell of Glengarry. Years later I visited her occasionally in Mussellburgh near Edinburgh in Scotland – a highlight on one of those visits was being given my first Crunchie! This was something special as sweet rationing had continued after the War for two or three years. We each had a coupon for 4 ounces of sweets a week. I usually bought boiled sweets as they lasted longest.

I did not return to Uganda for 55 years and when I did none of the people I was lecturing to had been around when I visited before. I felt like Methuselah!

Two of the earliest European settlers in the Nyeri district were George Maxwell and his brother who took up coffee farming about 1906. They had several farms apart from the home at Maxwellton in Nyeri. One was Ngondi, on the edge of the forest at the foot of Mt. Kenya on the west side.

We had several enjoyable holidays there. The house was wooden and covered with slats with a verandah along the front. It was situated on top of a ridge facing out over Ngondi hill to Mt. Kenya. The coffee plantation reached up to near the house on the south side. To the west the hill sloped down to the Thego River still surrounded at that time with native forest. At one point there was a dark, deep pool with flat rock along one side which we called the Black Pool. We used to swim there although I found it a bit eerie as it did not have a smooth bottom. Further upstream there were pools where brown trout could be

4.6 Douglas Maxwell and his mother, George's wife, at Ngondi. (1950)

caught. Beside one, a large rock protruded which we called the Rock of Gibraltar because of its resemblance to the great rock at the entrance to the Mediterranean. Beyond this the road crossed the river and wound up the hillside towards the house. I did my first landscape painting of the view of Mt. Kenya from Ngondi – I did not realize then that this would become an important hobby in later years.

Once we went for a picnic up a track leading upstream from the bridge. It was there that I had my first near drowning experience – I took a step backwards over a sheer drop of nearly two metres into the river. It was when I was small and before I had learnt to swim. I was blowing bubbles in the bottom when my gallant sister leapt in and dragged me out.

In September 1946 we had a holiday there. Monty went out hunting buffalo when he was only sixteen and I spent hours collecting butterflies – there were masses of them of many different varieties, including beautiful swallowtails, yellow and black with tails on their wings. It was an entomologists dream. The garden was laid out in front of the house and on two sides of the lawn which ran down the hill. There was a profusion of flowers and on one side a cactus garden. (4.6)

In the middle of the lawn was a rain gauge – an important item where so much depends on having enough rain. In later years one of the sons, Douglas had this farm. One time after he had been away he went out to check if there had been any rain – to his surprise the gauge was full but it did not seem that there had been so much rain. When he made inquiries of his houseboy he replied "Oh, I filled it up because I know you are always so happy when it is full!"

Sojourn to Scotland – 1947

In August 1946 my father went back to Scotland to see his father who was terminally ill. My mother stayed behind until we finished our school year. Sadly her father died shortly before we left. She had not seen him for 7 years. So towards the end of that year, 1946, both my grandfathers had died – my grandmothers lived till they were 86 and 94 respectively, so that I became well acquainted with them when I later went to Scotland as a student.

In January 1947, when I was 11, we traveled back to Britain on a British India line ship called the Modasa . It and its sister ship, the Mantola, on which we returned, travelled via the Suez Canal from Mombasa to London. They were relatively small passenger liners of about 9000 tons and took about three weeks for the journey – enough time for plenty of games such as deck tennis, played with a ring quoit, deck quoits which was rather like bowls played with quoits, and swimming.

My most vivid memories were our passage through the Suez Canal , built by the French engineer, Ferdinand de Lessups; Port Said, at its entrance, where Egyptians swarmed around trying to persuade the passengers to buy all sorts of goods from their boats and where some of them dived for money thrown for them into the sea, usually after they had dived off the boat deck on the ship – no mean feat. In Port Said I had a special treat – I was allowed to buy a small Dinky toy Packard car. When one sees the number of toys children in our affluent society have today it is hard to comprehend that during and immediately after the war such toys were rare and something to be treasured.

A terrible storm in the Mediterranean made me seasick for the only time in my life.

The style of our arrival at Tilbury docks near London made us wish we had never left Kenya or, at least, that we were going straight back. It was just after World War II and things were still disorganized. We dropped anchor at 2pm, had to wait until 6pm to disembark and it then took 4 hours to get through customs. The train to London took two hours – twice the usual time. From the station we took a taxi to our friend's home in Croydon but the taxi driver became lost and we finally arrived at 4 am on what was the coldest night in London for 80 years! Can you imagine the misery of this family arriving on such a night from the tropics! No electric blankets in those days – only stone hot water bottles in the beds – we called them 'pigs'. I still have a clear recollection of getting into a freezing bed with one of these providing the only warmth.

4.7. Monty with one of the violins he made.

We soon went north to Scotland where we spent several months in Edinburgh. We stayed in a house in Blackford Glen, Liberton which was not far from the Braids Golf course where we sometimes played. It was here that Monty made his first violin. He had gone to see a violin maker, Mr. Montgomery, off Leith Walk, about buying one but then became intrigued and decided to make his own. Monty had inherited, from both sides of the family, great skill as a woodworker. Mr. Montgomery gave him moulds and some instructions. He made three during his University holidays. Twenty years later I met someone in Auckland who had bought a cello from the same man.

4.8 George Heriots School in Edinburgh – my classroom was top right. Edinburgh Castle is in the distance on left.

I went to school at George Heriots – a castle like building to the south of Edinburgh Castle and across the road from the Royal Infirmary.

The school was founded by the goldsmith to King James VI of Scotland and James I of England, for boys who had lost their fathers. Even when I was there such boys were called Founder pupils and received free education.

After the summer my father had to return to Kenya so I went north with my mother to stay with my grandmother at Strathpeffer. I attended school at Fodderty Primary School, but not for long. By the end of the first week I decided that I wasn't learning much there – our teacher was almost blind and we did little real work so on the Friday I informed my mother that I was not going back to that school! Fifty years later I watched the boys from Fodderty School win the County Primary schools shinty cup just before the school was closed.

Shinty is a great game played only in the north of Scotland – 12 a side spread the length of a field 160-200 yards long with hails (goals) 12 feet wide and 10 feet high. It is played with camans (clubs), shaped like an old hockey stick, but with a triangular shaped head. The ball is like a miniature baseball. It can be stopped with the caman or the feet but can only be propelled with the caman. It is a fast and exciting game which requires a very

4.9 Fodderty Primary School near Strathpeffer.

good eye to stop the ball. My Uncle Kenneth Macmaster was a legend in the game having led the local team to victory twice in the main competition and then as a coach and administrator. He coached the Fodderty boys team until he was over 80 years old! After my Uncle Kenneth, his son David continued the family involvement in the local Caberfeidh Shinty Club. I played in the fields with neighbours, Sandy and John McGregor, when I was small and retained a life long interest in the game.

After my transient attendance at Fodderty School I returned to George Heriots School in Edinburgh. I was at the headmasters office by lunchtime on the first day – not to be reprimanded but to request my promotion to the top class as that was where my former teacher had told me I would have gone if I had stayed. I had been put in the second class with a rather unpopular teacher. I was promoted! Maybe this was the unwitting beginning of following *the principle that one should ask for what one wants because the worst that can happen is to be refused and you have lost nothing, while often one's request is granted.*

Heriots was a great rugby school but I didn't play there. However, at lunchtime, we played soccer in the playground. One of my friends who played was Ken Scotland who later became famous as Scotland's international rugby full back. I met him again in Vancouver, Canada in 1963 when he played his last match in the Scottish team.

My sister Catherine and I had stayed latterly at Home House, Duddingston in a home for missionaries children in Edinburgh. Thirty years later I found that the lady sitting next to me at a dinner party in Melbourne had also lived there just after I had left but while my sister was still there. Three weeks later she phoned to tell me that she had found three others who had been there with her who were now living in Melbourne – an amazing coincidence.

In November 1947, while I was at Home House, Princess Elizabeth, later Queen, and Prince Philip were married. We climbed the nearby Arthur's Seat, which was the large hill on the east side of Edinburgh on a cold November evening to watch the firework display celebrating this Royal event. It was a grand show.

Return to Kenya

In February 1948, when I was twelve, my mother took me back

to Kenya on SS. Mantola. My primary schooling was finished. I had been to four schools but the grounding that my mother gave me in my early years was the basis for a sound education.

My older brother, Monty, stayed to study science at St Andrews University and my sister, Catherine, finished school and went on to train as a nurse at Edinburgh Royal Infirmary.

CHAPTER 5

SECONDARY SCHOOL – 1948–1953

I arrived back in Kenya to start my secondary schooling on an auspicious day for the school. There was great excitement as the first XI hockey team won the Craig Cup final 5-4 in extra time that afternoon. This was a competition open to any European teams, so for a school to win in open competition was a unique occasion.

My school was the Prince of Wales which had been founded in 1929 with an ex-sea captain, Nicholson, as headmaster. His naval influence was reflected in the prefects badge which was an insignia worn at the left wrist! School prefects had a crown in the middle.(5.8) It was a European government boys school with about 500 borders from all over East Africa and about 80 day boys. Although most of the pupils were of British extraction boys of 28 nationalities attended the school including sons of many Afrikaans and Greek farmers, the latter mainly from central Tanganyika.

The main school building was designed by a famous British architect, Sir Herbert Baker. (C1.6) It was an impressive building with columns all round the covered walkway on three sides of a quadrangle. It included two of the original boarding houses.

5.1 Prince of Wales School quadrangle

The remaining six were scattered around the 70 hectares of the school grounds. Some of the buildings remained from the time of World War II – *temporary* wooden buildings, some of which are still in use half a century later! After I had left school, a chapel designed by the Archers, was built on the fourth side of the quadrangle. There was plenty of room in the grounds for masses of playing fields, classrooms and teachers houses.

Although the school was a government school, it was regarded as one of the English Public School Conference, an unusual situation. Our teachers were mostly British but some came from Canada,

Australia or South Africa. Most were good teachers, some brilliant, like Jim Duff. He was a small ex pilot with red hair, who was always immaculately dressed. He came from Sydney and taught us Maths. Geometry was a practical subject when he described how the equilateral triangles were used in bombing key dams in Germany during the War. He had complete control of a class without ever raising his voice – a look was enough. I had the privilege of maintaining a life long friendship after meeting him again when I eventually went to Australia. He was also a great organist and a wonderful gardener – he introduced me to growing Cymbidium orchids.

There were some amazing nicknames for the teachers which described something about them – "Pull through", an instrument for cleaning rifle barrels was given to Bill Liversidge, a tall thin man who was my housemaster and for whom I developed great respect; "galloping tapeworm" for a tall man with a gangling gait and "dudu', the Swahili for an insect, for a little, rather obstreperous man. We also had our bad egg who used to read from his "book" of obscene tales. He ended up in jail, but not before he had taught me French so badly that I just failed my final exam.

There were no airlines with regular flights and planes flying all over the country in those days so it took some of the borders from central Tanganyika a week to get home and a week to get back to school. Most of them came from Greek sisal farming families. They travelled up to Lake Victoria by train, caught the lake steamer around to Kisumu and then took the train from there to Nairobi. Half their holidays was spent travelling.

I lived only 150km by train from Nairobi but even that took from 11am to 5.30 pm to reach our nearest station, Karatina, 7km from home. But then the last 25km from Sagana involved climbing almost 600m. We had an extra engine to help pull the train for this stretch! (C1.7) At times the train would be travelling so slowly that some of the boys jumped off the train and ran along beside it.

Occasionally my parents would come to the school sports at the end of the second term. This delighted me as we left after the sports on Monday evening. People didn't just jump in the car and go and collect the children as they do today. Usually we went on the train and as our train on the Nanyuki line only went up on alternate days returning the next day we had to wait in the boarding houses for a night longer than anyone else. Our train ran on Wednesday and school always finished on Monday. In our earlier years this resulted in the opportunity to pile all the mattresses in the dormitory on our beds, sometimes sleeping on a dozen or more!

On one occasion I travelled home with "Bung" McLeod Young, who had his driver's licence because we could obtain one at 16. He was a bit of a mechanic and had an early 1930s Ford. It had a wooden body replacing the cab and a square wooden box on the back. There were no doors and the dust flowed freely through the floor-boards and out the open window at the back. We put our trunks in the back and tied my bicycle on to the running board on the side. He had three spare tyres as punctures were common in those days of unsealed roads and his tyres did not have much tread – they were totally unroadworthy by today's standards! But then there were not so many vehicles on the road. We left school at 6.30am and travelled through a relatively deserted Nairobi along the 48km of "tarmac" (sealed road) to Thika where we stopped for breakfast with a school friend, Miles Coverdale, whom I met again 47 years later. By 10.30 am we were on the unsealed road again chugging along with dust flowing through the car. We had just passed Sagana, about 28km from home when bang! We had a puncture. Bung did not just change the tyre but felt the one with the puncture was so superior that he would repair it. However he also decided it would be wise to put a gaiter (a segment of old tyre used to re-enforce the outer tyre) in it. To do this he had to let down one of his spares and take the gaiter out – a time consuming business. Finally all was fixed, the tyre pumped up and we set off up the hill to Karatina and hence the last 7km to Tumutumu. We arrived about 2.30pm –eight hours for 135km. At least I got home a day earlier and it is not every day one has such an memorable experience – in fact, I have never had another like it. It provided material for a story for my children and grandchildren which I called "old jallopy".

5.2 Tana Falls

Bung lived about 8km further on where his father ran the local power station. It was built at a waterfall on the Tana River – a distinctive fall which partly went through a hole in the middle. It was said that in the old days criminals were thrown through this hole and over the fall – an unusual way to finish them off. When I was small we drove across the river just above the falls on two steel girders placed the width of the car wheels apart.

It seems that this waterfall was formerly much wider – on the other side there was an underlying large cave which was occupied by hundreds, maybe thousands, of bats – and it smelt like it! We sometimes had them in our attic at home – at dusk one would see them emerge like a squadron of aeroplanes taking off on a raid – whoosh and they were gone. Sadly my chauffeur had a short life, being killed in a car accident in Britain about four years later.

The railway to Uganda used to pass by the school much to the delight of the train fanatics like Peter Rushworth who knew each engine by its whistle. He was very musical, even writing some music, and was a keen cricketer who captained the school team. He eventually spent his life developing navigational equipment. I met him again in London 50 years later.

Holes were bored in the walls of some classrooms to enable students to watch the trains go by. A certain element of mischief prevailed. Sometimes coins were placed on the lines to flatten them or grease was put on the tracks so that traction was diminished on the uphill slope causing the mischief makers much amusement as the engine wheels spun. We think of people who play such pranks nowadays as thugs but maybe they are not so different except nowadays they sometimes cause willful, permanent damage.

Smoking was prohibited except for prefects who, with their parents permission, were allowed to smoke in their common rooms. The idea was that they would police the smoking of the other boys who received a six of the best caning if caught. By and large it didn't work and many boys smoked – in fact if one didn't smoke at all one was regarded as a bit of a freak. Some smokers were very ingenious, smoking out in the middle of the playing fields. They selected a spot where the lawn mowers cut off the top of developing ant hills. These had holes going into the ground. Sitting there they could see any suspicious teachers approaching and could dispose of the cigarettes down the holes so they were never caught. My brother didn't smoke so I did not see any need to either.

I did not regard my schooldays as the best days of my life. I tolerated them mainly because of my enjoyment of sport. Hockey was my forte and I played for various school age teams and eventually captained the school team.

Tennis was not an official sport but we played matches against other schools, including girls, and clubs. I was also tennis captain and managed to introduce an inter house competition. I had some success in my last year being runner up in the Kenya Junior Boys Doubles with Gil Stanley with whom I next played tennis in Perth, Western Australia 47 years later. In 1953, I also won the singles and was runner up in the boys and mixed doubles in a European tournament run at Parklands Club. I always entered the mixed doubles without a selected partner and in each of the three junior tournaments in which I played I ended up partnering the girl who had won the previous major singles tournament. The first one, Julie Swain, was small and said to be rather volatile. My friends warned me to play well or she would throw her racquet at me – the joke was that her racquet did slip out of her hand accidentally while she was serving and flew across the court towards me, much to the amusement of my friends!

5.3 School tennis team , 1953. (Back) Michael Leete, Monty Yeger, Griffiths, John Winter, (front) Neville Jones, Kester Brown, George Mowat.

5.4 Gil Stanley

I learnt to hit the tennis ball against a wall and on the court but I learnt to play the strokes by studying a little book written and illustrated by the Wimbledon coach, Dan Maskell. There was a series of nine sequential pictures illustrating the six basic strokes. I practiced these in front of a window which functioned as a mirror until the strokes became second nature. Jack Kramer won Wimbledon in 1947 and went on to start the professional tennis movement. I also studied his book, "Winning Tennis", and another written by his coach, Bob Harmon, called "Use your head in tennis". These were my main tutors apart from my parents who taught me how to hit the ball. At one stage

5.5 Wearing a head-band to keep sweat off my glasses – 1953.

the Kenya Tennis Association decided to promote youth tennis and several times a couple of leading players came to the school to give us some coaching. One of these was Stan Thatcher who had a high, kicking serve. Another was called Barrett who unfortunately succumbed to poliomyelitis only three weeks afterwards. It was at the time when the polio pandemic was causing deaths and crippling many around the world. What wonderful discoveries were made by Salk and Sabin when they developed their vaccines to prevent this disease.

I wore glasses and found it distracting when I got sweat on them so I wore a headband nearly 30 years before Pat Cash popularized them in professional tennis.

During my last year at school I coached a young 13 year old, Monty Yeger.(5.3) He used my mirror method to practise his strokes. Later that year he partnered me to the finals in the Parklands tournament as my former partner had turned 18. He also won the under 14 singles, an omen of success to come, and played in the school team that year. Later Monty went on to become Kenya Junior tennis and squash singles champions and won the boys and mixed doubles in tennis as well. He eventually went to Oxford and gained a hockey blue. He was a brilliant sportsman. I was sorry not to hear of him again after that.

Free afternoons in the soccer term were often occupied playing a game called "three and in" with five others. We played soccer in pairs, one pair defending the goal while the other pairs were trying to score, having to contend with their opponents and the defending pair. When a pair scored three goals they became the defenders. It certainly helped teamwork in serious games and on one occasion three of us who played together scored five goals in eight minutes.

We played hockey in term 1, rugby and athletics in term 2 and soccer, cricket and cross country in third term. In senior school we had to choose between soccer and cricket. I elected soccer and played in most positions on the field. On one occasion I scored direct from a corner by putting an inswinging spin on the ball. I avoided cross country whenever possible – in fact the only time I did my piano practice was to get out of cross country. Finally I had to run the trials and the race – 5 1/2 miles – I was so naturally fit that I managed to come in twenty-eighth out of sixty. The course went out of the school grounds through some nearby coffee plantations.

In those days sport was largely race segregated but we played select Indian and African schools occasionally. Most of our school sport was played against the Duke of York School which was founded in 1949, and various clubs around Nairobi. The buildings for the latter school were not ready in time for the opening so the Governor moved out and let them use Government House for the first term. I played in the first ever hockey match against them at Nairobi Club. We won 6-2.

Cadets occupied one afternoon a week in the more senior years. I eventually became a sergeant. I resented time spent on it when I could have been playing games. Before my final examinations I managed to avoid the practice and final parade so that I could study!

I had some other experiences which helped to develop leadership skills. I was a prefect and I also had the unusual job of running the school tuck shop. Our major profit came from selling ice cream during the interval at the school play which was a bright idea of mine. I remember buying Bassett's Liquorice All Sorts for 88 cents and selling them for a shilling. (100 cents =1 Shilling. 20 shillings =EA£1) Maybe the experience helped me with budgets later on.

Our 1948 Christmas holiday was the first without Monty or Catherine. We went across the southern border of Kenya into Tanganyika and camped on a farm on the lower slopes of the 4300m volcano (inactive), Mt. Meru.

5.6. Our camp on Mt. Meru – 1948

Two days before Christmas an Afrikaans farmer from the next farm, whom we had never met, came over and invited us for Christmas dinner with them. We accepted. It was a big family gathering to which we were made most welcome. They even had presents for us, complete strangers. I have always thought that that was one of the great kindnesses shown to me – to be invited, a complete stranger, for Christmas dinner. It happened once again in 1960 when I went to Canada. Christmas dinner is a special family event in Christian communities – it is something special to have someone who is on their own, maybe from another country to join in. I am sure that I learnt this lesson on that holiday.

During my holidays at home, when I was about 14, I used to accompany my mother to the hospital once a week when she went to supervise the *lepers* receiving their medication and having their blood test for haemoglobin. They were receiving treatment with new anti-leprosy drugs and depression of the bone marrow where red cells are formed was a potential side effect. The test was done with a drop of blood on blotting paper which was checked against a colour chart.

The leper camp had its own building and gardens within the hospital grounds. It housed about twenty lepers suffering from all degrees of the disease. Some were hideously deformed by leprous nodules on their face and ears. One was blind. Another had lost all his fingers except two small stumps. He was a bright young man who became their teacher. He held chalk between the stumps of his hands so he could write on the blackboard. The loss of fingers is due to injury to the numb hands. They can lose sensation in them and so cannot tell when they are being damaged. It was a terrible disease made worse through the centuries because they were treated as outcasts even though the disease was not very contagious. These drugs were the first really effective ones and they changed the whole outlook of leprosy.

I also went to see occasional operations. The first was an infant with intussception where the bowel telescopes within itself causing a bowel obstruction and the danger of gangrene in the gut if untreated. These experiences undoubtedly influenced my decision to do medicine.

My parents went on home leave to Scotland in 1952. Would I accompany them and finish school there or stay in Kenya? I elected the latter. It was not the only time I had some say in where I went to school. Although this democratic approach caused some difficulties later, when I had my own family I believed it was reasonable to let children have some say in where they go to school.

It was arranged that my holidays would be divided between staying with an old family friend, Hilda Lyne Watt in Nyeri, Douglas Maxwell on his farm at Ngondi and my brother at Sagana. Douglas Maxwell and I occasionally played tennis in Nyeri. On one occasion the rain approached from the Aberdares on one side and Mt. Kenya on the other. We went ahead and drove in the 20kms in the hope that we would still be able to play. It stopped about a hundred metres on each side of the courts. Squash was an alternative which we could play in Nyeri. Douglas introduced me to it on another occasion.

My brother, Monty, lived at Sagana where he ran a fish farm growing tilapia.

5.7. Netting tilapia from the fish ponds at Sagana – 1952

His house was on the top of a little hill, overlooking the ponds. This was an advantage as it caught the breeze which provided some relief from the heat. They had a small group of very keen tennis players including the Indian stationmaster and engine maintenance mechanic. One holidays I joined them in a team which challenged Nyeri Club (European only) to a match. It was unusual for two reasons – that mixed race matches were still uncommon and I played doubles against two old fellows, Macnamara and Brady, aged 77 and 63 years, the latter smoking throughout, even when serving! They thrashed us. A great lesson on the power of cunning placement over brawn – it was a lesson I never forgot!

Sagana was at lower altitude, 1400m and was thus affected by mosquitoes which unfortunately gave me two doses of malaria which only became apparent after returning to school.

Academically I was diligent but not brilliant usually coming 20-26th in my class (A form) of 28. However, when the Cambridge School Certificate exams took place I did well, coming 9th in the school. I had decided that I wanted to follow my father and do medicine but at the end of form 4 my science teachers did not think I was good enough to do science subjects. The headmaster interviewed me and I insisted on doing science. He asked if I had been concentrating on anything else so I told him "Latin", which was true. I had improved my performance from 19% the for set book paper in the trial exams three months before to gain a credit in the Cambridge School Certificate due to the encouragement of my teacher, Teddy Boase. He had taught me in standard 3 at the Primary School and somehow arranged that he would teach me all the way through forms 1-4. He was a good teacher and mad keen cricketer but sadly died when going on home leave to Britain some years later. I was allowed to enter the science stream. It doesn't bear thinking about what would have happened if the headmaster, Percy Fletcher, had not supported me.

I was ultimately in the Biology class which also did physics, chemistry and French. There were ten in the class. I subsequently met five of them in later life, three nearly fifty years later.

John Winter was head of school and a special friend of mine. He went to Bristol to do science but, after a year, decided to go to New Zealand where he worked as a shepherd, bee-keeper and carpenter's assistant before returning to study. He eventually became a well known zoologist in Queensland, becoming an expert on possums and animals of the tropical rain forests. He was the only one of our class with whom I maintained contact – irregularly. Edward Lugard, nicknamed Slug although he was a very good runner, had a special interest in grasses at school. He went into the Army but was killed while young in a motor accident. Nearly 50 years later I found that Richard Powles had lived for 30 years within 2km of my home. I had only maintained contact with four school friends for years but suddenly after over 40 years I have become reacquainted with several others.

5.8. John Winter wearing a blazer with a school prefects badge.

The day before my final Physics exam in Higher School Certificate I was vaguely studying when my house-master, a physics teacher appeared. He had been an examiner in England and knew the commonly asked questions. He told me six likely topics for the exam. I knew little about them all but studied hard that day. All six appeared constituting four and two half questions on the paper of which we had to do five questions. I gained a credit – a big surprise for a poor physics student. And so I scraped through the university entrance requirement, having only had a subsidiary pass in chemistry because our teacher failed to cover all of our syllabus.

About 30 pupils completed sixth form and most went on to University mainly in Britain – several went to Oxford or Cambridge – and a few went to South Africa. There was no University in Kenya in those days. Overall many old boys from the school did well in their chosen fields. One of the less academic became a leading restauranteur in London's West End. Roger Whitaker became a famous singer and whistler, Terry Dalley an outstanding art teacher at Wimbledon, one of Britain's leading Art Colleges, while others did well as lawyers, scientists, agriculturalists, engineers and many other fields. What made them achieve their success? Maybe their parents set a pattern by their getting up and going to a newly developing land where they had to be resourceful to survive and succeed? Maybe the education we received helped? It is an interesting matter to speculate about.

Schooldays over, I left to join the Kenya Regiment as I had turned eighteen and the Mau Mau emergency was on. We had to do National Service. In January we left for six months training in Salisbury, Southern Rhodesia.

Chapter 6

Kenya Emergency and National Service

The population of Kenya when I left school in 1953 was about 5 million Africans, 60,000 Europeans and 160,000 Asians.

Before World War II Kenya, like many others, was a peaceful country which was governed by the British. There was no university and many of the people had only primary education, if any. While the Africans were mainly subservient, some fulfilled roles such as teachers, nurses, medical assistants and clergy and they had their own tribal leadership structures. There was an Indian population who initially came to help with building the railway but soon became the shopkeepers, businessmen and many other intermediate tasks such as running the railways, mechanics etc. Goans, of which there was a sizable community, were often accountants and worked in the banks. Their ancestry was part Portuguese.

The war changed attitudes because Africans participated as troops and in that environment they found that, while they were not high ranking, their fighting contribution could equal those of other races – they were not necessarily inferior and so why should they be subservient? Gradually attitudes changed. Men like Jomo Kenyatta went overseas to the London School of Economics and to Russia where they learnt about revolution and rights. And so trouble brewed and the emergency developed – the Mau Mau, whom the government and European population branded as terrorists, with good reason, but who the Africans have subsequently regarded as freedom fighters, which they may have been.

Nowadays we are used to hearing about terrorism, ethnic cleansing where thousands and maybe millions are killed but back in placid Kenya in late1952 we did not expect that sort of behaviour. Some later commentators have suggested that the Colonial administration had it all wrong and were the aggressors. These people did not live through the times when apparently innocent victims were brutally murdered, like the European who was buried alive with only his head above ground, although he was regarded as looking after his employees well, or the family where the husband and child were murdered in front of the mother who then had her womb opened, the fetus removed and left to die. They killed hundreds of their own Kikuyu people, often brutally, like the one who had the tendons severed at the elbows and knees and then, unable to move, was thrown in a fire to burn. I saw his body in the hospital mortuary. The Mau Mau oaths were, to our way of thinking, vile and disgusting. They were aimed to ensure obedience to the cause which included, on at least one occasion in our area, a son having to kill his father, who was a minister of the church. Failure to take the oath often led to death. What a terrible choice for thousands of innocent people who would not have wanted to be involved. At Lara in March 1953, Chief Luka, who was sympathetic to the administration, and many of his people were killed and their village burned. Is it any wonder that they were regarded as terrorists, because terrorise the whole community they did.

Mau Mau involved mainly the Kikuyu tribe who occupy the centre of the country and were a largely agricultural people rather than herders as their major rivals, the Maasai, were. Jomo Kenyatta was a Kikuyu, originally a trained teacher. He was arrested and accused of masterminding the whole uprising. He was valiantly defended by D.N.Pritt QC, an eminent British barrister. The case went on for months. An old friend of ours who founded Tumutumu, Ruffelles Barlow, who had written the Kikuyu Grammar, was the interpreter for much of the case. (2.2) It was hard for him, because he was not young and the defence frequently tried to say that the interpretation was misleading. In the end Kenyatta was sentenced to 7 years jail, almost, it seemed, a prerequisite in emerging Africa for a future president. Within 10 years he became President of Kenya when it gained its independence on 12 December 1963. He, like Mandela, took a conciliatory line and allowed members of the occupying races to remain and become citizens because he appreciated that they could be helpful in building the new country. (In contrast, Idi Amin who drove them all out of Uganda.) Kenyatta became one of the best regarded post-independence Presidents in Africa.

Kenya flourished and for many years was regarded as the most successful transition to Independence in Africa. It is a pity that corruption, greed and overpopulation (estimated at over 30 million) had an adverse effect on this once beautiful and peaceful country. Tourism, based largely on the wild-life, became its major source of income but increasing violence has deterred the tourists and the country has suffered.

We lived in the middle of the Kikuyu country and so the problem was all around us. Our servants used to warn us not to open a door to them at night because it is possible that the Mau Mau would force them to do it so that they could gain access. We had four Kikuyu boys from the local high school live in a room behind our house because my mother realized the danger it was to them to have to go home. One of them, Eustace, who did well in later life, took my mother, my twin daughters and I to the Ark, a game watching place in the forest, 25 years later. This was an expression of his gratitude to my mother.

One man was found hanging, partly strangled in a tree on the hill behind us. He was admitted to my father's hospital but that night gangsters came into the hospital and killed him. Our head hospital medical assistant was head of the local home guard but was also found to be treasurer of the local MauMau. One couldn't be sure what side people were on.

My father had to attend to his patients throughout all this. It often meant going to the hospital at night to deal with a difficult obstetric delivery. He trusted his faith and never carried any arms to protect himself.

The Mau Mau killed many more of their own African people than they killed Europeans and more Europeans in the security forces were killed accidentally than by the Mau Mau. Several boys who had been at school with me were among these – killed by grenades or accidentally shot. After most wars those who participated don't talk much about it. Those in the security forces missed some of the valuable years of their youth and their experiences undoubtedly affected them for life – seeing friends and colleagues killed is not pleasant and can easily leave bitterness and resentment. Four Kenya Regiment soldiers were killed in one encounter – few compared to modern wars but significant when the total European population was only 60,000 and so many knew each other. I remember that night listening to the news as they read the names out. When the initials J.M. were read out I shuddered as those are my brothers initials – John Monteith (Monty) – but the name that followed was Dowey, a fellow who had been two years ahead of me at school. One of them, Baillon, lived long enough to reach hospital in Nairobi – he was taken to the European Hospital but they would not admit him because he was not a civilian. The tragedy was that he died during transfer to the military hospital.

Unfortunately, in all conflicts injustices occur, and it can be difficult to determine who was the initial perpetrator. History is usually biased by the point of view of the writer, whose information may often be only second or even third hand.

By 1959 relative peace had been restored but the road to independence lay inexorably ahead. The freedom fighters were given recognition when the country became independent and many of the main streets in Nairobi are named after them – Dedan Kimathi Avenue is named after one of the well known and crafty forest gang leaders.

Military Service – 1954

We had cadets at school. Although I became a sergeant I was not an enthusiastic cadet, especially as it prevented us having sport that afternoon. My brother persuaded me to go to a cadet camp for a week in the Ngong Hills. My enthusiasm for such occupations did not match his. My most vivid memory was always feeling hungry. We could buy bread for a shilling a loaf, which I did daily. I can remember ripping the soft centre out, eating it and then munching through the crust. I must have been desperate!

6.1 Dakota (DC3) preparing to leave for Salisbury with Kenya Regiment recruits – January 1954

On completing school all 18 year olds were called up. I became a private in the Kenya Regiment (KR 3435). We were flown down to Salisbury, Southern Rhodesia (now Harare, Zimbabwe) in Dakotas (DC3) for 6 months training at King George VI Barracks.

We had some rough customers training us. "Rumble Guts" Cameron, Scots Greys, was our sergeant major. He succeeded in making us a very proficient group at drill. Our Barrack room sergeants were "Wee Robbie" Robertson from the Black Watch who was said to be able to drink 20 pints of beer in a day, not put on weight, and wake on time every morning to shout "Wakey, wakey" to us. The other was John Bull from the Royal Warwickshire Regiment. (6.3)

Kenya had a relatively small European community so many of us on the course knew each other from school. But there were others, some who were older and some who were of a poor white class. One had worked in the mines. He was a rough diamond and an unattractive character and gained a reputation for being "light fingered" – people always went to him and his neighbour to look for their equipment when it was "lost". Pat Colquhoun was a mischievous character who was always in strife with Rumble Guts and frequently had to run round the parade ground with his rifle above his head for giving him cheek. He suggested that the comedian Bob Hope, who was in town, should be invited to our passing out parade – a suggestion Rumble Guts was not impressed with! He certainly livened up otherwise tedious parades. Unfortunately, he died young after being stabbed in the neck during a pub brawl.

There were some more interesting aspects to the training such as map reading schemes out in the country, and shooting on the rifle range. I qualified as a first class shot with the rifle – probably a genetically inherited ability as my brother, Monty, was the best shot at school and we had uncles who used to shoot rabbits in Scotland. Unfortunately, the day we had to do the Bren Gun test I was in the butts checking everyone else's scores all day before shooting, so that I didn't perform well – only second class!

The final episode of our training was a 56km route march through the night to Inkomo where we camped for a week. Our accommodation was trenches in the ground which we had to dig where two of us slept under a ground sheet (a bivvy). I had a double when in uniform – Michael Crouch. I suffered as my name was easier to remember than his and so when either of us made a mistake on the parade ground I was shouted at. Then if I made a corrective move I was shouted at again! The final bungle occurred when Crouch became ill and was hospitalised while we

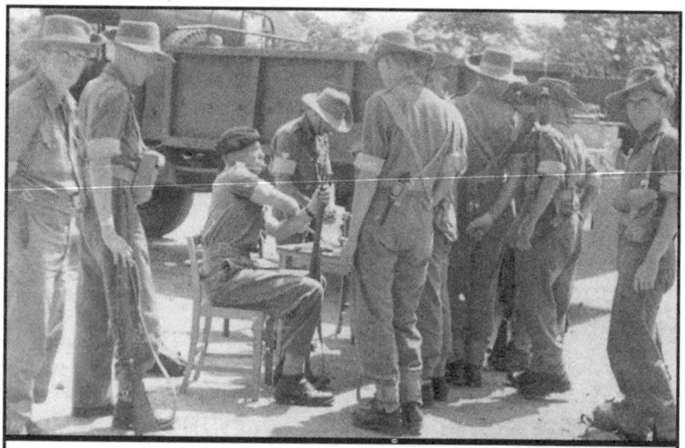

6.2. With my "double", Michael Crouch, at the rifle range.

were at Inkomo – when the next inspection took place they couldn't understand how I was at my bivvy– I was supposed to be in hospital! He had gone to hospital with my name!

6.3. Passing out parade.
Leading- Sgt. John Bull. Front row from Left – Sgt. Robertson, Pat Colquhoun, Dewar, Terry Clegg, KB, Tony Cartland, Andrew Hitch, Campbell,?.
Behind and visible – Alex Forbes Watson, Gordon Bell, Tim Heine, Bruce Low, ?, Aimable, J. Branson.
Behind and not visible – Terry Dalley, Faulkner, Heine 2, Dicky Hall and Botto.

By the end of our six months we were a very well drilled group as can be seen from the photograph taken at our passing out parade led by John Bull and "Wee Robbie" at the side.

I became the barrack room barber by easily out-classing the other two contenders. The job carried no benefits but was good experience. It was not without difficulty. One night I had to cut the hair of a very small fellow called Bruce Low, whom we nicknamed "Mighty Mouse". He was very drunk and kept waving his head around creating a moving target, but the hair had to be cut before parade the next morning. On parade sometimes he became tired supporting his rifle on his shoulder with his left arm, so would put his right arm across to hold the rifle and swing his left arm – an incongruous sight! The other difficult occasion was cutting Sergeant Bull's hair before the passing out parade. He had very fine hair and I had trouble getting a tapered edge. The cut gradually went higher and higher, and higher, up the back of his head. Fortunately he didn't seem to mind so long as it looked all right with his beret on. It seemed like unintentional revenge but was really the result of technical difficulty. Not all hair is equally easy to cut.

We were appointed lance corporal in turn for a week during the first half of the course and then permanent appointments were made for the remainder of the course. Dicky Hall was rather inept but we set up a whisper campaign saying "Dicky will be a lance corporal". Inappropriately, he was appointed. We must have been heard. Such is propaganda!

The positive aspects of the six months were the opportunity to travel – *Nyasaland* for Easter weekend, Victoria Falls, the scenic Eastern highlands and some more local trips.

The Nyasaland trip resulted from meeting an old family friend, Andrew Doig, when he was preaching in Salisbury. He was a missionary in Zomba, Nyasaland. He was an outstanding man, recognised as a leader in central Africa and later in Scotland. We had first met him when he visited us on his way to the Northern Frontier in Kenya in 1940-1 as chaplain to the South African troops who were sent to repel the Italian invasion from Abyssinia (now Ethiopia) during World War II. In 1954 his standing in Nyasaland was such that he was nominated to represent African affairs for Nyasaland in the European dominated Central African Assembly. This was a transient, unsuccessful experiment by the British government to improve the administration of the three central African countries – Northern and Southern Rhodesia and Nyasaland (now Zambia, Zimbabwe and Malawi). Later he was to return to Scotland where he became Moderator of the Church of Scotland and took part in Prince Charles' wedding to Diana.

He took me to Lake Nyasa – sandy beaches, palm trees and dug out canoes are what I remember.

I also hiked up the local mountain much to the consternation of the locals because there were leopards up there –

6.4. Lake Nyasa (now Malawi).

Fortunately, I didn't know and I didn't meet any. It was one of those climbs where the next horizon would be the top but it wasn't. So after reaching several "tops" I turned back.

On our mid course break I accompanied Richard Carles, who farmed at Timau on the northern slopes of Mt Kenya, on his motorcycle to the *Eastern Highlands*. We passed through a region with rocky hills before ascending into the highlands. Black clouds appeared, it grew darker even before nightfall, and then the skies disgorged buckets of rain. When we reached Inyanga we were wet and miserable. We had intended sleeping out but decided to try for a room at the tempting looking Inyanga Hotel. Fortunately there was one so we spent some of our hard-earned meagre salary (50 shillings per week) to have a warm room and hot bath. Next day was fine and we had a marvellous time visiting scenic spots – Pungwe Falls sliding down over a great sloping rock into a great valley heading east, the Mtarazi Falls tumbling about 650m into the Hundi valley, and then Troutbeck where there was a lake and a rather grand looking hotel, a fishing resort.

6.5. Pungwe Falls, Eastern Highlands

Access to some of these places would have been impossible by car as the roads were washed away – with a motor bicycle one could manoeuvre round the deep ruts. That night we slept in our sleeping bags in a pine wood near a little waterfall under the clear African night with its magnificent array of stars and the Milky Way glowing through the tree-tops above us.

Next day we made the trip back to barracks. Travelling by motor cycle was a more interesting way to travel as one was closer to one's surroundings when not inside a car. In those days back in 1954 it was less dangerous as there was much less traffic on the roads. Many country roads were not sealed and there was so little traffic that some just had two strips of tar for the wheels to travel on when nobody was traveling towards you!

The other major trip was to Victoria Falls, one of the great natural sights of the world.(Cover) Rumble Guts chartered a Dakota – DC3 to take about 30 of us for ten pounds each. It was amazing to see the cloud of spray over the falls while still many miles away.

We had a weekend there and slept under the stars out in the bush

6.6 Victoria Falls from the air showing the spray and the winding gorge below the falls.

– something which would not be safe to do today. Victoria Falls is a mile (1700m) wide and tumbles 120m at the greatest fall into a gorge which then zigzags through half a dozen sharp bends. There is an incredible bridge round the first bend from the falls. Why incredible? Well, it was built in 1902 when the area around was completely undeveloped and there was practically no European intrusion – the bridge is 200m long and is nearly 100m above the river. It carries a road, a railway and a footpath. It is incredible because it was built under primitive prevailing conditions with no loss of life. Of course, to most people it is just a bridge. (pictured on the cover)

The falls themselves are best seen in the morning from the Zambian side with its palm trees and in the afternoon from the Zimbabwe side as the sun forms rainbows on the spray. The volume of water, and hence the amount of spray, varies according to the season. The rains occur in December when the maximum flow of 80 million gallons a minute cascades over a nearly continuous width of the falls, producing so much spray that the falls can hardly be seen. It is difficult to approach the viewpoint opposite the fall because falling spray is like being out in a thunderstorm. On the other hand, being there before the rains can be disappointing, because the flow drops to 4 million gallons a minute and the falls become a series of trickles, so much so that someone once attempted to cross by jumping from one rock to the next – he made it for three quarters of the way! In the middle of the year when we went we had magnificent views with enough water to make a great show. It is the second biggest fall in the world after Iguassu in South America.

We also had a launch trip up the huge Zambesi River for a few miles. At one point we landed on an island and I took a photograph of the reflections of the overhanging tree rippled in the water.

It was to become my first photograph to receive a commendation

6.7. Zambesi reflections.

when I entered it in the Physician's Art Salon in Canada some years later. Its success was very significant to me as it was taken with a baby Brownie box camera. This disproves what is so often inferred when people say to me when I show them a good photograph – "you must have a good camera." Artistic photographs are produced by the eye of the photographer. A good camera and quality film certainly help the reproduction but do not compose the picture.

The course ended in June. We had a few days before we returned to Kenya. I spent them at the Rhodesian tennis championships. I became involved as an umpire and linesman when they came round looking for people with previous experience. Jean Forbes, a 16 year old, who later reached the fourth round at Wimbledon, was in the first match. Being a service linesman for the men's singles final between South Africans, Ian Vermaak and Derek Capell, gave me a taste of the difficult challenge that job provides.

Return to Kenya – June 1954

And so we returned to Kenya but not without a final episode to remember. Our plane, a Dakota or DC3, started down the runway to take off when the pilot suddenly braked – the plane was overloaded and he didn't think he would get off the ground! Fortunately, he was able to stop before the end of the runway, return and off-load a couple of fellows and some luggage. We then made a successful take off. Back in Nairobi we were given a few days leave before taking up our military duties.

I was posted to 'B' company which was stationed at a place called Kairo in the Fort Hall district at the foot of the Aberdare mountains. Because I was to be allowed to leave to go to university shortly, I was allocated the Bren gun to carry on patrol – all 13 kg of it plus my sleeping bag and food. It was a hard slog up and down the sides of steep ridges on the Aberdares, often through thick forest or bush.

6.8. On patrol in the Aberdare forest.

On one patrol we were being guided by an "informant" but were led to a camp which had not been occupied for some days. We crossed a stream and almost stepped on a corpse lying on the track. That night, darkness descended before we reached the top of the ridge, so we bivouacked half way up the steep slope where there was a flattish area inadequate for us all to lie. Despite tying our sleeping bags to bamboo some slipped several feet down the hill until they came to rest against another one. We did not find any MauMau on that trip. The density of the forest and their skill at melting away was considerable. Unless fresh tracks were found and could be followed we had little hope of finding them.

Because of his great skill at tracking, my brother Monty was later deployed to teach at the tracking school. He had learnt this by spending many hours from the age of sixteen tracking game, even buffalo, in the forests while out hunting.

We were often transported in open Land Rovers, overcrowded with some of the troops even sitting on the bonnet. It amazed me where some of the drivers made these vehicles go – straight down hillsides and along very rough and wet forest tracks.

They were very tough and versatile. So after a few weeks of spending days in the forest and some cold nights lying out in ambushes I was discharged from the army and soon after left Kenya for Scotland and university.

6.9. Travelling in the Aberdare forest by Land Rover

CHAPTER 7

MOUNTAINS – KENYA AND KILIMANJARO

My parents were passionate about mountains. My father was one of the earliest members of the Kenya Mountain Club but unfortunately he was foiled on the mountains because he developed mountain sickness when he approached 4000m. The common features of this condition are headaches and nausea, sometimes with vomiting.

I was born looking out on Mt. Kenya which is a magnificent volcanic mountain rising symetrically in solitary splendour in the middle of the country. (C1.4) It must have been very high before the cone eroded away leaving the main peaks, which were formed from the plug of the old volcano. Its glaciers, which have been steadily receding, are within ten miles south of the Equator. It was first climbed in 1898 by Mackinder but it was another 30 years before the famous mountaineer, Eric Shipton climbed it again with Tilman. Shipton paved the way for Hilary's successful climb of Everest. Tilman became a great adventurer who finally disappeared while sailing in the South Atlantic to the Falkland Islands. Now, like so many other mountains, Mt. Kenya is frequently climbed. By chance, I met a man on a plane flying to Dar es Salaam who had climbed it about sixty times. By strange coincidence I met him on the return flight and again two weeks later when we were having lunch in the Nairobi Club! The main peaks require some skill as a rock climber.

In 1928 my parents made a trip with several others up a recently built road from Chogoria on the east side of Mount Kenya to a hut which was built at 3,300m, just after the road emerged from the forest on to the moorlands. It was beautifully built with cedar by Mr. Carr who had the Ford dealership in Nairobi. His daughter married the doctor at Chogoria, Clive Irvine, who was a colleague of my father and a cousin of the famous climber who disappeared on Everest in 1924. I visited what remained of the hut nearly 60 years later and one could tell how well it had been built.

Vivienne de Watteville spent two months there in the early 1930s. She describes her adventures, the most graphic of which was being awoken early by her alarm because she planned a big hike to visit some lakes up the mountain. It was brighter than she expected. When she looked outside she saw a huge fire was coming down the mountain towards them. With the help of her two servants they rapidly back burned a protective strip around the hut. But the fire kept coming. Even their back burn did not seem to be stopping it. When all seemed lost, the wind suddenly changed and blew it back up the mountain. It is a hair raising, touch and go tale wonderfully described in her book.

My father had bought an old car for 40 pounds for this trip. It made it up but a major breakdown on the way back at Meru rendered it useless. Somehow he managed to sell the disabled car for a profit. People were very versatile at fixing cars in those days. It was easier because of their simple construction.

7.1. Cars emerging from the forest on the Chogoria (Carr's) road – 1928.

7.2. Car crossing one of the rivers – 1928.

The party climbed Point Lenana (5200m) which is at the top of the Lewis Glacier but my father could not make it with the others beyond its lower reaches and my mother gave up her chance to keep him company.

When the photographs of the glacier taken then are compared to the view today one can see how much it has receded since. They made another trip in 1934. My first mountain expedition was when I was two. My only recollections are from photographs at our camp and beside our old car on the moors.

7.3. Party at the foot of the Lewis Glacier – 1934. Father is middle right with mother in white hat next to him.

By the time my parents arrived in Kenya great expeditions were being mounted to try to conquer the high mountains such as Everest. Mallory and Irvine of the 1924 Everest expedition had disappeared without trace – only recently Irvine was found by a Japanese climber who unfortunately died himself on the mountain before giving the exact location of the body to anyone. Subsequently Mallory was found. Did either or both of them reach the top? We will never know for sure but many think Mallory did. He took a photograph of his wife with him which he told her he would leave at the top if he reached the summit. It was not among the photos found on his perfectly preserved body after all these years.

7.4. Our family beside our old car on my first safari, aged 2.

Percy Wyn Harris, whom I met as a child, was our Provincial

7.5. Camped in the forest beside our car on my first safari up Mt. Kenya – 1938

Commissioner and later became Governor of Gambia in West Africa. He was a member of the 1933 Everest expedition led by Shipton who pioneered the subsequently successful route. It was still another twenty years before it was conquered by Edmund Hilary of New Zealand and the Sherpa Tensing in 1953 – an event I remember well as a schoolboy because the announcement that they had reached the top coincided with the coronation of Queen Elizabeth, for which we had a holiday. I was hobbling around on a sore foot at the time having just had an abscess on the sole incised two days before with ethyl chloride spray to freeze the skin for anaesthesia. Ethyl chloride could also be inhaled at the beginning of an anaesthetic as it quickly made one unconscious.

When I was at school it was possible on very clear days to see both Mt. Kenya and Kilimanjaro, small and faint away in the distance, from high points around Nairobi. Maybe that is no longer possible with pollution over the city. These are the two highest points in Africa.

I was brought up looking out on Mt Kenya and I have been up three sides of it to various heights. In 1958, I went with several others, including my friend from Rhodesian days, Richard Carles who lived on the north slopes of the mountain. I was always intrigued that his mother was born on the Falkland Islands. We went up the Naro Moru (west) side and managed to reach the top of Point Lenana, the highest point which can be reached without being a rock climber. We camped the first night among giant groundsel which look like prehistoric trees.(C2.3) We had time on the second afternoon to climb up to Two

7.6 Mt Kenya peaks, Batian and Nelion, from Two Tarn Col – SW. Point Lenana at the top of the Lewis Glacier on the right.

Tarn Coll at the base of the Main peaks (SW) with Arthur's Seat and Point Piggot close by.

We descended back into the Teleki Valley and spent the night at the hut. My clearest recollection was sleeping furthest from the door making escape difficult and waking up with a terrible thirst and dry mouth. This results from over breathing, which is a normal response at high altitude to the low oxygen tension and breathing through the mouth. The next morning we climbed out of the east side of the valley to the Curling Pond where some of the party enjoyed their first snowball fight.(C2.4) As we climbed on up the ridge I took my pulse – it was 195 per minute, something I thought would be impossible then. Later I found out that this was below my maximum heart rate. We then traversed onto and up the Lewis Glacier to the top of Point Lenana (4940m) where we had a magnificent view down to the northern frontier, across the lesser peaks of Corydon and Delamere, and south over the Kikuyu reserve. It was a thrilling moment for me as I had looked out at this point since the day I was born. Fortunately, I was not troubled by mountain sickness.

In 1985 I reached a low ebb of physical fitness. I was invited to attend the East African Anaesthetic meeting in Arusha in Northern Tanzania. My sister had some friends who wanted to climb Kilimanjaro, so she arranged for me to join them immediately after this meeting.

7.7. Icicles on the track, about 3cm high, formed by freezing dew.

I arrived in Kenya a few days early so that I could visit Monty, my brother, and his wife, Barbara, at Naro Moru. He suggested a couple of days on the mountain. It seemed a wonderful idea as it would acclimatize me a bit and give us an enjoyable outing together. He is six and a half years older than I am and much fitter. We drove up to 3500m on the Timau (North) side and made a pleasant camp on the moorlands. We had a gentle walk up to about 3800m in the afternoon. After dinner I was amused listening to our Kikuyu cook, Ndeke, our Turkana helper, Lasekeria, and Monty conversing in Kikuyu, Swahili and English all mixed up, even in one sentence! Lasekeria also spoke Turkana and German.

Next day we started early. There were masses of tiny pillars of ice on the track, about 3cm high, formed as the water vapour condensed when the temperature dropped below freezing during the night. It was intriguing to watch these little ice pillars fall over and melt as the morning sun struck them.

Lasekeria was a Turkana, a tribe that lived on the relatively flat, hot deserts in the north so this was a very different experience for him. He and Monty sped on ahead as I, like the tortoise, struggled behind. They would stop to wait for me to catch up, but barely giving me time to catch my breath, they would be off again. The track took us up over the moors passing, from time to time, some interesting plants – giant groundsel (C2.3), lobelias (C2.5), thistles growing with flowers close to the ground, and others.

7.8. Glacier near the top of Kilimanjaro.

Gradually we trudged on, intermittently catching enticing glimpses of the peaks. We passed a little stream where some climbers were camped. At about 4,300m. we came on to a ridge which looked down into the Mackinder Valley with the main peaks rising beyond and the subsidiary peaks, Sendeyo and Terere over to the left. It was a deep valley. We decided not to descend into it as we would just have to climb out of it again on our return! I painted the view.(C39.4) After our lunch we walked east along the ridge for two or three km stopping from time to time to enjoy the views. Then it was time to start down for camp. We passed through an area with many groundsels and flowers. I was becoming weary and asked Monty if he could carry my camera. "No,"he said. "He was feeling terrible." He had broken the rule – pole pole (slowly) unless one is acclimatised. He was now 56, not as young but still fit at lower altitudes.

Next day we returned to Naro Moru and soon I set off for the meeting in Arusha convinced that I should cancel the Kilimanjaro trip as I felt near the limit of endurance at 4300m. I thought I had little hope of reaching the top at 5900m. In the end I decided to go as it had been a lifelong ambition to climb it and even if I only went part of the way it would still be interesting.

One morning at Arusha we had a wonderful view of Mt Meru rising nearby, blanketed in snow which is unusual as it is only about 4300m.

We travelled to Moshi where I visited Kilimanjaro Christian Medical Centre (KCMC). It was well known for training medical assistants in the basics of anaesthesia using ether, ketamine and local anaesthesia. The centre was run by a very able Irishman, Eugene Egan, who could cope with the attitude that anything which cannot be done today can be done tomorrow! The trainees spent one year there and for some years they received an EMO anaesthetic machine to take home so that they could continue giving anaesthetics. This was a very practical form of help given by the Irish Faculty of Anaesthetists.

Next stop was Marangu Hotel where we spent the night and where our party was organised. Miss Lany, a wiry, little, grey-haired lady had been there for over 30 years sending parties up the mountain. Her advice was "go pole pole" which is Swahili for slowly.

We were driven to the National Park gate around midday and after a short walk stopped for a picnic lunch. We then had a gentle walk up through the forest to the first huts – a climb of 1000m to 2800m in about 10km. The tropical mountain forests are dense with large trees, vines and other plants. They are beautiful, especially when one comes to a little stream which we did just before emerging on to the heathlands.

The next morning I was in for a surprise. I was presented with a meerschem carving of a little man which the donors, my companions, felt looked like me climbing the mountain. It was my 50th birthday present from them.

The group was very international. Glenn and Sue Gordon were from Oregon, USA. He was a retired surgeon, a caring dedicated man, who was working at the University in Dar-es-Salaam. Before the Arusha meeting I had visited Muhimbili Medical Centre and saw Glenn working with a Russian anaesthetist, something which was virtually unheard of at that time when the Cold War was still in progress. Larry was the American embassy doctor who was accompanied by his wife. There were two Germans, one of whom was a photographer, a slightly older Danish couple, a young English lady who looked like a student but turned out to be a bank manager with two degrees, and Ola Relling, a Norwegian who was working for four years on an agriculture project in Tanzania. Ola and I travelled at a similar pace so we walked much of the way together.(C3.3) He came to visit us on his way home at the end of his contract and later I visited him at Valldal in Norway. Attached to our group but travelling independently and carrying his own pack was the grandson of the first European to reach the edge of the crater. He was a student. Our baggage and sleeping bags were carried by porters, who went up and down with ease.

The second day was a 20km walk through some wooded areas, then through the heath country where we also saw flowers which I was told were unique to Kilimanjaro. One particularly pretty spot was beside a little waterfall where we rested for a while. At each stop I did a quick watercolour sketch which I later used in conjunction with some photographs to paint one of my large composite paintings. This was the biggest (75x50cm) and shows various features on the trip up the mountain.(C3.1)

The second huts were at about 3800m and the nights were becoming cold. We were nearing the top of the moors where the tussock grass thinned out before coming to a bleak moonscape-like region where vegetation became scant. (C3.3) What special features do these plants have to enable them to adapt to wide diurnal variation in temperature? At the top hut altitude began to take its toll. Altitude sickness prevented one of the group from proceeding and two others decided not to go further. Appetites had waned. I enjoyed large quantities of soup because dehydration is a problem due to the dry atmosphere and over-breathing to compensate for the low oxygen tension – at that altitude it was about 80mmHg.I had little desire for anything else.

We slept until midnight and set off shortly after with the aim of reaching the rim of the crater by or soon after sunrise. It took me until 9am. The cold during the night was extreme. I had three thick layers of clothes on but still felt cold. Two of the party stopped at a cave at 5,200m. and two more at the edge of the crater. One had been vomiting but was determined to reach that far. I struggled on and was pleased when the sun began to rise and warm things up. The mountain was engulfed by a radiant orange glow for a short time. During the day, by contrast, it is hot and one tends to burn easily. I reached the edge of the crater just in time for a short break before the surviving members of the party headed for the top. This involved going round the inside edge of the crater for a distance, across a stretch of snow and then up and along the last stretch to Uhuru Point, the top of Africa. We had a splendid view of the glaciers in the crater which, unfortunately, are diminishing and may disappear altogether.(C3.2) The reason for climbing early was to be there before the snow softened and became too slippery.

I was becoming more and more hypoxic. The oxygen tension in the atmosphere was reaching a low 70mm Hg. As only two thirds of the air we breathe reaches the alveoli in our lungs to allow gas exchange, the tension in our blood dropped further to about 50mm Hg. Normally we exist with over 100mm.Hg. I reached a point where one step of about 30cm upwards completely exhausted me. I was miserable and was prepared to give up – only 200m from the top. Christopher, my porter told me I could make and to keep going. After a rest I did and was the last of the five to make it. I was thrilled and surprised to have achieved my ambition. The photographs at the top are unrecognizable because of my dress and protective clothing. After a short rest the descent began. It was 10am and we had to descend to the second huts at 3800m.before nightfall. I had enough energy left to admire and photograph more glaciers on the way but my over-riding thought up there was "how could I be so crazy as to perrrrsssecute myself with this missseraaaabbble exissstaaance!" The low oxygen tension was making me miserable!

7.9. Kilimanjaro after a heavy snowfall.

The descent became more and more enjoyable and easy as the oxygen increased. We rose the next morning at the 4,000 m huts to see the magnificent sight of the whole cone of Kilimanjaro covered in fresh snow down to about 5000m. It would have been impossible to have reached the top that night, and also the night before we went, due to blizzards. We were back at the Park gate by 2pm.the next day.

We had been extremely lucky to reach the top. I had a new lease on life. I figured that if I could survive those low oxygen tensions my heart must be in good shape so I began playing hockey again!

We were awarded certificates which varied in colour depending how high we had reached. Back at the hotel I was pleased to see Catherine and Bob, my sister and brother in law who had come down from Kenya to collect me. They had known Miss Lany for years and she had arranged that they would pay the bill in a very practical way with electric light bulbs, toilet paper and packets of soup! At that time these things were very scarce in Tanzania which was going through a most depressed period. Things like light bulbs, bath plugs and toilet paper were taken by departing guests because they were difficult to obtain.

I luxuriated in a hot shower followed by a good dinner and a deep sleep.

I returned to my brother's place for a few more days. I thought it strange that he did not ask me until we were having afternoon tea how far I had gone. I don't think they even considered the possibility of me reaching the top. Eventually he asked " How far did you reach?" There was disbelief when I told him and his wife, Barbara, who always regarded me as an overweight degenerate individual! Luckily I had my certificate. Their cook immediately made a cake decorated with icing sugar showing me struggling up the side of the mountain, maybe the highest in the world, from its lowest base level on the north side of about 500m to the top at 5900m.

7.10. Cake showing me climbing Kilimanjaro!

I was 50! I thought I had done as much by then as many people do in a lifetime but I think the new lease of life enabled me to do as much again in the next 15 years when I stopped full time work.

I later returned to Kenya in 1989 and 1999 and had two further trips on Mt Kenya, going up the Chogoria track from the east side. In 1989 my son Ken accompanied Monty and me. It is beautiful up on the moorlands but the peak is less spectacular from that approach as there are no glaciers on that side. But there were good walks and plenty of wildlife to be seen – elephants, buffalo, bushbuck, monkeys and others. Buffalo left evidence that they had wandered very close to our tents during the night! A short distance from camp was Carr's cabin which I have already mentioned and which we visited. Our major walk was up the track towards the peak. We could see down into the deep Gorges Valley but we did not reach far enough to see into the cul de sac containing Lake Michelson. Monty's photographs of it taken on a later trip show the beautiful lake surrounded by spectacular cliffs, some dark and some brown and a little stream leaving the lake over a small waterfall. The weather turned bad – rain, then hail so that by the time we reached our vehicle I felt as if I had mild hypothermia. The second day we did a walk around on the moors visiting Lake Ellis.

The next trip in 1999 was different. We camped a little higher and did some walks. We saw animals – elephant, buffalo, bushbuck. But then the rains began. The road was much worse than the previous time and with the rain it was very difficult, even with Toyota four wheel drive trucks with chains. Several times one had to pull the other out including once near the camp where we had a short steep incline which an elephant had slithered down in the early morning leaving a very smooth skid mark. Fortunately we had two Toyotas so that they could help each other. (C2.7) At one point one had slipped into a deep rut and was leaning at a precarious angle. I was pushing from the side until I slipped into a muddy water-filled rut much to the amusement of the others. It took 4 hours to travel 24 km!

Although the peaks are much less interesting viewed from the east, the moorlands and forests lower down are beautiful. It was sad to see illegal cutting down of beautiful, very old camphor trees in the forest.

Our tents were pitched in clearings among magnificent nagenia (C2.6) and cedar trees, many with old man's beard hanging from them giving an appropriately ancient look. The moorland flowers reminded me of our childhood holidays on the Aberdares. These trips were enhanced for me by photography and being able to paint some of the beautiful scenes.

Elsewhere I have written about our holidays on the Aberdare Mountains which are a long ridge rising over 4000 m. They were formed when the Rift Valley developed and molten rock poured up from the fissure that developed

Kenya has other mountains – the extinct volcanoes in the Rift Valley like Longonot and Kulal (C19.3) and Mt. Elgon in the north west.

It is not surprising that I love mountains. I have seen many great ones – Machu Pukara in the Himalayas, Mont Blanc in the Alps in Europe, Mt Cook in New Zealand, Aconcagua, Cotopaxi and Osorno in the Andes, Torres del Paine in southern Chile, Mts Lister, Minto and Erebus in the Antarctic, Mt. Robson, the highest point in the Canadian Rockies – the latter mountains stretch for hundreds of kilometers with a grandeur which almost causes visual indigestion when one drives through the National Parks among them. I have looked at all these mountains, photographed and painted many of them and had some great hikes among some of them.

Chapter 8

The Voyage to Britain

8.1 A narrow Zanzibar street – 1954.

Travel was more leisurely in the 1950s. There wasn't the mad rush to reach everywhere in the shortest possible time. I travelled by sea, the long way round by South Africa on the Dunnotter Castle, a Union castle ship of about 14000 tons. The Union Castle line had a monthly sailing to Britain around southern Africa. Every third one stopped at Ascension and St. Helena which I would like to have visited but unfortunately we missed out. It was a great trip as there were four of us who had been at school together and there were other young people on board. I shared a cabin with Terry Dalley who was going to London to study art which he did very successfully at St. Martins School of Art and then the Royal College of Art. Most of his career he taught at Wimbledon Art College. We had been in the same class in Grade 4, then at the Prince of Wales School and finally in the same barrack room in Rhodesia.

8.2. Policeman directing traffic in Zanzibar in 1954. Where is it?!

The voyage took five weeks, with about fourteen days spent in various ports down the east coast of Africa – Tanga with its attractive beaches; exotic Zanzibar, with its narrow streets and old Arab buildings, where cloves and

8.3. Sleeping giants – cranes in Beira Docks.

coconuts grew in abundance; Beira which was the main port supplying Mozambique and the hinterland – Rhodesia and Nyasaland. Its giant cranes reminded me of sleeping giants when they were not working.

A group us went to a fine beach and while waiting for a return bus, a pick up stopped and gave us a lift. Terry sat in the front. Coincidentally, he had met the driver previously in the middle of the night during our final army training exercise in Rhodesia where we had a mock attack on the Rhodesian Regiment which was also on exercises. It was one of the first of many amazing coincidences in my life.

Next we stopped at Lourenzo Marques, which had a radio station that we used to hear broadcasting when we were in Rhodesia. We proceeded to Durban where some of the rickshaws were still drawn by Zulus in their decorative tribal dress. We went on a tour to the Valley of a Thousand Hills.

My only recollection of East London was watching a snake charmer. Then to Port Elizabeth and finally, after a very rough passage round the Cape of Good Hope, we reached Capetown, situated in its spectacular setting beneath Table Mountain. From there shipboard life became dominant as our only other stop before Britain was an afternoon in Las Palmas in the Canary Islands.

Capetown was a spectacular city but one of the days we were there was Sunday and it was dead – nothing was going on. We took the cable-car to the top of Table Mountain where we had wonderful views. However, the most entertaining episode was late in the evening when we wandered down to the end of the pier to find some people who had been fishing packing up. Then suddenly the last person fishing hooked

8.4. Rickshaw in Durban with driver in Zulu dress – 1954.

something. As he began to reel it in it became apparent that it was something big. He had to strain as he wound the line in. The rod began to bend under the strain. The excitement grew. Everybody was watching and much encouragement was given. Slowly, slowly the line was wound in, the rod bent more. It was flexible and strong. What had he caught? We were all intrigued. Slowly, slowly, with the rod bending under the strain, it appeared without a fight – a bucket off a passing ship, weighed down with the water it contained. Howls of derision. Much amusement for all except the poor fellow with the rod. What an anticlimax!

We now had two weeks sailing without interruption – swimming, games, dancing – to the music provided by one of the most bored bands I have ever seen!

There were several memorable features of that trip. Being young, with voracious appetites, we frequently ate through the whole seven course menu. Dressed cabbage followed by soufflé every day became rather tedious items after five weeks! The fancy dress parade produced some exotic outfits – Terry won with a crepe paper suit dressed as a cavalier. One chap, six feet seven inches tall (203cms) made a very glamorous 1920s lady!

Musical talent abounded with a professional singer and a professional violinist amongst the passengers, so they had a concert. Terry, who also has a very fine singing voice, gave an outstanding rendition of *Wonderful, wonderful Copenhagen*, so much so that the singer suggested that he should become a professional singer. He didn't but one of his daughters became an opera singer, so the talent was passed to the next generation.

Approaching Las Palmas we had early lunch as we were able to go ashore at 1pm. Then around the tables came a fellow we had nicknamed "Bong", a crazy guy, informing us all that there was to be a public hanging in the market square at 2pm! It was nonsense. Las Palmas in 1954 was like a museum of pre-war cars, all shining and beautiful. We hired a magnificent yellow one that took six of us around for the afternoon.

That evening we set sail for our final destination. Such trips are no longer the usual way to travel except on cruises. It is a pity we don't have time for such slow travel.

Arrival at Tilbury again had its setback. I had bought an Agfa camera at the great expense of £10 with my savings from my army salary.

8.5. Las Palmas taxi – the author with ?, Terry Dalley, Jem Holmes, Margaret Wright and Peta Thomas

Now the customs demanded duty because I had not had it for a year! That was an expense I did not need then as I had little money.

I had a few days in London where I visited the Kenya students office near Trafalgar Square and was taken to the ballet for the first time in my life. Tamara Tomanova was the prima ballerina but I have no idea which ballet I saw. Anyway I thought it was a very grand affair.

I was glad that I was not going to study in the huge city of London and that I had opted for St Andrews. I had been offered the place at St. Thomas' Hospital in London which was allocated for the Prince of Wales School in Nairobi each year. I was the only one in my year who chose to do medicine. After a few days seeing some of London and enjoying the kind hospitality of my father's friend and my namesake, Kester Wilson, I left for Scotland where I would spend the next six years.

Part 2

Scotland – Student Years

CHAPTER 9

STUDENT YEARS IN SCOTLAND 1954–1960

I don't remember many details about my arrival in Scotland but I was stunned on my visit to the Scottish Universities admissions office in Edinburgh where I had the horrifying experience of being told that as they had not heard from me accepting my place it may have lapsed! What a disaster that would have been having come so far. Fortunately, after some discussion and telephone calls the problem was resolved. I could proceed to St. Andrews to study medicine after all. Some mail may have missed me while I was at sea for five weeks.

An old family friend in Edinburgh gave me an introduction to the Forresters at 64 South St. in St Andrews which proved invaluable. He was a professor at the Divinity College, St. Marys. His wife was a sister of two well known Church of Scotland ministers – John and Donald Baillie. Duncan , their youngest son, was still at home. He was about to begin his honours year.

When I arrived before term and began to look for lodgings, Duncan kindly took me to the appropriate office that looked after enrolments for the University Residences. This was the beginning of a lifelong friendship. By a stroke of luck I obtained the last room – in Hamilton Hall which had formerly been the Grand Hotel situated across the road from the 18th green of the famous Old Course and the Royal and Ancient Golf Club. My room was not so luxurious – it faced into the well in the middle of the building. It had two advantages – it was not affected by the howling winds off the North Sea and so tended to be warmer and secondly it was cheaper, a major consideration when one only

9.1. The author and mother with Duncan, Professor and Mrs. Forrester at St. Andrews.

had £300 to survive the whole year. It cost £96 a year for the three terms. My fees were £60 so there was not too much for everything else. It taught me Scottish thrift!

The Scots are often considered mean and tight fisted. They are just thrifty (careful) because people who live further north have long hard winters and therefore have to save in the summer if they are going to survive. In contrast, the people living around the Mediterranean and in tropical climates, where food is always available, spend more freely. The Scots are, in fact, very kind and generous people.

I returned three weeks later with my trunk, which contained most of my worldly belongings, to start the long and sometimes arduous six years as a medical student. Certainly, by the time I reached my third year I wondered if I would really last the distance so far from my tropical home. My academic progress may have influenced my feelings as I always found it a struggle, particularly in the earlier years.

St Andrews thrived on the University, golf and being a summer holiday resort. It had a population of about 10,000 at that time. It was an old and very historic place having been the ecclesiastical and educational centre of Scotland in medieval times. It is on the North Sea and to its north west the West Sands run for about three kilometres to a point where they turn into the estuary of the Eden River. The sands slope away gradually so at low tide they stretch a long way out. They were firm enough to play hockey on, when our pitches were snowbound. It is out on this dunes area that the famous links golf courses are situated – the Old, New, Eden and Jubilee courses existed at that time but now there are three more in the vicinity. It is regarded as the place where the game was invented and as the home of golf with the Royal and Ancient Club determining the rules of the game. When I was there students could obtain a season ticket which allowed them to play on any of the courses between October and June for two pounds, or for one pound if you excluded the Old Course! How times have changed. A round on the Old Course for visitors now, if they can get a tee off time which are sometimes balloted, costs about 50 times or more for a round.

St. Andrews is a University town during the winter and a holiday resort during the summer. The University was founded by charter granted by Bishop Henry Wardlaw on 28th February 1412 and confirmed by Papal Bulls issued by Pope Benedict XIII in Avignon and promulgated in 1414. For two years before that academics had gathered there to teach. It was the first University to be established in Scotland. Before that Scottish scholars went to Balliol College, Oxford or to Paris or even Bologna.

The older part of the town is steeped in history and dominated by the ruins of a huge medieval cathedral which was consecrated in 1318, an occasion attended by King Robert Bruce. It and its precincts suffered after the Reformation, many of the old houses in the town being built from stones from the cathedral.

One fascinating wall in the ruins of the cathedral has the design of curved Norman arches interposed with another similar line of Norman arches, resulting in Gothic arches.

9.2. Norman arches super-imposed on each other to form Gothic arches – St Andrews Cathedral.

The castle is now also a ruin, its ramparts and tower still standing over the sea. It made an impressive setting for the performance of Shakespeare's Macbeth when I was a student. It is said that there are tunnels under the town to it. It has a bottle dungeon – a round cavern with a narrower circular entrance above so that it is impossible to escape without help. During my first year at St. Andrews the Bejants (first year students) captured three second year students and, having bribed the keeper to obtain the keys, imprisoned them there for a few very cold hours on the November evening when the annual first v. second year student pranks took place. (C8.2)

The University Chapel was originally constructed in 1460 while St. Mary's College and St Leonard's Chapel predated 1560. A reminder of the turbulent religious history of St. Andrews can be seen in the initials of two great church reformers, Patrick Hamilton and George Wishart, marking the spots where they were burned for heresy. They preached on reform ideas which they had acquired on the continent. Though they died their ideas lived on and their deaths fueled the desire for change – the Reformation followed.

The undergraduate students wore red gowns, a tradition going back over three hundred years. They were very practical as they provided warmth in the winter. One tradition was the pier walk when the students in their red gowns who had attended chapel on Sunday walked down round the end of the pier and back. It was said to have begun in the days when the congregation went to see the preacher off in his boat but I am not sure if the preacher came by boat in those days. Anyway it made a magnificent sight. (C8.1)

9.3. Kate and Bishop Kennedy, 1955

The Kate Kennedy procession, held each spring since 1926, recalls the history of St.Andrews and the University by the representation of the main historical characters accompanied, where relevant, by someone carrying their coat of arms. (C8.3) Members of the Kate Kennedy Club, who are senior students elected on the basis of interest in the traditions of the University and contributing usefully to university life, took the parts. Each year they selected seven bejants (first year male students) following interview from whom one was chosen to be Kate, supposedly the niece of Bishop Kennedy, the founder of St. Salvators College in 1450. It is uncertain whether or not she was mythical as there is no firm evidence that she really existed.

The selection of the bejant for the role depended on having good knowledge of the University and its traditions, a breadth of interests and abilities, and being a generally high quality and good looking person. Kate, dressed appropriately, travelled in a horse drawn carriage with Bishop Kennedy at the end of the procession surrounded by the six unsuccessful finalists who carried the University Shields. (C8.3) On one occasion I was Bishop Wardlaw's shield bearer and on another Bishop Wardlaw.

9.4. The author as Bishop Wardlaw (1959).

St Andrew's Day, 30th November, is Scotland's National day and was a University holiday when I began in St.Andrews. The only problem was that falling on a different day each year it upset the lecture programmes and so the

University Senate decided to discontinue the holiday. What sacrilege! But they were very cunning about it. They instituted the change when it fell on a Friday because the next year it would be on a Saturday. Rebellion occurred. St. Andrew's day began with a mock funeral for "St. Andrew" who was carried on a horse drawn hearse around the town starting at 6am. Then the students boycotted classes. But the authorities won in the end as by the next time it was on a weekday too few students remained who remembered having the holiday.

In those days St Andrews University was composed of United College in St Andrews and Queens College in Dundee. They were split into two Universities in the 1970s when Britain underwent an expansion of its Universities.

It was a wonderful place to attend university. It was small, historical, most students lived in residence and it suited me well. I was there to study medicine. That involved being in St Andrews for our pre-clinical part of the course (first three years) and moving to Dundee for our more practical clinical training for the last three years.

Duncan Forrester became my senior man which was a great help and privilege. He was entering his honours year in Arts and was a well known figure in the University. The role of the senior man was supposed to be to mentor and help his bejant (first year student). On Raisin Monday in November the bejant was supposed to give his senior man some raisins or an appropriate alternative gift for which he had to get a receipt. Duncan, being steeped in the traditions of the University, and also knowing Latin, gave me one in Latin.

His parents always welcomed me to their home, as they did many other students, and made me feel that it was a "home away from home". Their house at 64 South Street can still be recognised by the two owls that look down from the lintel over the front door. They were wonderful, kind people – she was a lovely, outgoing, dynamic and motherly person and he, rather more professorial but with a wonderful sense of humour with which he entertained me and many others until his death at the age of 93. He even made it sound funny when he told my brother that in the Highlands there were signs on the road saying "Beware of sheep"! Mrs. Forrester also had a sense of humour. She told me once that she had walked to the end of the West Sands where she found seals close by in the Eden estuary. She had heard that seals are musical and so she sang some well known Scots songs. They came closer. They seemed to enjoy them but then she switched to some hymns at which point they left! Obviously they were not religious seals!

Duncan was always active and on Sunday afternoons would drag me out for walks all around St. Andrews, which was to my benefit! He also included me in many of the most enjoyable adventures that I have ever had such as grouse beating and visiting islands, which I will tell about later.

He had his father's sense of humour and fun. When he finished his degree in St Andrews he and a distinguished friend presented the University Library a copy of their letters to the St. Andrews Citizen, the local newspaper. They carried on some amazing correspondence on such topics as sighting the great auk, a bird already extinct for a hundred years, the philosophy of Dr Hons, an idea for replacing the cobble stones in Market Street with fictitious tar Maccobble, because it would softer to ride ones bicycle on, and others. His final letter, written from Chicago the following year when he was doing a post-graduate fellowship in politics, brought fifty two replies. His letter said that he had been to some museum where the entrance drive was made up of sections of many famous roads – eg the Appian Way, the Boston Tea Trail and other equally ridiculous names and suggested that if they sold the cobble stones in Market Street to this museum they would probably get enough to pave it properly. Then he added that he had seen Dr Hons, had reminisced about St Andrews with him but sadly Dr Hons had recently died – hence the large number of bereavement letters, too many to be genuine. The St. Andrews Citizen had figured him out at last! A polite note from the Principal of the University told him that he should use either his correct name and address or false ones but not to mix them.

The next year he worked in shipyards on the Clyde, incongruously reading the Glasgow Herald while his colleagues poured over the Daily Express, News of the World, and other less erudite papers, and then in the steel mills in Sheffield so that he would get raw life experience before doing theology in Edinburgh. During his time in Edinurgh he worked in the poorer areas near Leith Walk with boys who were often delinquent. It was challenging but sometimes rewarding work. Subsequently he went to teach at Madras Christian College in India. After seven years he returned to be chaplain at Sussex University. I was on my way to visit him and his wife Margaret there when I met Spike Milligan's friend at Victoria Station. Later he returned to New College (Theology) in Edinburgh where he eventually became Principal. He had an outstanding career and was awarded Doctorates in Divinity at Glasgow and St Andrews Universities. His wife, Margaret, served for many years as a very enlightened and progressive minister to St. Margaret's Church in Edinburgh.

Duncan procured me a 1/6 (£2) share in a rowing boat which was tied up in the harbour. I had many happy trips in it. Once a friend and I took two girls out for a quick trip but found when we were at sea that the tide was still going out to an extremely low tide. It was four hours before we could enter the harbour again! On another occasion Duncan and I were out in the late evening and towards midnight the tide was still low but we re-entered the harbour. Unfortunately we became stuck on a sandbank in the middle – Duncan generously went overboard to push us off.

Although I am told by some of my colleagues that I was a bit shy and uncommunicative at first, I rapidly came to enjoy the social life at university – there were many clubs and social functions, Union hops (dances), the Celtic Society ceilidhs with country dancing, Afro-Asian Society and SCM meetings on Sunday evening which could occupy ones time. Girls also became of some interest although I followed the principle that there is safety in numbers until well into my second year.

The temptation not to work is great for young students so I resolved early on that I would do a quota of twenty hours study per week outside my fairly long hours in classes. To gain maximum benefit from my evenings at work I learnt to sleep for twenty minutes before dinner so that I would be more alert in the evening. It is an ability that has proved useful all my life. Social life reached a crescendo in second year when I seemed to attend Balls almost every week and on one occasion had two 21st birthday parties one evening followed by a Ball on the next. Cat naps were useful for survival on such occasions! Fortunately there were no degree examinations that year.

Much to my surprise I was elected as first year representative on the Bute Medical Society committee – I never understood how this happened as I do not remember displaying any feature which would make me stand out except that I came from the colonies and had done some national service. I was not on the committee in second year but was again elected as third year representative. We had interesting people come to speak to the Society each month but only three have survived in my memory – Roger Bannister, who ran the first sub four-minute mile; the first lady surgeon who struck me as a rather formidable lady, which she probably had been to survive; and Professor Ritchie, our professor of physiology. He spoke about the sensory area in the cortex of the brain. Only recently, at that time, had it been shown that some areas of the body were better represented in the brain than others. Those which are more sensitive such as the tongue and the pulp of the thumb have larger areas. Forty years later I returned to St Andrews and spoke to the same Society, only now the wine and cheese tasting received more prominence than the lecture on the promotional notices! Rather a sad reflection on modern society.

Hockey became a priority. During the first year I played for the United College (which was the St. Andrews half of the University) with occasional games in the University team. Then for the next four years I played regularly as right back for the University team. In my third and fourth years I was captain of hockey and also played for and captained the Scottish University team against the English and Irish Universities teams. That involved trips to Liverpool and Dublin. In addition we had a University tour to the North of England to play Manchester, Leeds, Sheffield and Newcastle. The highlights were staying in Durham Castle, then a University residence, and attending a dance at the Newcastle Union where I met several old school friends for the one and only time I ever saw them after school.

The following year we were Scottish University champions – there were only four universities then! We went to Belfast, travelling steerage on the overnight ferry. We lost to Queens University but the fellows saw their girls team playing- our fellows were so impressed that they decided that we should ask them for a social game which they accepted!! They were a good team, having the Hopkins sisters who both played for Ireland. One of them, Thelma was at that time the world high jump record holder at 5 feet 7 inches (167cms) – how things have changed. At that time the Fosbury flop, the technique used now, had not been invented and the best jumps

9.5. Ian Macfarlane using the Western role high jump technique at school in 1953.

were achieved with the western roll, and other less effective techniques.

Eight years later I found myself playing beside one of the Queens University players, Brian Lowry, in Vancouver. He became a geneticist. We went on to Dublin from Belfast where we played three matches, two of which we won. We lost to Trinity College Dublin, which had one of the best teams I played against while at University.

We had several overseas players mainly from Kenya. In fact we had enough East African students of all races to challenge the rest of the University. The only problem was that it snowed heavily the night before making the ground unplayable. Never to be put off we went down to the west sands (it was low tide) and marked a pitch out on the sand. At half time we moved along and marked out another so that we would have a smooth surface – to start with at least. Despite having four in the University team and a former University goal keeper we lost 5-1. At least it was a memorable occasion. After Kenya became independent in 1963 Mohamed Hyder became professor of zoology at Nairobi University, Khamis Jeneby joined the Foreign Office and represented Kenya at the United Nations and Duncan Ndegwa became the Governor of the Bank of Kenya. I lost touch with the others.

Tennis, my other main sport, was a summer game and as I usually had to study for my examinations during that term I rarely played competitively.

My achievements at hockey, which included a Blue, and the fact that I was at University for six years led me to prominence in the University Athletic Union where I became President in 1958-9. My name is recorded on the Presidents Board in the Sports Centre. Being President involved chairing the Athletic Union meetings, being on committees, representing St. Andrews on the Scottish Universities Sports Board and at the other Universities' Sports Union Balls as a guest. Fiona, my partner on those occasions was a science student who had half blues for fencing (foil) and athletics.

I participated in a number of less usual games. Carpet bowls were popular in our residence where there was plenty of space in the large lounges. So one day a group of us decided that we should play real bowls. We went to Kilburn Park and hired the bowls and special rubber shoes so that we would not damage the greens. In those days bowls was very definitely for the elderly. Anyway we had a good time and we did not have to dress in white as is customary in Australia!

Then I played croquet against the Staff. The only requirement for selection was to have played before. I think some of our team had very limited experience. Our opponents were very serious and competitive players. I remember one old fellow lying on his stomach as he lined up his next shot. Croquet is a game where one has to hit large hard balls through hoops with a mallet. It can be particularly vicious if someone near you decides to dispatch your ball to the other side of the ground. Strangely, we lost all the games!

I had been a first class shot in the Army so I tried for the shooting team but the range was indoors under lights. I found it difficult to see well enough with my glasses so I did not pursue that sport.

Our girls lacrosse team were the best in Scotland. The men's hockey team thought that we should challenge them at lacrosse. I knew a several of the team so the match was arranged. Our only hope was with the ball on the ground when we could push it. The girls did try to teach us how to catch and carry the ball in the cross but we did not master the skill adequately.

The captain of the lacrosse team was Margaret Lutley. Our paths crossed twice in later years – once in Chile where I met up with her briefly in Vina del Mar where she was teaching, and the second time through coincidence rather than in person. Margaret was born in China where her father had been a teacher. Over twenty years later my secretary, Pam, asked for a day off to meet her mother at the airport. She had been to China with a group to visit their old school at Cheefoo which, by strange coincidence turned out to be the school where Margaret's father had taught and also where two uncles of my brother in law had spent time. The daughter of one of them turned out to be the best friend of Pam's mother in England! Later we met Pam's mother and found out that she had worked with my father in law and his father. So many connections!

The first eight terms of the medical course at St. Andrews University in those days was spent in either St. Andrews (45students) or Dundee (28 students). After Second MB examinations we went to Dundee where the classes were combined for the remaining three years clinical training. The University was half in St Andrews (1200 students- Arts Science, medicine and theology) and half in Dundee where they had Engineering, Law and Dental faculties as well. In the 1970s, when university expansion was fashionable in Britain the University was split and after that the St. Andrews pre-clinical medical students went to Manchester to do their clinical studies.

I lived in Hamilton Hall, which had formally been the Grand Hotel and hence had beautiful Lounges and Dining Room with high ceilings. Some of the rooms had magnificent views out over the Old Course, the Royal and Ancient Golf Club or the sea but these were often large and shared by two students.

9.6. Hamilton Hall Men's Residence (right) and Royal and Ancient Golf Club overlooking the Old Course at St Andrews.

My first two years were in room 48, which looked out on the light well in the middle of the building. I then moved for my third year to room 73, which was on the fire escape. That was useful if one was out after the front door was locked at midnight but had the disadvantage that other late entrants also came through after midnight.

Eight others in our medical class lived in Hamilton Hall. Several of these have remained lifelong friends with whom I have been able to keep in contact. Bob Coulthard, became my first partner in practical classes – Physics.

9.7. Bob Coulthard

He came from County Durham and as they had relatively few university students he had a more generous grant that most other students. This enabled him to either run a little car or a scooter during our years in

Dundee which was a great help as we were usually in the same group in clinics and we shared lodgings in our final year. He was one of the top students in the year but eventually had to forego his original desire to do surgery and went for eighteen months on a cable laying ship off Brazil as ships doctor. He returned to Scotland with a Brazilian wife and took up psychiatry, later emigrating to Canada. While working in a provincial mental hospital he was asked to help in the criminal division which led him into Forensic Psychiatry. Later, he was head of the Clark Institute in Toronto, a leading centre in that field. In our year book the quotation about him was "that he always says that which creates the greatest stir" And he did. After a long cross examination in a multi rape case he said that he thought that rapists should be castrated. That caused a stir on television across North America that night!

9.8. James Forrester and his wife Carolyn at their son's wedding in 2001.

James Forrester was another top student who became a surgeon and eventually returned to settle in Dundee after some post-graduate years in San Francisco where he met his wife, Carolyn.

While there he undertook some important research on wound healing which showed that when a wound was re-sutured it healed more strongly, presumably because the fibroblasts which form the new healing cells had already been stimulated to grow before the second incision was made or dehiscence occurred. His father was the chief anaesthetist in Glasgow at the time and I had the privilege to meet him once in Madrid many years later after I myself had become an anaesthetist.

Years later when I visited James, he told me that his son, Andrew, was going to take a year off in the middle of his medical course and would be going to Australia. As Andrew and I were both driving to St. Andrews that afternoon I suggested that we should meet. I remember the occasion well because we met on a lay-by on the road near Guardbridge on the way to St. Andrews – anyone observing such a meeting could well be excused if they thought it looked rather suspicious as two cars arrived within a few minutes, the drivers emerge and engage in an intense conversation, return to their cars and drive off. It was also an unusual place to meet. In fact, it was an easy place to define and we knew it might be easier to meet there than find somewhere we could both easily park in St Andrews! We had the pleasure of having him to stay for a while some months later and he was able to get some benefit by accompanying me to the hospital. James was one of only four in the year of those still working who attended when we met for our Year's 40 year reunion. Later we had a sentimental journey back to St.Andrews for Andrew's wedding in the Chapel.

9.9. E.O.A.(Ernest) Bucknor from Nigeria.

Ernest Bucknor was a Nigerian whom we all felt was destined to become someone important in his country.

He was a politician and was treasurer of the Students Representative Council. He taught me something which proved very useful later in life when I became a member of many Hospital and anaesthesia related committees. It was how to win people with opposing ideas round to your point of view. The approach was always to recognize and make positive comments about good points in their arguments or their presentation before gradually working round to your point of view. Being complimentary to your opposition often defuses an otherwise very unpleasant situation. Ernie did reach a prominent position in the Nigerian Health Department. I met him 29 years later in Lagos where he took me to their Museum and introduced me to the sculptures of ancient Nigeria, many of them in copper – a history much further back than I had known about.

9.10. Tim Osafo from Ghana.

Tim Osafo was a Ghanaian who played hockey in the University team with me.

He was notable on the field as having boundless energy, using the heaviest stick (24ounces) of anyone I ever played with and not always using it gently. I met him once, quite by chance, in 1974 at Hammersmith Post Graduate Medical School in London where he was studying clinical Biochemistry. I lost touch with him after that but I met a Ghanaian in St Andrews during our 40 year reunion who knew him. He told me that he had migrated to Sweden.

Ivan Mannall became a paediatrician and practiced in Halifax. He was one of a group who lived in Newport and crossed on the ferry each day with me to Dundee during fourth year.

9.11. Ivan Mannall

He played hockey and obviously a little golf as the quote in our final year book about him was that "it is better to have golfed and lost than never to have golfed at all." He is now an addicted golfer!

Several times over the years I have visited Derrick Sapsford and his wife Vanessa who was a student at the same time. Derrick was a successful General Practitioner in Ashford, Kent. We last met in strange circumstances – for afternoon tea when they happened to be on holiday in Mauritius the same week as I was there teaching.

Another friend, Lachlan Mackenzie was not in residence with us as he was a native St. Andrean. He was tall, athletic and a javelin thrower. He went to work in New York. At 7am one Sunday morning, when I was interning in London, Ontario, I received a phone call to say that Dr. MacKenzie was there to see me. There were six Drs. MacKenzie at the Hospital so I was a bit puzzled which one this might be. It was none of them. Lachlan had decided the evening before to drive up from New York to see me and had driven overnight – several hundred miles! We had a wonderful day together and then he drove back. I was not surprised when he told me that he had written off two cars in the previous few months. I saw him at New York Airport three years later. We continued to write occasionally until about twenty years ago he sent me a card from the Safari Club in Nanyuki in Kenya which said "Don't know why you left here. Regards Lachlan". He didn't say why he was there, what he was doing and gave no address. For years I wondered what had become of him, even asking someone to try to track him down in New York through the phone book or the medical registry. He had disappeared out of my life. I did not even know if he was still alive. I related these stories when I spoke about various absent friends at our Forty Year reunion in 2000. Shortly afterwards one of our group met an older man in the lift who was at a simultaneous fifty year Reunion. When told that our colleague was there for the Forty Year Medical reunion he said that his brother was in that year. Coincidence, coincidence – it was Lachlan's brother who was able to give us his address. He is now a retired otolaryngologist /head and neck surgeon. And so contact has resumed after all these years.

The quota for girls then was 25% of the year. Now there are a much higher proportion of females. I went out with one of them, a small, dark haired, blue eyed girl called Elizabeth Jamieson, on and off for over two years. She was from a medical family. Her father, uncle, brothers and cousin were all General Practitioners near Glasgow. She left St. Andrews at the end of my third year and transferred to physiotherapy in Glasgow. I only saw her occasionally after that.

St. Andrews was a small town so we could easily walk to classes. Most of these were held in the Bute Medical Building. Many of the buildings in the old part of town were built of stones taken from the Cathedral ruins such as the one shown in College Street.

9.12. Bute Medical Building.

After our second MB examinations we moved to Dundee for our clinical training. For the summer term of third year we traveled by train from St Andrews. I was fortunate in having a friend in final year, Andrew McAdam, who arranged for me to take over his lodgings in Newport on Tay. My landlady was Lilian Scott, who was an elderly, petite spinster who had lodged medical students for many years. She was a kindly lady who treated all her students over the years as if they were family – many of them continued to visit her when in the area. She recounted the tale told to her by her father of the Tay Bridge disaster in 1879 when part of the railway bridge collapsed. She had the upstairs and basement of a large house that had been divided. Newport was across the Tay River from Dundee. As this was before the road bridge was built we traveled by ferry. This was a pleasant means of transport except when the cold winter winds were blowing. The trip took a variable time depending on the tide as there were sandbanks in the river. At low tide we were always a few minutes late for lectures. Four of us stayed in Newport – Ivan Mannall and John

Grainger in a "bunk"(lodgings) and Bob Coulthard in the pub near the ferry.

In fifth year I shared a bunk (as lodgings were called) with James Forrester. We lived in relative luxury with Rev Donaldson, a Congregational minister, his rather humourless, austere, large hypothyroid wife and their long time maid, Lizzie. They lived in a large manse in Douglas Terrace, very close to the Dundee Royal Infirmary. (C8.7) I had a large bedroom and a study to myself. They had had students since after the war when accommodation was in short supply. People did not have washing machines then. I can remember washing my clothes with a corrugated washboard which was very effective at getting the dirt out. Last time I saw one someone was using it as a "not so" musical instrument rattling out sound on it with thimbles on his fingers.

Mr Donaldson was a wonderful man with a mischievous sense of humour and a great understanding of human nature. By making outlandish comments he could break down barriers so that he could open communication with anybody. I learnt a great deal from him about people and how to deal with different types. For instance, when he met a Catholic who seemed rather reticent about meeting a Congregational minister he would ask why the Pope wears red socks? I don't think he did! He regaled us with many stories such the one about the student who had left his wardrobe full of empty whisky bottles when he left them. He was still wondering whether the fellow had drunk them or did it as a joke, because he had come home drunk one night.

We often made reference to a certain professor, who later became Dean of another Medical School, despite having been declared redundant in the Blood Transfusion service during the war. Mr Donaldson engineered a consultation with him just to find out first hand what this man was like!

I think the many discussions I had with James about his father's field, anaesthetics, may have contributed to my developing an interest in this specialty. It was with regret that I had leave Douglas Terrace at the end of the year because Mr Donaldson retired and left Dundee.

I moved to Broughty Ferry and shared with Bob Coulthard for our final year. We lived with Dr Chalmers, his Flemish wife and their four children in Fort Street House. It was large and we lived in style sharing a bedroom and a large study. He was an elderly General

Practitioner (69 years) who retired the next year. It was also a great experience and I learnt much from him about his work and his patients. On one particularly bad winter's day when there had been a heavy snowfall I went on his round with him in case he became stuck. In those days doctors still did home visits.

He had a fascinating photograph album with pictures taken by his uncle who had been the skipper on the first lake boat on Lake Nyasa (now Malawi). This steamer was shipped out to Beira in pieces and transported overland to the Lake where it was assembled, long before the advent of huge transportation trucks. What incredible achievements helped to open Africa up in the early years of the twentieth century. Imagine carrying sheets of steel all that distance.

Mrs. Chalmers had a sense of humour and enjoyed a good laugh. We certainly had one when we went with her to see a film, The Bridal Path, set in the western isles and around Oban. A young islander was very fond of his cousin but when the local minister came back from the mainland denouncing consanguinity he was told to go to the mainland to look for a wife. After many amusing scrapes, including being mistaken as a salmon poacher, he returned home without one to be told that actually his mother's husband had been at sea when he was conceived so his girl really was not his cousin!

It was during a stormy night that winter that we were awoken by the lifeboat siren sounding – it had to go on a rescue mission for a boat in distress. It never came back. All those brave men gave their lives to help others. It was a national tragedy. The lifeboat house was at the end of the street so we felt particularly close to the sad event. The scene of an old man smoking his pipe on the cover is across the road from the lifeboat house.

These great years were enhanced by some wonderful vacation activities. My medical course was hard work for me but in the long run I think that because I had to struggle a bit it has helped me to achieve what I have in later life, particularly as a teacher.

Chapter 10

Learning to be a Doctor

My academic career was not distinguished but, with some good fortune, I did pass all my degree examinations (the ones that count) first time. This, in itself, was an achievement as it was only managed by a quarter of the class. When I qualified I certainly never thought that I would become a specialist – that was for the bright people! I thought I would end up as a General Practitioner in the country.

My progress seemed to be a mixture of disasters and close shaves, but finally just making it each time when it really counted. In Botany only a few of us had to do an oral examination. The opening comment by my examiner was, "I don't know why you are having to do this." Obviously I created a better impression in the paper than I had done in class.

In second year I struggled with Anatomy and Physiology, which included biochemistry that was poorly taught or I found boring. One term, in Anatomy, I made a big effort to swat at the end and stayed up too late so that when I went to the oral examination with Professor Walmsley, a man with a beady eye that looked right through one – or so we felt – I knew the answers but couldn't express them. I was dumb. It was very embarrassing. I was, and still am, astounded by the sequel. He called me into his office a couple of days later and said he thought that I had been working too hard and that I should buy a fishing rod and go up into the Highlands to relax and do some fishing! What a wise man. How did he know? He was a great embryologist. Some years later I was able to repay his remarkable gesture.

The end of second year Physiology was also a disaster. One question was on ketosis, a metabolic derangement that can occur in diabetes. I could not remember what it was so ended up with only 25%. Threats were issued to a number of us who performed poorly and we had to write an essay over the summer on the physiology of human survival, a topic which fascinated me then and ever since. I am still amazed how some people survive high altitudes, low oxygen, very low temperatures, starvation and extremes of weather.

A visit to Perth Royal Infirmary early in third year was a day of enlightenment. Until then I could not understand what endocrinology was about. It is the study of hormones and how they adjust our bodily functions to maintain a very fine balance. On this occasion they sat three ladies in a row – a hyperthyroid lady (overactive gland – agitated, overactive metabolism and rapid heart rate, etc), a hypothyroid patient (under-active gland resulting in a low metabolism, a slowing down of many body functions, obesity and mental dullness) and a normal student. They represented the range of *thyroid* gland function. Suddenly I understood. Later, I worked in an endocrinology unit and became fascinated by the subject. Finally, when I was studying for my post graduate examinations I was taught by two brilliant physiology teachers from Melbourne University – Professor Doug Coates and Dr Kenny who both presented the subject with great clarity. I eventually went on to teach anaesthetists about the subject. Frank Netter, an artist who illustrated the Ciba Symposia with his brilliant, clear explanatory diagrams provided me with visual aids which made the subject easy to understand and remember.

These glands orchestrate the functions of the various organs in the body. An area in the brain called the hypothalamus has many vital control centres which communicate. The thyroid hormone levels, for example, are sensed there and thyroid stimulating hormone releasing factor (TSHRF) is released which then acts on the anterior pituitary gland situated in a small cavity in the base of the skull. The anterior pituitary gland is the control centre for the secretion of several endocrine glands, among them the thyroid. It produces just the right amount of thyroid stimulating hormone (TSH), which is carried in the blood to the thyroid gland in the neck, to cause the release of the appropriate amount of thyroid hormones to help maintain the correct metabolic rate and cell function. This is called a negative feed back loop because when the thyroid hormones levels rise the TSH decreases so that a constant level is achieved. The metabolic rate is related to the amount of oxygen the body consumes. The more that is required the more the oxygen that has to be taken up by the lungs and pumped around the body by the heart. Hence the volume of each breath, the rate of breathing, the heart rate and volume of blood pumped each beat depends on the oxygen requirement in the cells. Many other factors affect metabolic rate such as exercise, which increases it, and temperature. Temperature also has control centres in the hypothalamus which can interact with the thyroid control systems in the long term adaptation to hot or cold environments. All these types of interplay, which make the body function normally, are fascinating, but I did not really appreciate them until long after university days when I was doing post graduate studies. I am now sure that many medical students the world over have suffered by not having teachers who explained how physiology applied to clinical situations.

I passed my second MB with help of some of my colleagues who showed me their previous anatomy papers. It became apparent that they included material that I had considered too peripheral to be relevant and had not included in my answers. In Physiology I was the only one of about ten who did not gain exemption from the practical exam who passed.

The struggle continued in Dundee with pharmacology, pathology and bacteriology in fourth year. The new drugs which we learnt about were the first oral diuretic (drugs which enhance urine production) and the first drugs to lower blood pressure in hypertension such as the ganglion blockers which have long since been discarded. The fundamental concept of receptors and the chemical transmitters that act on them such as nor adrenaline, acetyl choline and dopamine, which is a key to understanding many drug actions, was just developing. Many drugs work by increasing or decreasing the neurotransmitter activity. This led to huge advances in pharmacology and drug treatment. Half a century later this seems so elementary compared to the detailed information of mechanisms of drug action we have now.

Our Pathology professor, Lendrum, came from an incredible stable of 28 professors trained by the famous Robert Muir in Glasgow. He was a rabid Scot and referred to England as the Southern Peninsula – probably correctly in geological terms as the oldest part of Britain is the north west of Scotland! Thirty three per cent in May Pathology exams was not encouraging but, as I had to explain to my examiners in the degree exam in June when I obviously did much better, the questions asked then were areas that I had not yet revised.

I was in fear and trembling before my Bacteriology exam but again it seemed that I was "supposed" to pass. Our old Professor, Willie Tulloch, was a great character. Having established that the question I had not done on the paper was one in which they hoped the students would discuss malaria I immediately responded to it with enthusiasm. When I knew that my time was nearly up I told them that I had suffered from malaria on two occasions. "You crook, you crook! Tulloch shouted beating his hand on the desk! Fortunately his co-examiner came to my rescue and asked what type of malaria I had suffered from. Then the bell went and I was saved. I passed and so two bouts of malaria had some benefit, although time seemed to stand almost still when my temperature reached 104°F (41°C). I felt utterly miserable. Some good comes out of most bad situations!

I learnt best by seeing and doing things. Listening to someone talking at me did not make as great an impression. I was fortunate to be able to gain a variety of good clinical experience.

I read William Osler's biography at some stage. He was regarded as one of the greatest physicians of the late nineteenth and early twentieth centuries. He worked at McGill University in Montreal, then Philadelphia, Johns Hopkins in Baltimore and then Oxford. He stressed the importance of pathology and of seeing patients when learning to become a doctor. I certainly agreed and gained my most useful learning experience doing locums in my later years for the resident doctors when they went on holidays. I also attended autopsies. In the summer of my fourth year I went home to Kenya and worked with my father and then in fifth year went to Labrador to work with the Grenfell mission at North West River and on their boat, the Maraval. These two summer experiences enhanced my clinical experience enormously.

East Fortune was a tuberculosis sanatorium near North Berwick. In my fourth year I had a job there as an orderly for part of three consecutive holidays beginning in the summer following third year. I learnt many useful, basic skills like how to wash and feed patients, give injections, clean bathes and toilets but probably the most useful was learning to talk with all sorts of different people. I also learnt to appreciate the role that nurses played which was invaluable later because I respected them for what they do. So many young and not so young doctors have lorded it over them. This has resulted in nurses respecting doctors less and what should be a harmonious team caring for the sick, functions less effectively.

Respecting people, whatever their position in the hospital is important. To greet them and thank them when they help gives them a boost and makes them happy. They respond better, work better and go the extra mile willingly if well treated.

I saw a few operations. One was a thoracoplasty aimed to collapse the ribs and chest wall so that the underlying heavily infected lung would be immobilised.

It was an exciting time when I arrived at East Fortune as effective treatment for tuberculosis had just become available with streptomycin, isoniazid and PAS. Tuberculosis was soon being defeated and disappearing – it was a disease that had gradually reduced thousands of people to skeletons as they coughed their lungs "out" before finally succumbing, often at a young age. The worst job I had was making cardboard cups for their sputum and then collecting them for incineration each day. By Christmas, when I returned, the hospital was already converting to a geriatric centre which provided me with some different, useful experience.

I well remember an old Mr Guthrie from Fife. He had been a fisherman from St. Monance, one of the delightful fishing communities along that coast. He had a fairly severe stroke and was hunched up, not able to talk. Watching different nurses washing and feeding him showed me that even someone who did not seem able to communicate verbally still had feelings. One of the nurses was a rough, harsh girl. One could see in his eyes that he resented this and was suffering unnecessarily. What a difference when a gentle, kindly soul was looking after him. He could not even smile but the eyes could tell that he appreciated her tender care. These are things that are not really taught to medical students and, nowadays, maybe not even to nurses studying in colleges.

I remember another old man who I had to bath and encourage to eat. His wife had recently died. I was very surprised to arrive one morning to find that he had just died. I think now that he just decided it was time and gave up living. Some people are lucky enough to be able to do that.

I went home to Kenya to work with my father at Tumutumu for the summer at the end of my fourth year. During that time I had the good fortune to be allowed to do the deliveries required as part of our obstetric training as medical students. It was a pleasant way to do it as they called me mainly when there were interesting cases at times that suited me. I saw twins, breech deliveries with the bottom coming first, babies coming the wrong way round, a girl with secondary syphilis. Many of the patients had had female circumcision or clitorectomy. It was a tribal custom but seemed to make little sense. In recent years there has been a movement to stop it in places where it is still practiced.

I was also introduced to anaesthesia by Epafara, one of the medical assistants who helped my father. The patients were rapidly induced by spraying ethyl chloride on a Schimmelbusch (gauze covered) mask. Anaesthesia was maintained by Trilene – ether delivered by draw-over vapourisers.

During that holiday we also had a good trip to Marsabit in the Northern Frontier. We went round Mt Kenya, descending from over 2000m to less than 500 at Buffalo Springs and Isiolo. Here the vegetation becomes sparse scrub before one reaches the desert. Northwards we passed some fine ranges of hills such as the Matthews Range. (C19.1) We passed Samburus with their herds of cattle and goats further decimating the land. They also had donkeys carrying the stick frames for their huts as they are nomadic. (C19.2) From time to time we would pass a herd of camels. Eventually we reached Marsabit which is an old volcano. In the crater was beautiful and aptly named Paradise Lake. There was plenty of game to be seen including Ahmed, a big elephant with huge tusks.

There was an entertaining story about the District commissioner who lived in Marsabit for many years. He used to go to Nairobi once a year. He had a suit which he placed in a 4 gallon paraffin tin when he returned and soldered it shut for another year – to keep the white ants from destroying it. They are one of the trials that can be encountered in Kenya. They build earthen tunnels to travel in. They have voracious appetites, even for books, which they can damage significantly.

It was wonderful to have had that time working with my father as after the age of nine I probably had less than three years with him in all. Despite that we maintained a regular weekly communication by mail. Each Sunday night he wrote to me, my siblings and his family in Scotland and I did likewise. I continued writing my mother regularly too as she also wrote until she was very old – in her eighties.

During my last two years I did several locums for the junior doctors when they went on holidays. During a gynaecology one I attended some sessions in the operating theatre. Not long before a patient had died during an anaesthetic so there was some reluctance by one of the patients to have a sterilization under anaesthetic. It was performed under hypnosis after several sessions preparing the patient to be hypnotised. It is the only time I ever saw this done. The major problem is ensuring that the patient is susceptible to hypnosis (not everyone is) and then practising to ensure that they are deeply hypnotised when the operation is performed. This locum proved invaluable experience and also saved the day when I sat my final examinations.

I did several other locums. Two were in paediatrics where I first developed my interest in children. Among my early patients were David, a little blue boy of five who had Fallot's Tetralogy. This is a condition where there is a hole between the ventricles, the chambers of the heart that pump the blood through the lungs or around the body. There is also a narrowing to the artery going to the lungs so more of the blood is pumped into the aorta and misses the lungs and is therefore not oxygenated. Our pink blood is due to it being well supplied with oxygen while passing through the lungs, otherwise it stays blue. Nothing could be done in Dundee at that time. Through the course of my career I have seen operations developed that allowed more blood to pass into the lungs allowing it to become adequately oxygenated, and then in the 1970s complete repair of this defect could be performed. David was not so lucky.

Mary was a lovely little four year old who did not mind having her finger pricked for blood tests which was unusual. They thought she had juvenile arthritis and put her on a course of cortisone. Two days after they stopped it I had to check her blood count. We had to do this ourselves – there were no laboratory with automatic counters then. I found her white cell count was almost 100000 instead of 5000. The consultant, who later became professor in Aberdeen, doubted my finding and thought that I had made an error. I repeated it and when I showed him the slide he acknowledged that I was correct. Poor little Mary had leukaemia for which there was no treatment then. Now she would have a good chance of survival from this dreadful disease which also took my sister in law that I was never to know.

Another 10 year old lad had cystic fibrosis, a disease which affected the gut but usually caused an early demise through its lung involvement. He was in the last stages of the disease already whereas today they usually reach adulthood and the outlook continues to improve.

At Easter I went to Inverness to work in the orthopaedic casualty department at Raigmore Hospital – it was the centre for the north of Scotland. There I learnt to apply plasters to broken limbs – I was taught by the nursing sister in charge who told me that she was the best in the north of Scotland. Maybe she was as I have always prided myself in my plastering technique!

We had a very rare and sad case of a man who was digging a ditch when the side caved in and broke his leg. He developed a fat embolism. This is a condition where fat from the bone marrow in long bones in released into the blood and is carried round to vital organs such as the lung, and sometimes the heart and brain leading to bad, and in this case, fatal consequences.

The final two locums were a week each in a general medical ward which was not too busy but each patient who was admitted had interesting medical problems. The consultant in charge was an old fashioned doctor who made one make a clinical diagnosis and did not allow one to order tests or x rays unless there was a clinical indication that something abnormal would be confirmed. Simple tests one could do in the ward. Although this is not accepted practice today it certainly made us good clinicians.

One old lady had a pneumothorax, a condition where a lung collapses. This leads to acute difficulty with breathing and is relieved by putting a drainage tube into the chest between the ribs. The only problem was that I had never seen this done so I had to read up my book and then find the necessary tubing and bottle for an underwater drain. Without the latter this problem could not be solved as air would still enter the chest. The tube is inserted between two ribs allowing air out if it is under pressure. The other end is then placed under water which forms a one way valve allowing air to come out but not to enter the chest. The job was accomplished successfully and the patient recovered.

After that I left for my next adventure – to work for the summer in Labrador on the north east coast of Canada, a tale which I recount later.

When I returned for my final year I decided that my first priority was to pass my finals so I retired from most social activities to study. My girl friend, Fiona, had moved to Aberdeen to work as a biochemist and so our relationship drifted apart as I could not afford to travel frequently. It was sad in a way, as she was a lovely girl. We had both been grousebeaters. That year I played hockey for the Queens College team in Dundee which played more locally and involved much less travelling.

I had to decide what I would do when I qualified. Medical students do not have to make many decisions about their course as other students do because the course in clearly defined. After graduation the big decisions begin. The choice of early jobs may determine one's future. I only expected to become a General Practitioner as my academic results were not outstanding.

I was offered the job as doctor on a St Andrews University expedition to Greenland which appealed to me after my experiences in Labrador the previous summer. Eventually I decided, with great regret, not to accept that offer because it would mean starting my internship at a time when most good jobs would not be available and secondly because I would not have been a registered doctor.

I had some friends who went to intern in Canada so I wrote to the hospitals where they had worked and also to the Royal Jubilee hospital in Victoria BC. St Johns, Newfoundland would pay $250 per month and a return fare on completion of the year but at that time it was not a University Hospital. Victoria Hospital, London, Ontario was a teaching hospital of the University of Western Ontario. They paid $145 per month and would advance my fare to be repaid from my salary. Royal Jubilee was ruled out because they would advance only $300 which was not enough to get there and I did not have the balance of the fare. So I selected London, Ontario.

Having decided to emigrate to Canada and not knowing where life would lead me and when I would see my parents again I decided to fly home to Kenya for the Easter holidays. My parents lent me the fare which I repaid when I was working. It was to be my last stay at Tumutumu. I had an interesting time helping my father at his hospital some of the time.

Unfortunately I was bitten on the arm and developed a big abscess which was treated with penicillin and tetracycline. Eventually it burst and drained pus. On my flight back to Britain we stopped at Khartoum where I saw a school classmate at the airport – that was possible in those days. Then a stop in Zurich where I had a drink of apple juice for the first time – we were served drinks in the waiting lounge during the stops. After that I began to feel itchy – I wondered if I was allergic to the apple juice. It gradually became worse. Fortunately I had arranged to stay with an aunt in London overnight. The itching became worse. Had I picked up a flea or something like that? When I arrived at my aunts I decided to have a bath and drown any such creature. To my horror, when I removed my clothes I found that I was covered with urticaria. I was taken to a doctor who gave me an antihistamine. During the night I became delirious so I was taken to hospital at St. Marys, Paddington where I was given adrenaline with some relief and ended up in hospital for two days, only six weeks before my finals – panic! Anyway I passed them much to my relief, especially after the fiasco of my final oral.

Midwifery (obstetrics and gynaecology) was my last exam. I was due to leave for Canada the next week so that it was vital that I passed my finals. We had our clinical examination in the morning. There were two external examiners and normally each student met one in the clinical and the other in the oral. I arrived at 2pm for my oral to be told that they had made a scheduling error – I would have had the same person examine me in both so they had reorganised the schedule. I would now be the last candidate, on at 5.50pm. That was a disaster. It was not worth going home and back again so I stayed around growing more and more fatigued as I watched my colleagues come and go. By 6pm I felt like a zombie! I went in to the oral and was asked quite straightforward questions. I realised that I knew the answers but I could not produce them. Disaster! I might fail and not be able to catch the ship to Canada. What a disaster! I left to find it was pouring with rain. As I walked round the corner to the bus stop the bus went by. More misery! Another ten minutes waiting in the rain. I had to change buses in the city centre and catch one to Broughty Ferry, about 8km out of town. As I left the first bus I saw the Broughty Ferry bus leave. Another fifteen minute delay. By the time I reached home I was totally despondent and in no mood to go to our Final year dinner. It had been one of the worst afternoons of my life. My friend, Bob Coulthard persuaded me to cheer up – he would wait for me and drive me in. And so I went and the next day I was greatly relieved to find that I had passed. I think Professor Walker gave me credit for the locums that I had done and considered my adverse circumstances.

I was luckier than a former brilliant student who failed. His colleagues were hostile at the injustice and organised for him to leave Dundee in a mock funeral. A large crowd followed the cortege to the station to see him off. He passed the resits but never again graced the University. This was sad as he became the pre-eminent authority on the eye producing Stewart Duke–Elder's fifteen volumes on that subject, probably one of the greatest individual medical works ever written. I well remember when he visited us at Tumutumu when I was a boy. He was a man with a mischievous twinkle in his eyes.

I had a few days before leaving Scotland after my finals during which Bob Coulthard and I went for a trip on his scooter to farewell my relatives in the north. I could not wait for my graduation as I was already late for my job in London – a pattern that continued for the rest of my life. I have only started one job on time since graduating and doing so, foreshortened my last holiday with my father. I regretted it but I could not have known that at the time. The next time I saw him was a few hours before he died two years later when he could barely communicate any longer.

I spent my last night in Scotland visiting my relatives in Stirling. Elizabeth, with whom I had been friendly in St. Andrews, came to see me briefly before I left. She was completing her physiotherapy training and not long after became engaged. I sailed on the Empress of France on June 18th. The voyage to Montreal took almost a week. I reached my destination with only about £7 to start the next phase of my life – my professional life as a doctor, which is mostly recorded in my medical memoirs – *Catalyst*. But there are many other interesting experiences to relate in this volume.

Chapter 11

Vacation Activities in the Highlands and Islands

During my university vacations I often visited my grandmother in the north of Scotland until she died in 1958, aged 85. She was a wonderful old lady who lived in Ardival cottage (C5.1) overlooking Strathpeffer with the golf course and Ben Wyvis beyond rising to a little over 1000m. (C5.2) In winter it is covered with snow and in the summer with open grass and heather. My grandmother's cottage was compact and had an open grate stove in the kitchen.

There were two narrow staircases up to the bedrooms. I remember admiring the board in my grandmother's room on which hung all my uncles' shinty and shooting medals. They were good sportsmen. The toilet was outside. It was a bitterly cold place to visit in winter, especially if it was snowing, raining or the wind was blowing. I have to admit to some youthful sloth in winter when it was much more appealing to stay in the warmth of the bed until late morning when sometimes the sun came up. During the warmer months the garden was a picture of beautiful flowers tidily arranged in their beds. Many tourists would stop to admire it when walking up the hill. My aunt lived with my grandmother and so I continued to visit after my grandmother's death. Strathpeffer was the home of the Macmasters and I have always had an affinity towards it. (C5.3&4)

11.1. Uncle Ken Macmaster with my mother on her 90th birthday, Uncle Roy's wife Ishbel, my cousin David Macmaster and my daughter, Catherine.

I had three uncles living in the district. Ken was a quiet, well respected man.

He had a significant influence on me as I spent quite a bit of time with him. He was a joiner and was

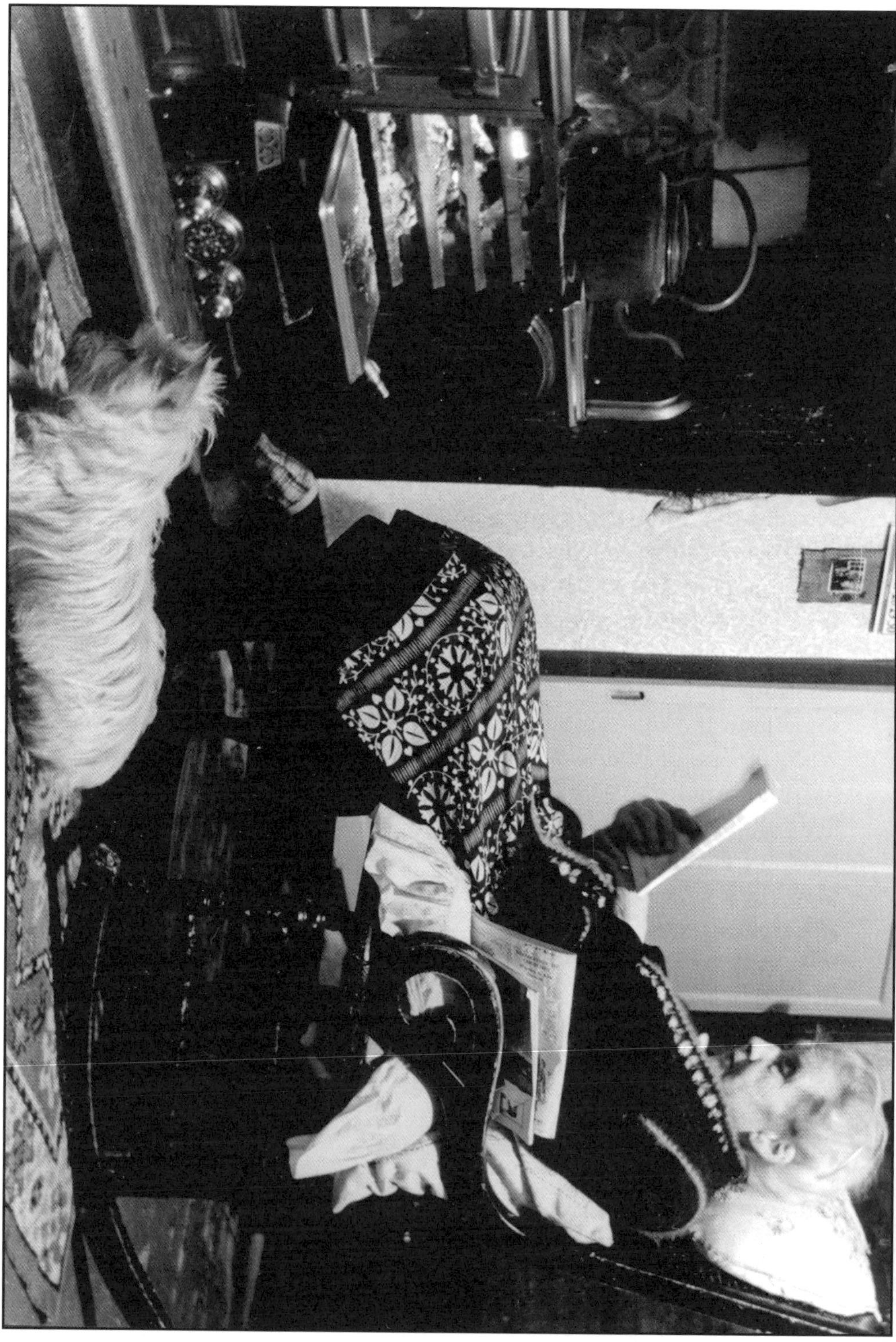

Opposite: 11.2. My grandmother by the fireside in her kitchen – 1957.

well respected for his carefully done carpentry. He used to say to me "that a job that is worth doing is worth doing well." One lady proudly showed me the kitchen he had built for her with revolving shelves in the corners so that space was not wasted, a slot under the cupboards below the bench so she could slide he feet under and so get nearer the bench as she was a small lady. He was a leading sporting figure in the community carrying on the family involvement in organizing the Strathpeffer Highland Games which are held on the second Saturday in August each year and differed from most others by having horse races as well as the dancing, bagpiping and athletic events such as tossing the caber. He was also a legend in the Highlands as a shinty player, administrator and coach. He continued coaching Fodderty schoolboys until he was over 80. It amused me when he and his brother Roy played golf that they often did not even take their jackets off to play.

Roy worked in an engineering plant at Muir of Ord and lived in Dingwall. His wife, Ishbel, outlived him by many years. (11.2) She is one of the kindest people that I have known and had an encyclopaedic knowledge of who was who in the district. She has celebrated her ninetieth birthday.

Don was affected by gas in the First War and was advised to have an outside job because his lungs were weak. He was a postman and a dedicated and enthusiastic gardener who lived until 23 days short of a century. He was the classic example of the contented gardener – they do not become depressed. At one stage after his wife died he lived in a little flat on his own in town in Dingwall and his mind began to wander. After he went to a retirement home with a big garden in which he could work his mental acuity returned so that he was still alert until he died.

I was also expected to visit my Grandmother and aunt in Stirling. That was not so enjoyable although they were kind enough to me. In the north men were not allowed to do kitchen duties such as washing up. In Stirling any visitor was expected to spend time in the scullery washing up. Can you imagine having a separate little room or alcove just for washing dishes? The misery was increased in winter by it being cold and lonely. I had to wash up while the ladies played bridge in the lounge. The house did not have central heating. The Scots did not go in for that much. The bed I slept in was like a board and cold so all in all the result was that my visits were usually just long enough to fulfil my duty.

My father's brother died with leukaemia when he was about 35. His wife and son, Alastair who was 6 weeks older than I, also lived in Stirling and provided some alternative company.

I had some wonderful vacation experiences, mostly in Scotland apart from a couple of sojourns to London, including Wimbledon, and to the South West of England, in 1955 with my sister Catherine and her husband, Bob Polhill and in 1956 with Monty and his wife Barbara. The traffic, even then, amazed me. We passed about one bus a mile between St Ives and Lands End on the narrow roads of the time! I saw some great players at Wimbledon – Art Larsen playing Gardner Mulloy who played in the US Open championships until age precluded him at 45, Neale Fraser who won Wimbledon later and became Australian Davis Cup captain for many years, and Jean Borotra, one of the four French musketeers from the 1920s playing mixed doubles at 53.

During my first Christmas vacation I delivered the Christmas mail in Strathpeffer. Imagine waking in the dark with snow outside. This is hard in most places where I have lived. Some mornings it was actually snowing! Although my aunt was up before me and had started the fire in the kitchen the house was still cold. The only inducement to get up was that I had to go to work. I would take my clothes into bed to warm them before putting them on. Breakfast and then down the hill and through the village to the Post Office by 8.30am. At least it was warm in there but it was still dark outside. The parcels had to be sorted into piles for each part of the village. Delivering them was not an easy task because there are very few streets with names (most of the houses are individually named) and the village had some quite steep hills to climb. Fortunately there were two of us. My colleague was a local and knew the names of the houses and who lived in them. I soon learnt many of them. In addition there were so many parcels to deliver that we took a sledge to carry them. I soon worked out that it was a good idea to reach my uncle's house at one end of Strathpeffer in the mid morning so we could have a cup of tea and warm up beside the fire! I was pleased with my pay – three pounds seven shillings and sixpence a week – 1.3% of my annual allowance. For some reason people coming from the tropics to cold places did not seem to feel the cold for the first couple of winters as much as locals. Thank goodness!

11.3. Campbell's croft at Loch Ussie.

Sometimes when I was at Strathpeffer I would hike through the wood and over the hill to Loch Ussie in the next valley to visit an old couple who lived in a croft. These are small holdings in the Highlands with a few fields where a few sheep or sometimes cows are kept and crops such as turnips, potatoes or corn may be grown in the warmer months. The houses are usually very solid stone ones with thick walls, small rooms with little windows, and sometimes they had an upstairs. They were often painted white and usually had grey slate roofs. Often the hearth was open like it was in my grandmothers. Kenny and Becky Campbell were a great couple and always gave me a cup of tea when I visited. Their croft was beside Loch Ussie. It had a nice unmade track bordered by trees leading to the house. The accompanying photograph conveys the wintery feeling on the path over. (11.4)

Sometimes there would be snow but regardless of the time of year it was a good walk and always ended with a warm welcome.

During the Easter vacation in 1955, Duncan Forrester organized a party to visit the Isle of May in the Firth of Forth for a week to ring birds as part of a migration study. There were five of us students and a very earnest schoolboy from Edinburgh who took his ornithology very seriously. We sailed from Pittenweem, one of the delightful harbours on the east Fife coast. (C8.4) The island was only about 8km away. We landed in a relatively protected alcove on the west side of the island.

11.4. Path over to Loch Ussie in winter.

11.5. Isle of May landing.

The Isle of May is rocky, with cliffs and stacks on the east side sloping down to a rocky coast on the west. It has the oldest lighthouse in Scotland. The modern lighthouse is a large rectangular building with a light tower on top situated on high ground in the middle of the island. There are ancient ruins and it was said that in old times pirates occupied the island – they lit fires strategically on it to attract ships hoping that they would run aground. There were remains of several wrecked ships but they may have been more recent.

11.6. Cliffs on the east side of the island.

Our accommodation was in a white building like a small light-house on the north coast. It was heated with a coal fire. One day it was very warm for that time of year – probably 15°C! Some of us decided to go over to the landing stage and maybe have a dip. It was certainly the coldest swim I have ever had – late March in the cold North Sea is not warm! George and Mac debated whether they would swim. Eventually George said he would go if Mac joined him. So they began stripping. Funnily, George became slower and slower than Mac. Then his evil plan became apparent. As soon as Mac was undressed George pushed him into the sea and then grabbed his clothes and ran back to our abode.

11.7. The lighthouses. The smaller building was the oldest lighthouse in Scotland.

Seals could be seen on the west coast – they seemed to enjoy the sound of whistling and would come close and listen for long periods. It was intriguing to sit and watch their roundish heads bobbing above the surface. The east coast seals differed from those on the west coast which had a more pointed snout. Occasionally from a distance we would see them basking on the low lying rocks.

There were crevices in the rocks and gaps in the cliffs where the big waves would come rolling in. I watched them with fascination and was rewarded by seeing the breakers crashing into the vacated hollow left by the previous wave receding. Sometimes this was like an explosion with water flying in all directions in the midst of thunderous noise. One of these I succeeded in photographing. The result looked like an exploding bomb.

11.8. Exploding wave.

We were there for a purpose, as Duncan reminded us each morning – it was to flag passing birds into a large netting tunnel which narrowed into a small opening into a box with a glass front. The idea of the glass was to not to frighten the bird before it was in the box. Once there we could remove the bird and place a ring around its ankle with identification and a number so that if it was picked up again its migration could be tracked. Sometimes the duration of its flight could also be calculated. Some birds migrate incredible distances each year. For instance, mutton birds which breed in Australia migrate up to Siberia and back each year. We had to record all the birds to which we applied rings and also any that arrived already wearing rings. Unfortunately, one blackbird flew in at high speed, crashed into the glass and broke its neck.

The days passed pleasantly and we had an enjoyable week on an interesting island. It was the first of several fascinating trips with Duncan, which were mainly to study birds.

The Outer Hebrides – they were enchanted, remote islands where few people visited. Mingulay and Berneray are the two southernmost islands of the group. These were the next islands on Duncan's agenda. Would I go with him at the end of June? How could I refuse when I had nothing more pressing to do? We took the train to Oban and boarded MacBrayne's steamer to the isles. Steaming out of Oban, passing the magnificent Victorian houses on the Esplanade with McCaig's Folly on the hill behind, through between the green islands to Tobermory in Mull was beautiful. It was a hive of activity there. A Spanish galleon was said to have sunk in the harbour centuries ago with gold bullion on board. Many attempts had been made to find it and another was in progress. It always seemed rather romantic to be looking for gold on a sunken Spanish galleon – I do not know if they ever found it but I suppose it kept some divers in profitable employment! The next stops were at Tiree and Coll, two long flat islands – there was no harbour so boats came out to meet us to collect passengers, mail and provisions. A few more hours passed before we sailed into the bay with Kismaul Castle and the Castlebay dock on Barra, the main island of the southern group in the Outer Hebrides. We disembarked. Duncan negotiated with the men taking the lighthouse relief boat out to Berneray to give us a lift. It was the most southern island and Barrahead lighthouse was situated on it.

11.9. The boatmen taking us to Berneray.

We left early next morning after camping in the village near a tranquil little stream which gurgled down to the sea.

There is a sloping landing place on Berneray, near the north east corner of the island. We decided to set up camp in the ruin of an old bothy (cottage) as the remaining walls would provide some shelter from the wind. The lighthouse was situated about 2km west from where we camped, 200 m. above sea level on

11.10. Barrahead lighthouse from the south east.

the top of some impressive cliffs.

We found the three keepers most hospitable. They spent two months on and one off the island. Their task was not onerous, each taking twelve hours on watch in turn. It was a quiet, relaxed life. Their light was one of the most powerful in Britain and being at such an elevation it could be seen for over 50 km. out to sea in clear weather. They gave us some guillemot eggs to eat which, not surprisingly, had a very fishy taste.

11.11. Barrahead Lighthouse 200m above the sea, from down the cliffs to the west.

The cliffs were steep and provided homes to thousands of birds such as puffins, guillemots, razorbills (aptly named as they could almost cut one's finger off if bitten), shags, and fulmars whose gracious flight one could watch, enchanted, for hours.

The puffins became my favorites, fat squat little birds which are probably better swimmers than fliers. To me, they represent the entertainment value and have life styles rather reminiscent of the penguins in the Antarctic. Of course they are much smaller and they can fly but they are blown around in the wind and often seem out of control. They are black and white and have large very colourful, striped beaks. The most amazing sight is when they are carrying fish – they seem to dislocate their jaws so that four or five little fish can be laid out neatly one behind the other, crosswise. They nest in burrows on the cliffs and I had many happy hours sitting near these waiting for them to pass in and out. I was able to photograph them less than a metre away.

11.12. Close up of a puffin.

It saddens me to hear that their numbers are diminishing because of the interference of commercial fishing. June is the best month to see them, as that is when they breed and are at their nests. Another site where they can be seen at the right time of year (June), which is more accessible, is Handa Island in Sutherland in the far north west of Scotland. It is a short boat trip from Tarbert.

Deep in slumber at 4 o,clock one morning we were rudely awakened by the hooting of a typical western isles "puffer," announcing its arrival with the year's coal supply for the lighthouse. I remember looking out of the tent to see a bright yellow and orange sunrise with a sheep grazing contentedly in the foreground and this old boat behind. The scene inspired a photograph.

After a week the lighthouse keepers rowed us one calm afternoon about a kilometre across to Mingulay where we spent the next week. It was a wonderful island with a beautiful white sandy beach spreading about 600m around a bay on the east side of the island. (C7.1) Inland from the beach there were the ruins of dry stone buildings that had once constituted the village. (C6.1) Dry stone building required special skill so that the stones were placed to make a strong, stable, draught proof wall. A newer, double storey building, which was the Catholic church and residence, stood on the hill behind the village. A little road led south from the village across a little stream bordered by blue irises to the old school house, a solidly built stone building. It was still used by the shepherds when they came out at lambing and shearing times. Initially we camped on a knoll near the school house looking down over the beach – a magnificent site. Bad weather developed and eventually drove us to set up our cooking facilities in the school house and spend some of the miserable days there.

We had some patches of good weather during which we roamed around the island, which was about 5km long and 3km wide. It sloped up to cliffs on the west with about 240m shear drop into the sea. (C6.3) A small island with steeply sloping cliffs nearly 200m high is separated from the main island by a narrow channel on two sides. Some goats lived on this island – I wondered who put them there and how many generations had lived in that harsh and isolated environment. I cannot imagine any human pursuing them now. All these cliffs also provided nesting sites for what seemed like millions of sea birds, including puffins although I was not able to get as close to them as on Berneray. (C6.2) We sat and watched these birds, especially the fulmars with their slender wings, and the gulls, catching the air currents, gliding by like ballerinas of the sky. Duncan was more focussed. He had a purpose for being there – to do bird counts. I contented myself taking photographs with my first colour film. Each picture was carefully composed as colour film was precious then.

The flowers were out in abundance, especially the sea pink or thrift (C7.2, C6.4). Sheep wandered unattended most of the year except for the few days when the shepherds came for lambing and shearing. We met one wild-looking creature which seemed to have escaped the shearing for three or four years – it was a wild, woolly creature. Maybe it wondered what this strange creature was sitting on the fence in an old raincoat.

11.13. The author sitting on a fence!

A "dun" is a word for a fortification derived from the Vikings. They raided down the west coast of Scotland ten or more centuries ago. Mingulay had a dun on the south west corner. It was a point with cliffs on three sides and a narrow connection to the main island on the fourth making it an ideal bastion to which the inhabitants could withdraw and defend themselves if necessary.

The island had been uninhabited since 1908. We heard various reasons why. One was that supplying the island was too haphazard in winter so the people moved to closer islands or Barra. Another, more dramatic story told to us by a girl who lived on Barra, was that all the people died of some strange ailment. When the supply boat arrived one man went ashore and found all the people dead. The others told him to stay there in case he was contaminated – they threw him a bundle of food and told him they would return in six weeks to take him off if he was still alive. He survived but the mystery was not solved – or was there one? Maybe it was just another grisly myth not based on fact.

Duncan and I returned two years later for another fortnight wandering through the Outer Hebrides. On that occasion we were given a lift by the shepherds and spent the first day on Berneray roaming our old haunts. In the evening we were dropped off on Mingulay where we spent the next three days, while the sheep were shorn. We camped on our old spot overlooking the long, white, sandy beach and during the day wandered over the hills and watched the masses of birds and admired the flowers again. The sea pinks were in bloom.

Near our landing place close to the beach I found a beautiful rock pool with colourful sea weed, sea anemones etc. (C6.5)

After these four enjoyable days we returned to Barra. We trudged off up the road and then across fields to the north side of the island, which is much bigger than Mingulay. It was a hot afternoon and I remember resenting Duncan's apparently unending enthusiasm to keep going. Oh for John Valentine and a big rock in Duncan's rucksack to slow him down – more of that later! About four o'clock we arrived at the point where boats leave for South Uist. We phoned for the ferryman to come and transport us across to South Uist, about five miles away. His wife answered in her soft spoken, slow island tongue: "He's awa today. He'll come for you tomorrow". Such a delay was rather irritating but while we sat contemplating the blue sky and deeper blue sea two young fellows arrived. It soon became apparent that they were making their boat ready for departure. They had sailed over from South Uist in the morning. We asked for a lift. "Yes, they said provided you help us to row the boat back"– it was a dead calm. So we rowed this boat, about six metres long, across to South Uist. It was not as strenuous as I had expected and we saved many hours not having to wait for the ferryman. We walked a short distance before setting up camp for the night in a field near the road. South Uist is a relatively flat, uninteresting island about 30km long. We walked into the town of Lochboisdale next morning and took a bus up to Benbecula, an island lying between North and South Uist.

We stopped there to enquire about the possibility of going out to the Monach Islands (also called Heisker) which are about 20km farther west in the Atlantic. We were fortunate that a boat was leaving shortly and the boatman was prepared to take us. He was coming back the same day but told us that there was a lobsterman on the island who stayed in the schoolhouse. He usually came in on Saturday and would give us a lift back. We were trusting fellows so set off to yet another island. The sea was relatively calm and eventually we reached the eastern of the two islands. They were low lying, sandy and connected at low tide by a sandy causeway. It was a strange feeling to be dumped on an almost deserted island out on the edge of the Atlantic with the hope but uncertain knowledge of a return passage. The island was a blaze of yellow with the buttercups in full bloom with a background of green from the grass. A few cattle grazed peacefully on the bright sunny, but breezy, day. (C.6.6)

There were five buildings remaining on our island and a lighthouse on the other one. We picked what looked like the schoolhouse and went up and knocked on the door. There was no apparent response so we opened the door and called in. Still no response. We were on the point of leaving when the old lobsterman appeared. Duncan said, "We are looking for a man named Wally Stewart." The old fellow replied in a slow island drawl "I aam thaat maan". He agreed to take us back on his return two days later and let us camp in the front room. Of course, there was no furniture. We slept on the floor but at least it was out of the wind. There was little other protection as there are no trees on these islands.

The Monach Islands were evacuated in 1942, during the war because, I think, there was a perceived danger for supply boats from German U boats. We did not make it to the other island as the tide was not low enough and we did not know how long it would be before it turned. The beaches were the home of Arctic terns which were nesting in hundreds, if not thousands. They are beautiful sleek birds, largely white but with black heads, which were a joy to watch flying and gliding immaculately through the air or sitting on the beach with their eggs. We kept away as they defend their nests by vigorously dive-bombing any intruders.

We returned to Benbecula with Wally Stewart where we had a drink in the pub with him. In seaman style he downed his tot of whisky in one gulp and then sipped his beer.

Next stop was Lochmaddy where Duncan had someone to visit before we caught the MacBrayne's steamer across the straight to Rodil in the south of Harris, part of the largest island in the Outer Hebrides. We had arranged to go with the local shepherds for three days out to the small islands in the sound when they went shearing. Alas! The weather turned foul, the cloud came down and it rained. The shepherds postponed their trip. We spent three rather miserable, wet days waiting for clearer weather. During some drier periods we visited the local church which had been visited by the Queen during a tour of the Western Isles. We walked along the road to a small place established as a processing plant for the Leverhulme company. It looked rather out of place in the old fashioned islands. I think its fortunes disappeared on the death of the well-intentioned, Lord Leverhulme

Finally we gave up waiting and hitch hiked up to Stornoway and caught the steamer back to Kyle of Lochalsh and hence I returned to Strathpeffer by train with two weeks growth on my chin. It had been a most interesting trip.

It is amazing that people lived their entire lives on these remote islands. Their diet, like the inhabitants of St. Kilda further out in the Atlantic, included birds and their eggs as well as fish and some vegetables that they grew in their little fields still marked out by stone dykes. They caught the puffins by sitting on top of the cliffs with a long pole. When the hapless birds were blown up past the edge of the cliffs by the updrafts they hit them from underneath in such a way that the birds were killed and tossed over their heads with one blow, to land behind them.

I never visited St Kilda but it is a very isolated island still watched over by the National Trust and at times occupied by British troops. The people were all re-settled on the mainland in the 1920s. In the late nineteenth century they had a terrible problem with a very high infant mortality rate. The problem was finally solved by a Dr Thompson from Glasgow, who happened to be the great grandfather of a friend of ours. He went out and found that they had a custom of wiping the umbilicus after birth with sheep's dung. This was contaminated with tetanus spores that opened when in contact with open flesh leading to infection and toxin production which caused lethal neonatal tetanus. It was a clever piece of deductive thinking at a time when microbiology was not very advanced.

Thirty two years later Duncan, my son Fraser and I made a sort of return pilgrimage to Barra and Mingulay. We took MacBrayne's steamer from Oban but did not stop at Tiree and Coll. We had a day trip to Mingulay – it was too short but we recaptured the isolation and spectacle of thousands of birds nesting, going fishing and just flying around. The sea pinks, irises and other flowers were all still flourishing. The Barrahead lighthouse, like most lighthouses these days, has been automated and the keepers have left.

Much had changed. Even bus tours came on the steamer and off loaded in the islands. When we had been there before there were very few cars, even on the island of Barra.

Duncan had to return before us – by air. The planes landed on the huge beach which had white, very hard sand and stretched a long way, especially when the tide was low. We went by bus to the beach "airport" to see him off and then walked back to Castlebay visiting some very old buildings including a little chapel with a very low ceiling.

There is something magical about out of the way islands – the peace that can be found, the isolation away from the intrusion of modern society with all its encumbrances – traffic, pollution and too many people.

Scotland provides many walks of the appropriate distance for one, two or more days through beautiful, sometimes majestic scenery. There can be a down side, as there are in many countries where walking is popular – insects such as midges which appear in great numbers at certain times in the summer to bite and irritate the hapless hiker. And then it can rain which it often does in Scotland.

Foolhardiness and danger are not apparent to the young. I went off on various hikes alone without any consideration of potentially bad consequences. One such trip was out west from Strathpeffer when I went off to climb Ben Dearg, one of the Munros, as mountains in Scotland over 3000 feet high are called. These big hills are mountains in Scotland! I had a lift to the nearest point across the valley. The walk was across heather and peat. Ben Dearg stood massive, challenging me to climb it.

11.14. Ben Dearg, Ross-shire.

I began the climb up a ridge. Suddenly the cloud came down but I went on. I surprised some deer. Then I came to a point where I suddenly realized I was near the edge of a sharp drop. The cloud rose a bit and I found that the drop was over a cliff for several hundred metres! Even then I did not consider the inconvenience it would have caused if I had fallen over it, although I did realize it was safer to keep away from the edge. The weather prevented me from reaching the top.

Shirley Martin was a fairly hardy, mountaineering, young lady with short curly hair who was one of the Abergeldie grouse beaters the first year that I went. She was doing honours geography. Her thesis was on Moidart, an underpopulated region on the west coast with only about 300 inhabitants, a consequence of the Highland clearances. This was a dreadful process initiated by wealthy aristocracy from the south who basically drove the crofters off the land, sometimes even burning their houses, so that they could rear large flocks of sheep. Many of the people went to Canada, (mainly Nova Scotia), Australia and New Zealand. A few remained, clinging to a subsistance fishing life on the coast.

Shirley wanted someone to go with her to Moidart, preferably someone who could take photographs for her thesis. Not everyone had cameras in those days. Her male friend was not free at the time so a couple of weeks after the beating I set off for Moidart. We met in Fort William, crossed Corran Ferry which was 17km south. We had 40 to 50km to reach our destination at Acharacle. There was no traffic. How long would we have to wait? The next ferry brought a Land Rover with only the driver. It looked hopeful but it was fully packed. The owner rather reluctantly agreed to take us provided we held his eggs on our lap. It turned out that he was going to fish for a couple of weeks. What did he do? Surprise, surprise! He turned out to be the owner of VAT69 whisky! We were very grateful for the lift.

We were dropped near our planned destination. We walked 2 or 3km along a road that ran through beautiful woods with oak, chestnut, sycamore, pines and occasional silver birch trees and rhododendrons which were not in flower at the time. The road was bordered by dykes running beside a tranquil river where one could imagine and, occasionally see, fish swimming peacefully. We crossed one of those old, arched, stone bridges that are common around Scotland. Eventually we came to an open grassy area beside the sea on an inlet across from Castle Tioran. It had been a solid stone building which was accessible at low tide.

11.15. Castle Tioran, former stronghold of Clan Ranald.

The inlet was surrounded by wooded hills sloping down to the waters edge. Beyond the castle lay Eilean Shona, an island where palm trees were reputed to grow because of the warm climate created by the Gulf Stream. We pitched our tents near some pine trees

11.16. Interior of Castle Tioran showing the thick stone walls.

and then made dinner using our small, methylated spirit stove. The next day, when the tide went out we crossed over to inspect the castle ruins. It had been well built, about three or four storeys high, but most of the internal structure was gone. It had been the castle home of Clan Ranald but had long been a ruin.

Our journey by foot continued along a narrow tar road around and over some small hills to Kinlochmoidart where there was a little shop and post office. When I visited it again about thirty years later I was served by a lady who had always lived there. I calculated that she had been two when I first visited. It is a shop no more having become a tea room for passing tourists who can reach it easily by car. We camped a short distance further on by an open ended boat shed beside the sea. That night I slept well and was totally unaware that during the night there had been a storm with high winds. Shirley's tent was blown away and she had to seek shelter in the boat-shed which is still there! It was calm again the next morning. The road ended here and from then on we had to follow a rough walking track over a ridge to the next bay. It was steep in parts but the views from the top made the effort worth it.

11.17. Looking down on Glenuig.

We camped again when we reached the sea. There was a large house nearby which was serviced by boat. About three kilometres around a point was Smearisary – a few small holdings, one large house, a few fishing boats, oak and other trees and bracken beginning to change to their autumn colours. It was so peaceful, nothing apart from the twittering of birds, the wind blowing through the trees causing the leaves to shimmer, and some sheep.

Our life was not so pleasant for the next day as it rained and a fine mist came through my tent giving it a rather damp feeling. Our final stretch was the walk along the northern shore by Loch Ailort to the road which joined the Fort William to Mallaig road leading to the ferry to Skye. Nowadays there is a connecting road through Glenuig to Kinlochmoidart making it easily accessible to tourists. Even so, I don't think many travel through this beautiful country. The isolation has gone. Years later, I made the circuit round Moidart by car in spring with my mother, when the countryside was covered with masses of daffodils making a cheerful yellow and green landscape.

We made it to Glenfinnan where we planned to catch the train to Fort William. There wasn't one until the next morning. It was still raining, a common occurrence in the west of Scotland. Where were we going to wait overnight? We asked the stationmaster if we could stay in the small station but, instead, he offered us a railway carriage that was parked on the side track – it was pure luxury after wet days in our small tents. Anyway, the objective of the trip was achieved – we had obtained a good set of photographs for the thesis on this sparsely populated district, whose population had been decimated by the Highland Clearances more that a hundred years before.

Walking round a district makes a much bigger and more lasting impact on the memory than driving through it. As a result I developed a great affinity for some of these places and am repeatedly drawn back to them when I return to Scotland. Moidart, Deeside and the Hebrides all have this effect on me.

When my parents were on leave in Scotland in 1957 we had several trips including one to Skye with its famous, rather formidable mountains – the Cuillans and Blaven and to Wester Ross and Sutherland with its increasingly bleak landscape littered with a series of impressive peaks such as Scurr Mor, Scurr Beag, Suilven and Quinnag. These great blocks of rock rise from the surrounding peat and heather lands. They are beautiful in September when the heather is blooming and the hills are purple, especially if the sun is shining. There are occasional small villages such as Lochinver and Kinlochbervie, mainly on the coast. (C35.5) Even when the clouds are down in the Scottish Highlands they create an ethereal atmosphere. It can even compensate for the disappointment of not having a nice sunny day!

Many people tell me they have been to Scotland – to Edinburgh, a magnificent city, or to Glasgow but if they haven't been to the north west they have missed the best. It is one of the most hauntingly beautiful areas in the world.

I had some holiday jobs, such as five weeks one summer when I developed photographs for a Polish photographer in St Andrews called

Tad. He had people who went out photographing holiday makers, especially on the beaches. It was long before automatic processing, which takes less than an hour. I developed and printed all these in the dark room, which was in a little house on a courtyard off South Street. It was said that this house was over five hundred years old and it was thought to be connected to the castle by an underground tunnel. It was also said to be haunted. Why wouldn't a house like that have a resident ghost or two? I don't know if it was or not and I did not meet any ghosts, but it could be very spooky when I was working late at night, with only the red darkroom light, to complete the printing of the photographs taken that day. Any creak or groan in the place could prey on one's mind! I stayed in two lodgings during that time, both very small and old houses.

I had a room upstairs in one in which I could not stand upright without hitting my head and I was only five feet nine inches tall (173 cm).

11.18. College St., St Andrews. The author lodged in the second house during one summer.

St. Andrews was a quite different place in the summer when the students were away and hundreds of holiday-makers descended on the town. Scotland was very organized – the major cities- Edinburgh, Glasgow and Dundee – had designated holiday fortnights so that industry all shut down at one time and the holiday resorts had the visitors spread through the summer. In August the St Andrews Fair was held for three days in South Street – 'dodgems', roundabouts, fortunetellers and lots more.

For three years I went grouse beating in September – the subject of the next chapter. During my last two summer vacations I went home to Kenya for one and to Labrador for the other, an experience which broadened my outlook and gave my life a new direction. During some of the other holidays I worked in hospitals and gained valuable experience.

Chapter 12

Abergeldie – Royal Interlude

In September 1955 I took the train to Blair Athol in Perthshire with my friend Duncan Forrester and another friend of his, John Valentine. We were going to walk for three days up valleys and over hills to Abergeldie Castle on Deeside on our way to two weeks grouse beating for Queen Elizabeth, the Queen Mother.

Following the King's death in 1952, the Queen Mother decided to continue the grouse shooting for her friends and her brother, David Bowes Lyon, with whom I had many conversations on the moors. King George VI had been keen on the sport and was a very good shot.

Duncan and another St Andrews University student, Alastair Morton, had responded to a advertisement for beaters and were asked to organize the party. Duncan, being my senior man at University, invited me to join the second party in 1955 and hence my arrival for the first of three grouse shooting seasons at Abergeldie. We did the beating on the Corndavon Estate on the other side of the River Dee and further west. If one drives from Tomitoul to Crathie it is on the right before one descends into Deeside – miles of rolling hills with a large hill called the Brown Cow on the north western skyline. The gravel road winds in towards and along beside the River Gairn to the ruins of Corndavon Lodge.(C8.6) Beyond that a track leads to Loch Builg and on to Tomintoul.

12.1. Grouse beaters lined out on the moors.

Grouse are small game birds that live in the heather in Scotland and some of the gentry enjoyed the sport of grouse shooting. Our job was to walk 10 to 15 miles a day over moorland hills waving white flags to encourage these hapless birds to fly down wind over the butts (earthen fortifications behind which the men with guns could position themselves) where they might be shot or escape depending on the skill of the shooters.

In those days conservation was not the issue it is today but the wisdom of the people took it into account. What many present day conservationists do not seem to realize is that culling is sometimes kinder than allowing the creatures to die of starvation when too many survive. This is a principle used in good game management, even today, because it prevents overstocking leading to destruction of the environment. There is plenty of evidence of this happening in sub Saharan Africa where the desert has been moving south for years. Many of the real conservation issues relate to loss of the creatures' natural environment, particularly associated with increasing human population. It is so easy to interfere with the chain of life. Remove one creature which is a predator and the next will breed in excess using the food reserves so that starvation occurs or they destroy excessive numbers of creatures further down the chain.

In our grouse beating days the people who controlled the shooting balanced the duration of the shooting season against the number of birds. Thus in 1955 we only beat for 2 weeks because there were fewer birds that year, while in the subsequent years when the birds were more plentiful we beat for 3 and 4 weeks, usually only 4 days a week. This helped to maintain a balance. I think this is an intelligent approach to conservation. I certainly believe in conservation but also in maintaining balances. I would not have approved of grouse shooting if there was any chance of the grouse being decimated out of existence. There wasn't.

We were paid £6 a week – a handsome sum in those days. We spent a quarter of it on food.

We became fit walking for two or three days before the beating, especially as we were carrying our needs for the duration of our time at Abergeldie – often 25kg or so. This gave us an advantage over the less fit beaters and made the days beating a pleasant 15 to 20km walk over the hills.

Glen Tilt is long narrow valley running north from Blair Athol towards the southern end of the Cairngorm mountains. After leaving the train in the late afternoon we walked about five or six kilometres before we camped for the night in a lightly wooded area. Further on the next day trees became fewer as we reached higher altitude. We followed a little road built by General Wade when the English were trying to control the Scottish Highlands in the 1700s. It even had a little

12.2. Our camp at the headwaters of the River Dee.

Wade bridge, characteristic of his roads, to cross the River Tilt. At the end of the day we crossed the watershed and camped at the headwaters of the Dee. It was fairly open moorland country but there was a small pine plantation nearby.

Duncan was always very enthusiastic, particularly in the morning, which was something we other young fellows couldn't understand. For some reason young men around 20 have a propensity to sleep in late in the morning. Have you ever considered why this might be so? Anyway Duncan had us up making our porridge with salt – it's a staple food in Scotland. When he went off for a few minutes John plotted a wonderful plan to slow down our slave driving friend. Put a rock in the bottom of his rucksack! At first Duncan's enthusiasm and early morning freshness were such that he did not notice. I don't recall exactly how long it took for him to realize that we had successfully plotted against him but we had a good laugh when he did!

The walk into Braemar was about 15km passing the beautiful Linn of Dee where the river fell through a small gorge before emerging into the wide valley with attractive silver birches and some Scots pines adding beauty to the valley. I remember arriving in Braemar and reading a thermometer – it was 80°F (30°C) in the sun which was regarded as very hot in Scotland in those days. We stopped to quench our thirst. After about ten more kilometres out on the road going south we turned on to the track to Loch Callater where we camped, ready for the meal cooked on our methylated spirit burner. It was a pretty spot with a grassy patch beside the loch. There were two small lonely silver birches near the loch (Scottish for lake) which were striking in the otherwise lonely, heather covered landscape. I used them to enhance my photograph.

Next day, we plodded up and over into the head of Glen Clova. It was hot again – I remember us all luxuriating in a cool deep pool in the burn (Scottish word for stream or small river). We descended into

Glen Clova and then began the steep climb out over to Glen Muick. I thought that I had fallen in with two madmen, or maybe two of us had fallen in with one crazy fellow. Why would one not walk or even take a bus down Deeside for 16km from Braemar to our destination, instead of trekking up one valley, down into another, on a very hot day, and then up what seemed a long, steep hill with 25kg on our backs to escape from Glen Clova into Glen Muick which eventually led, after several kilometres, to our destination? At least I can say that I have done it and we did get fit. A destination usually seems more attractive if one has to strive to reach it – so it was with Abergeldie Castle. (C8.5)

12.3. Abergeldie Castle, where we lived for two seasons.

This was a castle which was unused except that a caretaker, dear old Maggie Robertson, lived in a small part of it. It was still furnished in very elegant Victorian style. How did we know it was Victorian? All the huge pots and pans were stamped VR meaning Victoria Regina. The kitchen had a high ceiling with a long table down the middle and a huge sink in the corner where we dutifully took turns washing up after meals.

It was in the kitchen that I had one of my meetings with the Queen Mother! She always came to visit her beaters on the Sunday before we began beating to ensure that we were comfortable and settling in well. She met most of the beaters in the Lounge room – an elegant room about twelve metres long with furnishings befitting to an old royal castle. She singled out one of beaters, Ian McPherson, to speak to specially – "I'm sorry we couldn't pick you up on the moors (he tried to hitch a lift with a couple of Land Rovers) because the cars were full with the children (Charles and Anne) and dogs" she explained. She had Corgis, the most famous one being called Honey. Ian was picked up later by some American tourists, who apparently fell for his yarn that a haggis is a bird with one leg longer than the other so that it can run round the hills easily – of course it can only go one way, clockwise or anti-clockwise, depending on which leg is longer!

The Queen Mother realized that we were not all there and those of us working in the kitchen didn't realize that she had arrived. It was an Abergeldie tradition that anyone who could bake would make something for Sunday tea. I was making shortbread while a couple of others were baking cakes. It was with some surprise to us when the Queen Mother appeared in the kitchen. I was working hard kneading the shortbread, the most important aspect of its production, sweating slightly, when she approached me and asked what I was making, what ingredients I used and how I made it. It is on the basis of this interview that each year I make "Queen Mother's Grouse-beaters shortbread" at Christmas, individually labeled. It was a demonstration of how interested she has been in all sorts of people and how easily she communicated with them. Another example of her consideration and generosity occurred when half a salmon arrived for us one evening. She was a very keen salmon fisher and she shared this one, which she had caught herself, with her beaters. One of the original beaters eventually married another beater and they received a gift from the Queen Mother for their wedding. So, when on her 100th birthday, the commentators mentioned this very personal side to her nature, I thought they were right. She was a charming lady.

Next day we began beating. We were dropped at an appropriate point and then walked out to our positions spread across the hillside.

We had white flags to wave at the birds to encourage them to fly down wind in the appropriate direction. Two beaters would have the job as flankers that guarded the sides to the row of butts and their job was to encourage any grouse veering off to fly on the suicide route over the guns. It was an easier job as one didn't have to walk so far. The old hands usually acquired these positions, having the advantage of local knowledge. Of

12.4. Walking out to our beating positions on the moors.

course we would make out that this position required special skill to divert the stray birds – actually the proximity to the guns increased the chance of collecting a shot which fortunately was a rare occurrence although one of the ghillies had lost an eye in such an accident.

Usually we did five or six beats per day. They were skillfully planned as we had to walk downwind, cover ground close to the previous beat and not repeat the beats that had been done recently. We had a little bus to take us to the moors. On the way home in the evening there would usually be joyous singing. "The wild colonial boy" was a favorite. Unlike gifts of salmon we never received any gifts of grouse. The only one we obtained was one that I caught with my hands in the heather!

One day things did not go as usual. We arrived on the moors on a miserable wet morning. There was much discussion on whether we would beat or abandon it for the day. We were asked if we would do one beat but ended up not doing any. Strangely, we were not allowed to travel back in our bus. Somehow, we didn't realize that this was significant and we greatly enjoyed the alternative which was on a tractor and trailer belonging to Willy Finlay, one of the local ghillies who lived in a cottage on the estate.

We eventually arrived back at Abergeldie, had lunch and I went off to have a sleep. A unique experience then occurred. When I awoke and joined the group downstairs I was told that we had all been sacked for not beating! However, after discussion with the man who had come from the estate office to sack us, it became apparent that there had been a misunderstanding – we had thought we had been given the option to decide whether we would do the one beat, but they had expected us to do one. We were reinstated. I clearly remember the date – *Friday 13th September 1957* –

12.5. Willy Finlay taking us back to Abergeldie by tractor after not beating on Friday 13.9.57. Willy driving, Duncan Forrester (became Principal, New College, Edinburgh) (L) and John Parker CBE., (cardiac surgeon) (R)

when I was sacked and reinstated, all while I slept. Few people could claim such a distinction!

On days when we were not beating we either worked on building tracks on the moors or else, more often, we were free to enjoy the surroundings and the benefits of being estate workers. We played golf on the Balmoral 9 hole course and on one occasion saw Princess Anne out riding – I wondered whether her horse on that occasion was the one trained for her by my Uncle Fraser in Dublin. He was always regarded as the black sheep of the family but in his own way as a riding teacher and trainer was successful as he was known internationally for his ability with horses. (24.1)

We were also taken in our little bus to the Braemar Highland Games, attended church at Crathie, the Ghillies Ball at Balmoral Castle and on other days climbed local mountains such as Lochnagar. It was like a wonderful paid holiday. We felt very important walking into the church passing the assembled crowds who had come in as many as 30 buses to see the Queen going to church. They would not have expected to see us and probably wondered who we were!

The Braemar Gathering is one of the largest Highland Games. Its importance is enhanced by the attendance of the Royal Family. The massed pipe bands, usually four or five Regimental bands together, makes a very impressive and moving spectacle.

In addition the traditional sports, such as tossing the caber, throwing a 28 pound hammer, throwing a 56 pound weight for height over a bar, attracted the greatest Scottish heavyweight sportsmen. Tossing the caber is a unique Scottish sport where the competitors have to heave a large log carried vertically so that it goes end over end like a somersault. Success is only achieved if it goes over vertically and forward. The winner is the person who tosses it closest to 180 degrees – that is directly over. Usually the log is of such a size that only two or three competitors are success-

12.6. Massed Regimental Bands passing the Royal Box at Braemar Highland Games.

ful. At Braemar the caber is larger than at most other games because all the heavyweight athletes are usually competing.

Other important components of the Games are the bag-piping and Highland dancing competitions. The venue in Braemar is very attractive in a slight hollow surrounded by low hills. We were very privileged as our bus was driven into the grounds and parked on the slope where we could get a good view. Another amusing aspect was that we followed the Royal entourage leaving the ground. Some of us had acquired the technique of the Royal wave and used it as we drove through the crowds.

12.7. The author tossing the caber with a relatively small log.

The Ghillies Ball was held in the Ballroom at Balmoral castle. The estate workers, the guard and Royal household attended. We had individual invitations which stated on the back "This ticket is not transferable". The Royal family participated and Alastair Morton was invited to dance with the Queen. As it was mostly Scottish country dancing we met up with several of them in the progressive dances such as the Dashing White Sergeant.

The third season that I attended we were housed in Abergeldie Mains, a large farmhouse near the castle (C8.5), because the latter was becoming unsafe. It was sad years later to find that the once immaculate gardens, with apple and pear trees which had been meticulously espaliated along the garden wall, had become neglected and the major part of the castle had been demolished, leaving only the tower with its clock standing still at 1.23. I often wonder whether the caretaker, Maggie Robertson, left her ghost to haunt the place. I wonder what happens to ghosts when their home is knocked down. There are records of one in Edinburgh who does not restrict himself to only one site but haunts the area around Greyfriars churchyard and the nearby district!

In 1956 and 1957 I walked through a pass in the Cairngorms called the Lairig Ghru between Aviemore to Braemar on my way to the grouse beating at Abergeldie. This was a good hike of 42km with a substantial climb in the middle. Descending into Speyside from Inverness the Lairig Ghru looks like a great wedge cut in the mountains. The walk up through the Rothiemurcas forest with the beautiful Scots pines, passing little burns (streams) and then on to the higher moorland with heather, purple in September, was very scenic.

12.8. Approaching the Lairig Ghru from Aviemore.

I particularly liked the old Scots pines. At the top of the pass at 860m the track crosses about a kilometre of boulders, many with a reddish hue and then descends down the valley with the great corrie of Brairiach on the right and Ben Macdhui, Scotland's second highest mountain, rising steeply on the left.

12.9. Crossing the boulders at the top of the Lairig Ghru.

On one occasion I was wearing shorts as I commonly did, carrying about 27kg in my pack, with only an ex army groundsheet to protect me from the weather. I never even considered the possibility of cold exposure as a problem. However, on this trip, it began to rain, then sleet and there was wind when I was crossing the top of the pass. The temperature dropped. My legs became cold and then began to seize up. Fortunately the cramp was not so severe that I had to stop. I might have been in trouble if I had. I just carried on down the valley to the bothy (shelter) about two or three kilometres

12.10. Crossing the burn (stream) on two wires.

further on. The most difficult part of reaching it was that one had to cross the river on two parallel wires. It required some technical skill to do so. One had to lean forward because leaning backwards meant that ones rucksack was pulling downwards towards the river – an undesirable situation!

I reached the bothy where I lit a fire and warmed up. Later three others arrived to join me for the night. The track then goes on down the gradually sloping valley and turns east along the lower slopes of Cairngorm to join the road near the Linn of Dee. Here the Dee rushes through a narrow gorge tumbling over falls as it goes. The road continues on through a wide valley, with silver birches and some Scots pines adding beauty to the landscape, to Braemar about 10km further on. I usually caught a bus from there to Abergeldie which was a couple of kilometres past Balmoral Castle.

After the first season's beating I walked through the Lairig Ghru in the other direction from Braemar to Aviemore, with two other beaters, Willy Thompson and Shirley Martin (with whom I later went to Moidart).

On another occasion, after the beating I returned to Aviemore via a track that follows the eastern rim of the Cairngorms – the Lairig an Laoigh, meaning the "Pass of the Calves" in Gaelic, because it was an easier road than the Lairig Ghru when cattle were being driven south. It eventually turns west past Loch Morlich, now popular for water sports, to Coylum Bridge and Aviemore where I caught the train to Inverness. This route does not reach as high as the Lairig Ghru because it avoids the main mountain mass of the Cairngorms. Some years later I had a day walk when four of us walked from Inverey Youth Hostel up the first part of this beautiful track winding through Scots pines and along the river bank. This burn (stream) comes down from the small, scenic Loch Etchahan at the foot of the ramparts of Ben Macdhui which tower above. Ben Macdhui has a rolling flattish top. A few hundred metres walk to the north of Loch Etchahan took us to an impressive view down into a deep valley with a long narrow lake, Loch Avon (pronounced A'an).

I greatly enjoyed these walks, even when I was on my own. I never felt lonely. I was young and the danger of being alone was never a consideration although I now recognize that it can be dangerous if one is injured or lost! My love of walking in the Scottish hills obviously came from my father who had three major hikes in the Cairngorms over the years.

Grouse beating was great fun largely because of the unusual opportunities it provided but also because of the life long friendships that were made with some of the other beaters.

Sharing an experience with someone when you are young, especially when it lasts more than a day or two, can create bonds of friendship that are easily renewed even if you don't see the people for 40 years. It is the shared experience that is binding. Inevitably, I lost touch with many of them but some have remained close friends. John Valentine drowned in Sydney Harbour when still young. Duncan Forrester I have mentioned elsewhere. John Parker, a Rhodesian medical student who became a well known cardiac surgeon in London, was awarded the CBE but died in his fifties; George Cockburn, who was also on the Isle of May with us, became Registrar of Lancaster University after a period in the Colonial

12.11. The 1955 group of beaters – front from left – Willy Thompson, Marnie Murdoch, Mary Catto, KB, John Valentine. Behind – M.Catto, George Cockburn, Shirley Martin, Dennis Smith, Leigh Paton, Jim Burt, Alastair Morton. With our transport.

12.12.The 1957 group of beaters. –front from left – George Cockburn, KB, Fiona Vine, David Duncan, Claude Taylor, Elizabeth Jamieson, Duncan Forrester, John Parker, Ann Graham. Behind – Noel Turnbull, Graham Baird, Archie McAdam, Nigel Thake, James Stewart, Judith Reid. Sitting – Gillian Richards.

Service. Many became doctors, teachers, ministers and one, Graeme Baird, an antiquarian book consultant to Sothebys. They worked all over the world. Alisdair Stewart and his wife Elma were in my medical year and later practiced in Harrogate. They had a Queen Mother's grouse-beaters tie designed and made. It is dark green with a gold crown and a red bird below it. It must be one of the rarest ties one could have – some friends thought mine needed replacing but were unable to find one in any of the famous tie shops in Britain. Alisdair later gave me a spare one!

Periodically when I return to Scotland I have driven by Abergeldie but it is now run down and does not have the grandeur it had when we were there as students. One time I was compensated by seeing a pair of capercaillie, a large game bird found in Scotland, in the grounds. And the tiny blue *forget me nots* still growing in profusion are reminders of romances among the beaters, some begun and others ended, in those carefree days.

Part 3

Summer in Labrador

CHAPTER 13

WILFRED GRENFELL AND LABRADOR

Labrador! Where is this exotic sounding place? There is even the suggestion of gold in the name. Is it the home of a breed of dogs? No, not really! It forms the north east coast of Canada stretching from the St. Lawrence estuary to the northern tip before the coast turns west into Ungava Bay, Hudson Strait and on to Hudson Bay.

It is a strange place – on the one hand it is rather desolate, very sparsely populated by humans, lonely and very cold in the winter and yet it has an attraction, beauty and appeal of its own. It has been referred to as "the land that God gave Cain." It is a vast area with undulating, mostly low hills with rocks and trees, but as one goes north even the spruce and fir trees become stunted and then disappear altogether. There are many low lying rocky islands off the coast, smoothed by the great glaciers of the Ice Age, with mosses and sparse cover – hardy, low growing plants. Ice bergs float by in summer.

Why would anyone live there? First there were Eskimos (now known as Inuits) and Indians and then the fishermen arrived via Newfoundland from Britain, particularly from Devon and Cornwall, and from France. Their language became isolated and did not develop as it did in England. The "Newfies" (as Newfoundlanders are called) have a dialect which is hard for outsiders to understand – it has retained many characteristics of the language that their forefathers brought 300 years before. They went to Labrador to fish and a few to hunt beginning in the later 1700s. They had tough lives, poor conditions and diet, and no health care. It was to this environment that Wilfred Grenfell was sent to investigate the living conditions among the fishermen.

13.1. Dr. Wilfred Grenfell

The story of Labrador would be incomplete without some reference to the life of this great man, his work and his legacy, the International Grenfell Association, which he set up to provide health care in Northern Newfoundland and Labrador. Late in life he became Rector of St Andrews University, elected by the students, and it was as a result of this that generations of students from St Andrews went to work as volunteers in Labrador. I became one of them. This was one of the great experiences of my life and I became a great admirer of the man.

Wilfred Grenfell was born in 1865 at Mostyn House School at Pargate on the River Dee near Chester in England. His father owned and taught at the school until the end of 1882 when he moved to the then desperately poor part of the East End of London, described by Charles Dickens in his novels, to become Chaplain to the London Hospital. Wilfred was a youth who enjoyed outdoor activities by the sea and in the country as well as sport. When eventually his father asked what he wanted to do he was somewhat surprised that he was actually going to have to train for an occupation. Those who were reasonably well to do did not really work!

He was influenced, by a doctor friend whom he respected, to study medicine and elected to do it at the London Hospital. He was not a very conscientious student until he came in contact with an unusual surgeon called Frederick Treeves. He was at the forefront of clean surgery and adopted the principle put forward by Lister and Pasteur to try to reduce infection which killed many of the patients who were operated upon at the time. The situation is epitomized by the story of a woman who, when requested to consent for her husband's operation, asked, "And who is going to pay for the funeral?" Treeves also appealed to young Grenfell because he was a sportsman and he sailed. He eventually became Treeves' house surgeon. Although he was a lively student he did not participate in the alcoholic debauchery of his fellow students. He saw too much of the desolate lives and violence that resulted from East Enders who were caught up with drink. At that time the famous American evangelists, Moody and Sankey, were preaching practical religion around Britain. He heard Moody speaking and was stimulated by his message. He was not a sudden convert but rather took the view that to live like Jesus and help the poor and down and outs was a worthwhile thing to do. He applied Christianity to practical living and doing good for his fellow men. He ran boys clubs and took young East Enders out sailing and thereby broadened their horizons.

In 1886 he was employed by the National Mission to Deep Sea Fishermen and was sent out to the fleets fishing in the North Sea as a doctor on a mission boat. The conditions had improved somewhat with the introduction of these boats, helping the seamen and supplying their everyday needs instead of succumbing to the sale of alcohol offered by boats from Holland which set out to ruin them. When Grenfell joined them things were still very tough. He gained the admiration of the men by joining in their work when he was not taking medical care of the sick. He himself was tough – he could withstand cold and regularly swam in the Serpentine in Hyde Park, even during winter, when he was a student.

In 1892 he was asked to go to Newfoundland to investigate the conditions there and up the coast in Labrador. He sailed on a ketch-rigged sailing vessel, *Albert*, which had been built and equipped as a hospital ship. They arrived at St. Johns to find a inferno – much of the town was destroyed by fire.

Grenfell was ideally suited to his task in Labrador. He was stirred and exhilarated by the country but what he found amongst the people was terrible – poor health, inadequate diet and dozens of hard working but run down fishermen and, in the coastal settlements, impoverished families without hope. They were far worse than the poorest of the poor in the East End of London. They were kept poor by the traders to whom they supplied the fish. It was the policy of these traders to keep these poor people in their debt so that the fishermen would keep working for their benefit. They received little more than enough to subsist through the winter. The arrival of Grenfell in 1892 gave them some hope – someone cared about them. When he returned to St. Johns at the end of the summer having travelled nearly 5000km up and down the coast, visited fifty settlements and treated over nine hundred people, he was met by an enthusiastic population who heard from returning vessels about his wonderful work. They wanted to help him to continue it. He was forthright in telling them what was needed and in criticizing those who profited selfishly to the detriment of the fisher folk.

The next summer he returned with two doctors (Bobardt, originally from Melbourne, and Curwen) and two nurses (Cecilia Williams and Ada Carwardine) on the Albert. He had also raised funds to buy another smaller boat, *Princess May*, which was 14 metres (45 feet) long and 2.5 metres (8 feet) wide. He travelled on this himself from St Johns to Labrador much to the consternation of the locals because the boat was not ideally suited to the wild conditions in which ice-bergs could often be encountered. It did however enable him to enter many little inlets which the larger *Albert* could not safely reach. The construction of two small hospitals was already under way funded from St. Johns. These were at Battle Harbour on an island off the south coast near Mary's Harbour, and at Indian Harbour on islands out from the entrance to Hamilton Inlet, half way up the Labrador coast. The latter was a two storey building which became the main hospital for many years.

Grenfell returned for several years each summer to work his way up and down the coast providing medical care, clothes and helping the people to keep going. He was an inspiration to them, giving hope when they had none. He was already a legend in Newfoundland and Labrador. He had boundless enthusiasm and followed his ideas to a conclusion, often to the consternation of the council to the Mission to Deep Sea fishermen in England. He lectured in Canada and USA and enthusiastic groups in many major cities such as Boston and New York set up committees to raise funds for his work. These became the continuing basis for funding the work of what eventually evolved into the International Grenfell Association.

Other doctors and nurses went to work in Labrador. Donors helped them to finance more boats and new hospitals were built with money raised by his supporters. His Christian beliefs were so strong that he believed that if something was needed it would be supported by someone although it was not always clear where the money would come from.

He was very forthright and it is not surprising that some of his activities impinged on others, eroding their influence or, more likely, their profits. But he did what he thought was best for the poor people on the coast to try to give them more independence. One example was the establishment of co-operatives so that the people became empowered to do their own trading at better prices. The people benefited but the traders did not and they became bitter about it. Grenfell did not mind because he considered that they had been taking advantage of the poor, uneducated people, which he regarded as un-Christian.

Eventually he was ordered to stay home if he wanted to retain his job as superintendent and so for some time he did but by then fishing methods were changing and becoming more efficient and the old trawlers were being replaced with bigger and faster ships. Many of the fishermen were growing old which was a matter of great concern to him because they had no pensions or income.

He returned to Labrador three years later. He could not keep away from the people who admired him and had relied on him so much. He had changed their lives. He had many ups and downs with the Board of the National Mission for Deep Sea Fishermen who were concerned that they could not control their superintendent. Eventually, after he had been back to Labrador several times and had made several successful fund raising tours in Canada and USA it was decided to split the work and have a superintendent for the work based in England and Grenfell would look after Labrador and northern Newfoundland. He settled at St. Anthony and each summer travelled extensively on the coast doing his medical work, opening co-operatives, schools and expanding the hospitals and nursing stations. The staff grew accordingly and as many as 4000 people were being treated each year.

He wrote a book "What life means to me" in which he said he believed in the "socialism of Christ … fraternity in action." He believed that intellectual testing of religion was futile as it would not help non-believers to see the benefits of Christianity. The truth was evident in the happiness and certainty that faith gave. He was also opposed to the fragmentation of Christianity and, at times, ran foul of the mainstream churches because of his extremely ecumenical approach. He basically believed in doing the best to help those in need.

The most dramatic story about him was on one occasion when he was going to help a young boy who had osteomyelitis and was deteriorating. This was a devastating infection in bone which was difficult to treat in the days before antibiotics. It was spring. He was warned that the ice was dangerous and that he should follow the shore but after a while his sense of urgency led him to cross the ice. It was dangerous and he found himself on a small floe that was breaking up. He saw a larger, safer looking floe but he could not get his huskies to swim for it. He also had a retriever with him. He threw something on to the neighbouring floe and told it to fetch it. It obeyed and the others followed. Then he had to swim himself which left him in soaking clothes in a low temperature and in the wind – normally a lethal combination if one has to spend too long exposed. He decided to kill two dogs, which grieved him considerably, to get their skins to provide some covering. There was great consternation when it was found he was missing. Then he was sighted but there were only five dogs and he had seven – they thought it must be someone else and that he was still missing. A boat went out, struggling through the melting floes. What relief when they found that it was him. Maybe his survival resulted from his habit of swimming however cold it was, to his faith and to his commonsense in using the dog skins.

He spent his last winter at St Anthony in 1918-19. After that he devoted his efforts to fund raising, mainly in North America. He made his last voyage to the coast in 1932 when he was 67.

In 1929, he succeeded the famous Arctic explorer and philanthropist, Fridjof Nansen as Rector of St Andrews University, the chairman of the University Court elected by the students.

Andrew McAdam was a medical student two years ahead of me who had spent a summer with the Grenfell Mission and had lodged with Miss Scott in Newport two years before I did. He told me that this "bunk" (student accommodation) was available but of greater long term significance in my life was his lighting the spark of interest that led me to apply to go to Labrador at the end of my fifth year for the summer as a volunteer. Student electives as an organized part of medical training did not exist then. I wrote away to the International Grenfell Association office in London offering my services and in due course was accepted.

Usually the students travelled by ship, signed on as supernumeraries so that they could travel free. Term ended and I waited and waited for my ship. I watched Wimbledon on television until my eyes were nearly "square". Television was a novelty then. Eventually, in desperation at having to wait so long, I did two week-long locum jobs in Medicine at Dundee Royal Infirmary which I have described elsewhere. It was excellent experience.

Then news came that as there were no ships I was to fly out with Len McBeath, a student from Glasgow, who was going to the main Grenfell Mission hospital at St Anthony in northern Newfoundland. This was an important hospital with an excellent surgeon, Gordon Thomas, in charge. They had staff and facilities which allowed them to provide a high standard of medical care. There was also a tuberculosis sanatorium as this disease was still widespread, although beginning to diminish at that time.

We flew to Gander in central Newfoundland. The airport had only recently been opened as a refueling stop for the trans-Atlantic flights. It was a fine airport with a magnificent 25m wide mural depicting progress into the air. It was there that I was first subjected to piped music – it nearly drove me crazy – one could not even escape in the toilets! We had to stay overnight in Gander. The accommodation was at one of two hotels which did not have catering so we had to return to the airport for meals! The airport is still there but its useful life as an international stop was short as soon after its completion the advances in aviation resulted in the 'planes being able to fly directly from Britain and Europe to Montreal and other mainland destinations.

That evening there was one of the most magnificent sunsets that I have ever seen. The sky was lightly clouded and the whole sky gradually turned a deep pink to red – add to that the smell of the coniferous trees and it made an everlasting memory. The saying " a red sky at night is the shepherds delight" proved correct. The next day was beautiful with clear blue skies.

We were picked up and taken shopping in town before setting off to the Pond where the Beaver, JAT, was waiting. (C10.7) These planes were the workhorses of the north – single engine aircraft which carried up to six passengers. In summer they were fitted with floats and in winter with skis. They were sturdy but only flew at 150 to 180kph. We took off and headed north-west over the woods and lakes of northern Newfoundland until we reached the coast. There was great excitement for us newcomers when we saw our first icebergs far below. What a thrilling experience to see these great white blocks floating off the coast with an unbelievable six sevenths under the water.

We landed at Rodicton, a small settlement on the coast of the northern peninsula where we picked up a patient and proceeded on to St. Anthony where we stopped briefly for lunch. Then we flew across the strait to Labrador heading for Cartwright. About half way there we came up to a huge bush fire burning out of control near Port Hope Simpson. We were flying at 1600 m. but the smoke reached twice that height, making it impossible to go through, so we turned back and landed at Marys Harbour, a small settlement with a nursing station where we spent the night. This settlement had been largely overrun by fire fifteen years before – all except the nursing station was burnt. That it was close one could see from the lesser height of the new vegetation growing only twenty metres from the building. In the evening, when I was out walking and inspecting a new dam which was being built, the sky suddenly became blacker and blacker when it should still have been broad daylight. It was the smoke from the fires which were ravaging Labrador that dry summer. It felt like the end of the world was approaching. The only other time I felt like that was when a massive dust storm engulfed Melbourne, almost blacking it out.

The interesting aspect of this visit was the visitors book. It had previously been at the hospital, later nursing station, at Battle Harbour on a nearby island. The book had been signed by Peary in 1909 on his return from his claimed success at reaching the North Pole with Matthew Henson who was a Negro.

Much controversy waged about who was first to the Pole as a man named Cook claimed priority. Eventually it was decided that he could not have done it in the time and the evidence from some Eskimos (Inuits) indicated that it was unlikely that he had reached anywhere near the Pole. Now there is debate whether even Peary reached the North Pole, or did Amundsen from Norway get there first, much later. Peary's claimed rate of travel with dogs might have been enough to enable him to have done so if it was true. Now many doubt him.

Next day the fire had subsided and the smoke had cleared so we were able to proceed north to Cartwright. This settlement was named after George Cartwight who lived there for 12 years from 1775 to 1786. He had previously been in the army in India – a great contrast. He was a brother of Edmund Cartwright who invented the spinning loom in England. George had taken about 400 people out there to fish and trap, sending the goods back to England. The settlement was on Sandwich Bay where fishing and wild life were abundant. Most of the people returned to England about sixteen years later when American privateers captured most of his ships during the war between Britain and the United States.

In 1914, Garland Lethbridge, who spent that year in Cartwright, showed Clarence Birdeye how to fast freeze fish. The latter went on to revolutionize the food industry with quick frozen foods. It is amazing that the idea came from such an isolated place.

The plane returned to St Anthony and left me to wait for transport to my destination at North West River. I stayed in the dormitory as the school children were on holiday. I had three days in Cartwright during which I walked up through the woods to the dam. I was attacked by mosquitoes and "blackflies" which are rampant in the north in summer. One can be unaware of being bitten until one sees the blood oozing from the bite.

I rowed across the bay from the Grenfell mission, which had a nursing station and a school and dormitory, to the settlement several times as it was only a few minutes away. There were several houses and a Hudson Bay store. The other store had recently burnt down but was being re-built. Many of the people were out at their fishing camps around Sandwich Bay for the summer. I watched the unloading of their catch for the day including plenty of beautiful salmon. Some they bottled for the winter. I had never had such large pieces of salmon as I was fed there. To think that people had lived there for nearly two hundred years – it did not seem that there had been much progress but then that was Labrador. The population was small and life was hard.

After three days the "Burgeo"arrived. It was the ship which travelled to North West River and Goose Bay, at the western end of Lake Melville, from St Johns. I finished my journey on it, eventually reaching North West River in late July. (C10.1)

This settlement was established in 1743 when Louis Fernel set up a trading post to trade with the Montangais and Naskaupi Indians who lived in the area. There was still an Indian settlement across the river from the main settlement. In 1959 there was no bridge across the river but one has been built since.

The hospital was a relatively new, long two-storey building situated near the wharf on the river where it runs through between Small Lake and Lake Melville. It had forty beds in three wards upstairs with a separate section for TB patients. There was an operating theatre, a small laboratory, an outpatient room and x ray unit, a dental suite, and the other usual ancillary offices, stores and accommodation completed the facilities.

The doctor in charge was *Tony Paddon* who had been brought up on the coast.

13.3. Dr. Tony Paddon.

His father, Harry Paddon, who had heard Grenfell speaking at his school in England, had devoted his life to Labrador, first working at Indian Harbour and then, initially during the winter from about 1912, at North West River. It eventually became the main hospital in the north.

Tony was trained in Boston and served in the Navy during World War II before returning to North West River where he lived the remainder of his life. He was a wonderful and very practical man who taught me many things, particularly how to extract teeth, take x rays and fit glasses. He told me many entertaining tales of Labrador, some of which I will recount later. He lived across the point from the hospital, in a white house surrounded by a neat paling fence looking down Lake Melville. He was a keen gardener, in this place where gardening was not easy. I remember him telling me that he grew potatoes and that these had adapted to the harsh climate by developing glycerol or a similar anti-freeze as the weather became colder, so that they withstood frost.

Tony Paddon's autobiography has many interesting tales and gives many insights into Labrador life and history. For instance, he describes a fire at the Indian Harbour hospital caused by a kerosene heated sterilizer being too close to a patient being anaesthetized with ether, which is flammable. He claimed that the patient apparently exhaled a smoke ring of bright flame but was rapidly removed from the theatre and suffered no serious consequences. Fortunately there had been a gale and dozens of schooners had been sheltering in the harbour. When the billowing smoke was seen men rushed with buckets of water to pour over the fire. There was no fire brigade. Soon they were joined by men from the schooners and eventually there were enough to form a human chain from the sea to pass water to the site. They had to and did save the hospital as it was the only one for over 300km.

He describes an occasion when an old Inuit approached to ask him to find another wife as his four previous ones had died from causes unknown. He humorously suggested that it was because they found him unendurable!

A quarter of a century later, on my way to St. Johns, I was told that Tony Paddon had become Lieutenant Governor of Newfoundland. I later learned that when Prime Minister Trudeau's office had called to inform him of the proposed appointment he told the man on the end of the phone to stop playing practical jokes on him. An indignant voice then repeated that this was the Prime Minister's office calling and that it was not a practical joke! Such was Tony Paddon – a humble man. While he might not have expected such a position his stature in Labrador was such that it was very appropriate recognition for all he had done for the people of the coast and I am sure he fulfilled it in a down to earth way. Regretably, I was not able to meet him during my visit to St. Johns in 1985, as he was leaving early the next day for Labrador.

The hospital had a small staff for forty beds – one other doctor, David Rees, two British nurses and five local nurse aids. (C10.2) A Filipino dentist arrived during my stay – there was plenty for him to do. There were also administrative staff and one incredible little Eskimo man called Natan, who was the janitor. Dr Paddon met him in the north at a summer fishing station called Slambang, when his wife was very emaciated from cancer and I think must have organized a job for him when she died. He was highly regarded by the Moravians and by his people. Flies were a pest in the summer. This man was the greatest fly hunter I have ever known! He had a long piece of elastic with which he could strike flies with incredible accuracy. It was certainly better than fly spray and any reduction in the fly population was a bonus. Slambang derived its name from the boats that were crashed on to the rocks there by williwaws – furious gusts of wind coming down from the hills. There are some wonderful names in Labrador.

My work was interesting – I did the simple laboratory work, looked after patients and saw outpatients. One of the remarkable problems was with Indian infants who were brought in their papouse –a swaddling wrapping. If they had an elevated temperature it was hard to know whether they were sick or were wrapped up too much in the warm summer weather. We had to undress them and then wait to see if they cooled down before checking the temperature! The papouses were also useful because the Indians could hang their babies up in their tents in them! We also had some deliveries and on one occasion I had to go to the settlement across the river to check an Indian woman who was in early labour.

It was useful to learn how to take x rays and then process them. By the end of the summer I was an expert on chest x rays having taken over 700 of them on nearly everybody in Northern Labrador. My letters home also tell that I fitted at least 29 pairs of glasses, immunized many children against polio and learnt to pull teeth. Dr Paddon thought he had pulled about 18,000 over the years because the people had very poor teeth. He pulled 180 in one day up the coast after the war when the people had received little attention during his absence. He told me that he had even filled his own teeth! I wonder if he was pulling my leg or was a man of great ingenuity! I saw one old Eskimo lady whose teeth were worn flat from chewing on seal skins to soften them when she was sewing them. I also learnt a bit about anaesthesia and how to do nerve blocks before extracting teeth, so all in all it was great experience.

The volunteers lived in a house near the hospital. There were two others, Sally Fowler and John Murphy, who were college students from

Chicago. John decided to teach the local children how to swim. It may seem strange that most of them did not swim when they lived by a lake. It was usually far too cold and much of the year it was frozen. It could be 50 degrees below zero in winter and the summer was short and not very hot. Anyway John persisted and had some success. I heard sad news a year later that his mother was murdered in Chicago.

The community was the largest in northern Labrador apart from Goose Bay, which was a combined American/Canadian Air Force Base, and its civilian neighbouring town of Happy Valley. Still, it was not a huge settlement. Further along the river-side was the Hudson Bay company store which provided most things for the community. There was a school and the High School for the northern half of Labrador. Many of the children came in from settlements along the coast and lived in the boarding house. In some cases, children from very isolated families on the coast could only come to school on two out of three years, if there were three children. The reason was that one always had to stay at home in case of sickness or accident so there was one person to stay with the sick person and one to go for help. Radio or telephone communication did not exist for these people. Few completed high school.

One of their most successful students gained entry to Queen's University in Kingston, Ontario. Tragically, within three weeks of starting his studies he was killed in a car accident. I attended his funeral.

The woods were mainly spruce, firs and silver birches but there was also an abundance of plants with pretty flowers and some of these bore fruit later in the season. The bunch berry flower had four white petals and then produced red berries. (C10.5) It was full summer when I arrived but the vivid golden and orange leaves of fall were there when I left ten weeks later.

A few days after my arrival Dr Paddon had to go north to do some clinics and to investigate a suspicious death. I accompanied him on the flight. We flew off over waterfalls, lakes, trees and muskeg calling in at Makkovik and Hopedale (C10.3), to drop off patients who were returning home, then north past Davis Inlet, to Nain and on to Hebron. (C11.1)

Hebron was the most northerly indigenous settlement in Labrador, 350km north of Nain. It had been settled by Moravian missionaries, who had come to work with the Eskimos in 1830. Their mission building had been constructed in Europe, dismantled, each piece numbered, and sent out for rebuilding. (C11.1) There were no nails. It was held together with wooden pegs. The church section was fifty feet long and was of particular architectural interest. It had no pillars to support the ceiling which was hung on two 16m long beams 100x30cm thick, which in turn were hung from the triangular roof frame which did not collapse because of the strong cross struts. A similar construction was used in the Hopedale church.

My notes, written at the time, comment on the variety of wild flowers – more than I had noticed anywhere else on the coast, and on the mosquitoes which were very bad at that time of year. These are amazing features of the far north – that there are so many flowers and mosquitoes in a land which is frozen up for about eight months a year.

For some years there had been discussion about moving the people south to more accessible settlements. When we visited there were signs of people preparing to move on the last two voyages of the summer by the Trepasse, the ship that did the Goose Bay to Hebron run.

After a short visit we flew off, passing over a grounded iceberg – beautiful white with blue tinges and magnificently sculpted by the wind and sea (C.10.6) – to the camp further up Hebron Bay where the dead man lay. (C10.4) It was a small encampment with about a dozen people and their dogs. The man concerned apparently did not belong to the same clan as the others. The previous night they had all been drinking and he had beaten up his wife. The question was whether there was foul play, especially as he was of another clan or had he been drunk and fallen into the stream or had the dogs attacked him or was it a combination of some or all these? He was found face down, dead and his face had been mauled by dogs. Resolving such cases was a difficult problem in these out of the way places.

We had to fly back over the Kaumajet Mountains which rise to about 1400m, over the Tessuiuk River, which I was told was excellent for fishing. Later I confirmed this. On the way south we stopped in Nain (C11.2) to do a clinic and immunize children and then proceeded on south over rocky country which gradually became increasingly forested as we approached North West River

Our pilot for the beaver aircraft was a Rhodesian called Jeff Henderson. He was one of those people one never forgets. He was an exciting, although rather hair-raising, pilot with whom to fly as he liked to fly low enough to see animals and things on the ground. He had spent three years in Australia, had been a Spitfire pilot and had flown during the emergency in Malaya in the early 1950s where low flying over the forests would have been necessary. He was a well read, very talented man with many interests. He made money to spend, not to save! On one occasion he had gone into the dorm at Cartwright and found a dozen children in need of new shoes. He took them all over to the Store and fitted them out.

There are *many interesting tales* in the north, some of which Tony Paddon told me. One was about a man in Hebron who did not have a dog team and did not go on long hunting trips. He was unconventional in his environment. This man was allocated one of four little houses (10x10 feet) set up under a government housing scheme. He moved in when many of the other people were away in their fishing camps. There are no trees within forty miles of Hebron so he chopped up the floor boards for his fire. When they were finished he took off the lowest boards on the wall and burnt them. To overcome the draft he cut the vertical posts down to ground level and then started on the next layer. The people watched this process wondering what would happen when the roof became too low to stand and then to enter the very low house at all. At that point he put up his tent and broke up the roof and burnt it! When asked what had happened to his house he said it had gone up in smoke! It was thought that he was probably relieved not to have the responsibility for a house which he probably never really wanted. Apparently he was a very talented man, a skilled ivory carver and an excellent shot, even with a rifle which others considered hopeless. He could adjust the sights so he could shoot accurately. There are all sorts of people in the world. Being unconventional does not equate with hopelessness!

Another story Dr Paddon told me was about an Eskimo man in Nain whose wife was murdered. It was generally considered that the husband had probably committed the deed. However, when the authorities considered the complexity of the case and the need to take the witnesses all the way to St Johns for the trial there was some reluctance because of cost. A medical check up was ordered and he was found to have tuberculosis. He was sent to the Sanatorium in St Johns for treatment. After a couple of years he recovered. Conveniently, the crime was forgotten and he was sent home on a TB pension. Was it a case of getting a pension for murdering his wife? Many thought it was!

The next trip was to Makkovik, a settlement at the head of a bay. The small Moravian mission there was run by Katie Hettasch, whose brother was in Hebron and later moved to Nain. We saw some patients and immunized some children. Katie lent me a copy of Peary's account of his trip to the North Pole in 1909 which I read with interest.

We had to transfer a patient to the main Grenfell hospital in St Anthony so I was assigned to accompany him. This was an interesting trip as we flew over Port Hope Simpson where the great bush fire had been burning when I was coming north. We could see how close it had come to the settlement which was out on a point on a lake – it stopped about 200 to 300m from the village. It had burnt a huge area but there is little that can be done up there. The expanses of forest in Labrador are enormous and there are hardly any people so the fires burn until the wind changes and blows them back on themselves when they die out. At St. Anthony I had the chance to see some of the hospital and meet Gordon Thomas, the surgeon in charge. I met him two or three times during the summer. My notes from the time say that he was a fine surgeon who did thoracic and even some cardiac surgery. He was keen on fishing. He did not seem to say much unless spoken to or one knew him well. I do not know whether my impression was accurate or not. He was certainly regarded very highly as a doctor and surgeon.

On the way north we had to call at Cartwright where we spent a night. Then Jeff made the trip really adventurous. We flew low along the North River so that we could see the moose – at times our wings were level with the tree tops. Then up and over the Meally Mountains rising over 600m, and back to North West River. Flying with Jeff Henderson was certainly exciting skimming across Lake Melville at 20m, over waterfalls and other interesting geographical features. He usually went by routes which had a little extra interest in that vast and rather desolate land of rocks, trees and lakes.

One evening we had a picnic on the shores of Small Lake. There was one of the most stunning sunsets I have ever seen turning from orange to pink and to gorgeous purple and indigo – another memory of a wonderful summer. (C9.2)

CHAPTER 14

NORTHERN LABRADOR ON THE "MARAVAL"

A month on a small ship going up the Labrador coast – what a great prospect!

14.1. Captain Small on the Maraval.

On 20th August, a month after I had arrived at North West River, I joined the *Maraval* for the Northern Labrador trip which took nearly a month. (C12.1) It was to be one of the most interesting trips of my life and made me a confirmed addict of the North. We sailed with Dr David Rees, the crew of four plus Captain Small, our experienced Newfie skipper and for a few days, we had John Murphy, one of the student volunteers. The chief engineer and the cook played in Salvation Army bands – the accordion and coronet respectively.

The *Maraval* was designed by a famous New England yacht designer, John Alden. It was like a New England beam trawler, was well equipped and had a good diesel engine. It was built of oak and other hard woods and sheathed with greenheart, a hard tropical wood that is not scored by ice. In addition, the prow was covered with steel to enable it to break ice. It was 23m long and had a shallow draft so that it could go safely into harbours in only a fathom (2 m) of water. It had two masts and could be sailed in the event of engine trouble. This had happened only twice. The dispensary on the deck housed an examination table, a sink, an x ray machine and a dark room. The Maraval had been in service for over 20 years when I sailed on it.

We had two lectures on Radiology as students in Dundee! The lecturer had invited anyone who was interested to visit the department. Knowing that I was going to Labrador I thought that it might be quite useful to accept. I was somewhat surprised by the royal treatment I received – I was only the seventh student ever to have taken up the invitation!

One of my tasks all the way up the coast was to x ray everyone as we were still surveying for tuberculosis (TB). We took the x rays and then I had to wait until we laid up, usually for bad weather, to develop them. It was not exactly exciting work but rather reminiscent of when I worked with Tad, the photographer, in St. Andrews developing photographs. It was not long before the developing began. And then they all had to be correctly named. Further north I had to learn the Eskimo (Inuit) names such as Igliliorte (means house builder), Tuglavina, Semigak, Onalik, Kajuiatsiak, Atseratatjok, Nogassak and others. It was not easy for one not very familiar with them!

Our first stop was *Rigolet*, a small settlement founded as a trading post in 1787 at the east end of Lake Melville, about 70km from North West River. It was a poor place which I had already visited by 'plane. Many of the children had chronic running ears and impetigo, an infectious skin disease covered with scabs. I suspected that there was significant interbreeding as there seemed to be a high incidence of abnormal children with sight and other problems. When we arrived many of the families were away fishing but we x rayed and immunized those that were there.

At the east end of Lake Melville we passed through the narrows to Hamilton Inlet where we anchored for the night at Collinghams Cove. An elderly couple, Arthur Rich and his wife, lived there in isolation. They came out in their dory (flat bottomed Newfoundland boat) for their annual visit with the doctor. They chatted for about an hour and then they left to return to their isolated life for another year.

The next night we anchored at Indian Harbour, the site of the former hospital, to shelter from a storm which blew up. We had to stay there for two nights during which I developed all the x rays taken so far. Unfortunately we did not go ashore but we had a visit from some of the fishermen. I remember one in particular because of the wild and wooly look produced by his long tousled hair – long hair was certainly not the fashion at the time. There were only a few fishermen then – nothing like the hordes that crowded the Grand Banks in Grenfell's days. Probably they had bigger ships that could ply back and forth to St. Johns more readily.

Heading north we stopped by Marak Island to collect water. We found masses of what the locals called "bake apples" but in other parts are called cloud berries. They are a pale apricot colour with a structure resembling a raspberry and are very delicious. We spent a couple of hours collecting them – we were glad of them because the cook made delicious bake apple pies, a pleasant change from the rather monotonous diet of grapefruit for breakfast; fish, mainly cod, and browis (off-white pork, potatoes and sometimes dry biscuit mixed together) and salt beef which constituted most other meals.

Strawberry was the next stop. It had a neat little harbour and was a summer fishing station for two families, among them several Andersens, descended from a Norwegian called Torsten Andersen who had settled at Makkovik, which was our next stop. Katie Hettasch gave us a warm welcome there. The boats came alongside the Maraval bringing the people to be seen and x rayed.(C12.2) We held the clinic and took the x rays in the dispensary on the deck. There was quite a festive atmosphere about our visits. At each place we immunized children, took everyone's x ray and dealt with any medical problems

Our journey took us out to sea again before heading up Kaipakok Bay to *Postville.* The first trader to settle there was D.R.Stewart in 1837. It was hard to believe that it had existed for so long, although there was only one house until they built a sawmill there 15 years before. The previous year disaster had struck and it was burnt down and with it an important source of work. I have a photograph of Postville taken in the very early morning when the sky was lightening and turning to a very delicate, pale pink hue. It just seemed to me that it was a small place that missed the main stream of even Labrador life. It didn't seem to have any indigenous population and the Moravians had not settled there. We had two days there as we were waiting for Dr Paddon to join us. During the time we did some fishing, I checked a contaminated well and visited some homes where I found children with impetigo and running ears that needed attention. So many children in this world live with these rather offensive conditions because of poor hygiene, lack of running water and inadequate medical services.

There was some additional excitement when the Trepasse arrived on its way between Goose Bay and Hebron. It was owned by Windsor brothers, one of whom was member of Parliament for Northern Labrador. That would make electioneering easy!

There are some funny uses of words in English. In Postville I realized how often we use the word "pretty" inappropriately – pretty good or pretty bad. While in most of Labrador "some" was used instead, in Postville they substituted "ugly". Isn't it amazing that something could be ugly wonderful or ugly good! No more ridiculous than pretty bad.

We arrived in Hopedale (C10.3) in the evening and immediately began work. It is a barren rocky place with only a few trees behind the settlement. It had been settled in 1782 and was the site of the first Moravian mission. Across the bay, on a large rocky hill, one of the American DEW line (Distant Early Warning) radar bases was situated. These were scattered at intervals all across the north as part of the North American defence system during the Cold War. Several of us visited it the following afternoon.

My notes describe "the general appearance of most of the houses is poor and it is an untidy place with old tins covering part of the shore. I was invited into one of the Eskimo houses. The furniture is sparse – maybe two beds, a table, one or two chairs and a few boxes as cupboards." I also noted, from photographs that I was shown by the Hettaschs, the darkness of the Eskimos skin in the spring which I presumed to be due to reflected light from the snow and possibly some dirt and smoke too!

Davis Inlet was different. The first European visitor was the English explorer, John Davis, looking for the North West Passage in 1586. It was a beautiful place with well wooded hills on both sides. The first trading post was established in 1831. It was an Indian settlement with a Roman Catholic mission, established in 1945, run by Father Peters, a Belgian. There was a double story mission house and nearby an Indian encampment of tents – again the conditions were crowded and poor. (C12.3) The Indians were mainly hunters and had little interest in fishing. I met Sam Nappeo, who was reputed to have threatened Father Peters with a gun when he was feeling the worse for wear. He sold me the skin of a black bear that he had shot for $4. I have a photograph of him paddling his canoe, reflected in the calm, deep blue water beside the Maraval.

It was here that Dr Paddon taught me how to pull teeth. I remember him telling me about his first trip north after the War when he pulled hundreds of rotten teeth from people who had been neglected because of the war.

The Indians spent much of their time out in the bush hunting. With little medical care, an itinerant life, drink and a tough environment infant survival was low. In the previous year, 1958-9, nine babies had been born and eleven infants had died – a terrible situation. They lived in tents. (C12.3) It is hard to imagine how they survive in winter with temperatures of minus 40-50°C.

Nain, which was established in 1771 (C11.2), was the next major settlement with a population of about 400. It is situated on the north side of an inlet with a large rocky hill on the opposite side. (C.12.3) There are still trees around although at that latitude they were becoming more stunted. The new hospital with eight beds was opened in 1956. It was through some trees to the west of the settlement. We arrived to find that a boy had just broken his leg, a spiral fracture of his tibia. We x rayed it and then set the fracture under anaesthetic on the Maraval. I maintained the anaesthetic while Dr Paddon manipulated and plastered the leg. It was the only time that I ever used Vinesthene (divinyl ether) which is a rapidly acting inhalational anaesthetic. It was all we had on board. The boy recovered.

A girl had died the previous day and we had to do a post mortem as the cause of death was not clear. It seemed possible that the acute illness was due to poisoning, maybe resulting from an attempt to induce abortion. She had been given intravenous therapy by the nurse but to no avail.

Many of the people went out to fishing places in the summer. The nurses taught some of the brighter young people some basics of medical care, especially the recognition of symptoms. They could radio telephone the nursing station, describe the patient's symptoms and be given instructions what to give the patient from their medical supplies. They even had a very capable fourteen year old girl doing this.

Nain was a relatively big place so there were many people to see and x ray. We had a long day not finishing work until 10pm. The following day we sailed around nearby fishing camps in the inlets – more x rays. By the end of it I was tired having taken 230 x rays in two very long days. The next day there were 100kph winds so we stayed where we were and I developed all the x rays.

Black Island was the next stop – a unique place because the buildings and landings were built on steep rocks which then fell sharply into the sea so that we could go alongside. (C12.5) In most places apart from Hopedale and Nain we transferred to land by small boats. When we finished taking x rays I pulled some teeth and fitted glasses while Dr Paddon went to visit an old resident, Willy Ford. There was a whole clan of Fords on the coast, one of whom, Dora, worked as an aid at North West River Hospital. (C10.2.) The crew jigged for cod and fed the dogs who were sitting hungrily on the rocks. I am sure they appreciated our visit. Jigging is a process where a line with big hooks is dropped into the sea and pulled up and down until a fish is struck and then pulled up.

Much of our passage had been in channels sheltered from the ocean by islands. This continued up Port Manders Run to Medusa Bay. (C12.6) What a beautiful spot! The big bay opened to the sea through a narrow channel while the rest of the ocean side was separated by a raised beach, flat on top covered with pebbles which looked spectacular in the low evening light. There was a fine view across to a large flat-tish topped mountain, Mt. Thorsby (1000m) to the south west. Inside a solitary deserted hut old magazines and newspapers lined the wall creating some historical perspective. I wondered who had lived there. What was his story? It had probably only been used in spring during the sealing season and in summer as it seemed too lonely in this isolated, quiet, peaceful place – except when the wind was howling – to spend the winter there.

We anchored for the night in the bay where we jigged for cod. The fish were so plentiful that they were hooked, often through the side. I caught about ten in as many minutes!

Now, the cod has been fished to excess and such an experience may be a thing of the past. Over-fishing on the Grand Banks is another example of how commercial greed has almost decimated a major source of food.

The 'plane met us here and Dr. Paddon returned home, being replaced by Paddy Roundhill, an Irishman who had been at St. Anthony. He replaced David Rees at North West River.

The next day we set off up a bay to Tessuiuk piloted by Fred Grubb, the Moravian missionary in Nain. There were two families up there. The skipper was cranky because he thought this was an excuse for a fishing trip. Maybe he was right but it was fortunate that we did x ray the five people there because one of them was the worst case of TB we picked up on the whole trip. Dr Thomas from St. Anthony reviewed all the films. It was an experience to watch this as he remembered all the patients and could tell at a glance, without reference to previous films, whether there were any signs of deterioration. I was very impressed.

After the x rays were taken, we rowed to the mouth of the river, beached our dory and set off to fish. I was very inexperienced in the art of trout fishing but was lent a rod with a spinner. It was an exciting afternoon. I caught several 1/2–1kg trout and char. The river was bordered by wooded hills on either side of the valley. We fished up the river to some falls where the salmon were trying unsuccessfully to jump to reach a lake which stretched several miles inland. We fished for about four hours and having caught all we needed and maybe more I can remember having fun watching the fish following the spinner and pulling it away when they tried to bite – a great fishing story with an unusual twist! Fancy trying not to catch the fish.

Okak Bay was to be our next destination but the weather was too rough so we sheltered in a safe harbour beside the former settlement of *Okak*. (C12.7) The wind died down sufficiently in the afternoon for us to go ashore. It was a most haunting, interesting place to visit because of what had been there – a thriving Moravian mission and a substantial, predominantly Eskimo settlement. Not much was left.

In the fall (autumn) of 1918 the *Harmony*, the Moravian mission supply ship arrived with a sick man on board. It only came twice a year so was an occasion of great excitement in these isolated settlements. Normally the people went on board to help unload the cargo and to load the fish and other goods that were being sent out to be sold. On this occasion the skipper told the people not to come aboard because of the sick man. They ignored his advice – how could they miss this occasion? He turned out to have the Spanish flu that caused a pandemic all around the world and caused about twenty million deaths. Within ten days the settlement was devastated – only 59 people remained alive out of 263 who were in the settlement at the time. Most of the men died. The indigenous population suffered most as they had no exposure to outside diseases and therefore had no immunity. The disease caused a fulminating pneumonia but there was no pain or discomfort in the death.

14.2. Doris Saunders, Goose Bay. Editor of Them days.

Decades later some of the survivors told their stories in *Them days*, a little magazine published by Doris Saunders in Goose Bay. This small, dynamic, wonderful lady published this quarterly with stories of old Labrador, thereby preserving some wonderful history. She was given an honorary degree from Memorial University in St Johns, not having had a university education, and then received an Order of Canada award for her outstanding work.

One lady told how her mother was sewing and just keeled over and died. Her father brought wood in and put it on the fire and lay down and soon died. All the people in her house died one by one until only she and her little cousin remained. They were weak. She could not feed him. She was just a little child herself. Then the dogs, which hadn't been fed because the people were all ill, became ravenous, broke from their chains and began eating the people. They broke into her house which had dead bodies all around and took her little cousin – she did not know whether he was yet dead. It was amazing that their lead dog protected her from the other dogs and she survived. Eventually some of the survivors recovered sufficiently to go to the help of the others and shoot the dogs which had become dangerous. It was only when she screamed that the people realized that she was not a dog when they came into her house.

Orphaned children were taken into care by others, some of whom were only young women. The mission people survived and eventually organized the burial of the dead in a mass grave. This proved difficult to dig because it was November and the ground was frozen below three feet. They had to pour oil on the ground to melt the ice so that they could dig further.

Some of the people were still out in camps around the bay and on the islands. One of the missionaries attempted to visit one of these places, Orlearsuk, but had to turn back because of bad weather. When no news was heard from there they assumed all the people had died. After some time two boys went out there to pick up a barrel of berries. When they arrived they saw someone moving in the window of one of the houses and thought it was a ghost. Who wouldn't? They left in a hurry. Three weeks later someone else went over to investigate and shoot the dogs and found a little girl on her own who had survived by melting snow with a candle and gaining sustenance from a tin of milk and some berries. She was living with the dead who were being eaten by the dogs. What a devastating memory to have to live with. These are only two examples of the tales recorded.

The *Harmony* had come from Hebron where it had also taken the disease. Only sixteen out of a hundred people who were there at the time survived. Many were away at the time but in the district only 70 out of 220 survived. Nain and Hopedale missed the 'flu but were devastated the same year with 23 deaths from measles and chicken pox in Nain and six from chicken pox in Hopedale.

Little remained in Okak to tell that forty-one years before it had been a thriving community. There were a few pier pylons remaining, the chimney of the mission house and further away a few gravestones in the original cemetery. But there was rhubarb such as I have never seen or heard of anywhere else. It stood about one and a half metres high. Needless to say we took some which the cook turned into magnificent rhubarb pies, a nice variation in our diet!

I walked up the hill to the south where we could look over to where another settlement, Nutak, had been while the other direction to the north and north east lay the Kaumajet mountains. When we left Okak for Hebron we had to sail through a great crack in these mountains which formed a narrow channel, Mugford Tickle, with towering cliffs on either side. It was a spectacular site with the strata of rocks sloping up to the north. Unfortunately the clouds were down and it was drizzling so that I was unable to photograph it. Beyond Mugford Tickle was White Island which was composed of grey rock. It has an interesting outline – mostly concave surfaces and pointed hill tops.

Having passed through Mugford Tickle we came out to the open sea. The ship rolled considerably more than when we were protected by islands which we had been much of the way. Dr. Paddon had joined us again and he told me that if I wanted to be seasick, which I didn't, I should try shaving using the mirror in the dispensary on the deck and watch the sea reflected in it through the window – this doubled the appearance of the roll. I immediately felt like vomiting but by use of considerable will-power I managed not to. What a challenge that was! That was the funny sort of thing he would tell me. We passed White Island and soon the Kaumajet mountains made a magnificent panorama with the Bishops Mitre (1200m) and

14.3. Sketches of Bishops Mitre and Mt. Brave.

Mt.Brave rising 1400m steeply out of the sea. Fortunately I sketched these grand mountains as the weather was not ideal for photography.

We soon reached *Hebron* which I have already described with its fascinating mission building and church. (C11.1) We did our x ray and medical work and then I had time to wander around and up the hill which was very rocky. Suddenly I came across stones laid in a line. I lifted one and found myself looking at a skull of a complete skeleton. Obviously it was too rocky to dig graves so they buried their dead under a pile of stones. There were several of these scattered over the hillside.

Hebron had a stone dog out on a little island just off the shore. Andrew Piercy, who had been a patient at North West River took me out in a boat to see it. There is a mythological story attached to it that the magician of Hebron turned the dog into stone to show that he was just as good as his counterpart in Nain.

14.4. The Stone Dog at Hebron.

Hebron was closing down. Supplying a settlement over 300km further north than the next place, Nain, was expensive and provided more problems in winter. Providing medical care was difficult and infant mortality was high. In addition the trees in the area had been cut down for firewood and they were having to travel long distances to obtain wood to keep them warm in winter. After several years discussion about resettling the people south in Nain, Hopedale and Makkovik it had at last been decided that over the next two years this would be done. However when the first group had left the remainder, except one family of Semigaks, decided that they did not want to be left behind so the move was soon to be completed. It was a privilege, rather sad really, to make the last visit to a community which would be a ghost village within three weeks – just deserted, with that historic, 130 year old mission building left to the ravages of nature. It is still there but its condition is deteriorating. It would be wonderful to have it restored as a historic monument. But then, how many people would travel to see it? The strange thing is that Hebron is still marked on maps.

Our journey south now began. First stop was Okak Bay where we had been prevented access because of bad weather. We arrived to find that the people were not there. We retraced our route to Black Island, September Harbour and Youngs Harbour as we had to repeat some of the x rays and pick children up to take them into school in Nain. In my notes I comment on "one little fellow of six who was wearing a new parka with a fur lining around the hood. It was a little too big and seeing his face smiling out from the hood was rather quaint."

They had recently introduced a better exporting system for the fish from Nain so that the prosperity of the community had improved and the amount of brewing and drinking had declined.

On 14th September we had our first snow at Davis Inlet.

I never expected to return to Postville but we did in the most unusual circumstances. Dr Paddon was on board. He said to me "I think we should go into Postville". I replied "Why? We have seen everybody going north and that we had already spent two days there." He thought about it but decided that we should go. We arrived to be greeted by some relieved people who told us that a boy had broken his arm that morning – I don't know whether that was before or after our discussion. It is an example of someone who is very in tune with his environment having a sixth sense – Jim Corbett, the man eating tiger and leopard hunter had many similar experiences while in the jungles of India. We took the boy with us back on the *Maraval* to North West River. After that we made a fairly rapid trip back with only short stops at Makkovik and Rigolet.

14.5. On the Maraval on arrival back at North West River.

The *Maraval* never went so far north again. Hebron closed down. Things changed. The greater use of air transport to carry the x ray machine into the settlements and the decline in tuberculosis meant that the *Maraval* was no longer necessary and eventually went out of service. It had served the people of Labrador well. I considered myself very fortunate to have made that historic last voyage north on it.

I was due to return to Scotland but they asked me to stay for another fortnight which I readily agreed to. It had been a wonderful experience and contributed to my decision to return to Canada.

Little did I realize when I left with the trees brilliant with gold and red leaves that the following year I would be asked to return to do a locum for two weeks. That was like returning home to the harsh land to which I had become attached. And so ended one of the most interesting and exciting periods of my life. But there is one more important story to tell!

Chapter 15

The Traverspine Monster

The story of the Traverspine monster was recounted to me by Dr Paddon as we sailed past Voisey Bay in the north. It was one of many tales he told me but for some reason I remembered it – maybe because I enjoy a good practical joke.

Years before, when Tony Paddon used to do dog team trips to the northern settlements during winter, he received a message that old Amos Voisey wanted him to visit. This involved an extra 25km up what is now Voisey Bay, a place which is now well known because of mineral discovery there. He arrived in the evening and stayed overnight. During their conversation Voisey told him he was old and deteriorating and that he did not expect to be around when he next came. He had something on his mind which he felt he should tell someone before he died as the other fellow involved was already dead.

When he and his friend were young they had worked in a lumber camp at Traverspine. One day they were left in camp to look after things. They decided to play a practical joke. They made large footprints which they tracked through the snow into camp. They then created the appearance of a scuffle and left the camp. They hid with the intention of coming out to announce that it was a joke. The problem was that it did not work that way. When the men returned from cutting timber and found these footprints they were terrified, grabbed their things and fled, never to return. The young fellows were now too embarrassed to admit their mischief and so the legend of the Traverspine Monster (or Devil) was started.

When Tony Paddon told me this I thought it was an amusing story and have told it many, many times over the years. I told it at a yarn night on a trip to the Antarctic. Afterwards a lady in the audience approached me to tell me that she had been for a trip to Labrador and had met one of Dr Paddon's sons. She had his autobiography and offered to lend it to me. When I read it I found that he had described this excursion in detail but had not included the tale of the Traverspine Monster. I wondered why? Maybe he had forgotten about it.

As I was going to Montreal the next year, 1998, I thought I might see if any of the Paddons were still in North West River and so I wrote to "any of the Paddon family, North West River, Labrador". In due course I received a letter from Dr Paddon's wife, Sheila, and then had an email from his son in Toronto. I decided that I would like to return to see what it was like after all these years.

When I was passing through Toronto I phoned Dave Paddon and told him the story of the monster. He said he had never heard it before which surprised me. He said I should visit Doris Saunders in Goose Bay which I did. Imagine my surprise when I told her the story and she replied that she had never heard it and furthermore, that she had planned to spend time at Traverspine that summer looking for evidence of this monster! "This is a big legend in Labrador,"she said. I was surprised. She then asked me to write the story for her so that evening, not finding much else to do in Goose Bay, I wrote about my summer in Labrador and called it "Myth exploded or tall tale".

Next day I returned to North West River after 39 years. Now there was a good road and a bridge over the river. The hospital was closed, the Grenfell mission had handed over the medical work to the Newfoundland government and while more houses were still being built the activity on which it had thrived had gone. I visited Sheila Paddon and she had never heard the story either. I suppose Dr Paddon told me not expecting me to remember. But why had he not mentioned it in his book? Was it that he had forgotten or did he not wish to expose the real story of the legend?

When I left Goose Bay I bought T shirts for my grandchildren. They had a midnight sun, a moose and a strange creature with very large feet printed on them!

And so it appeared that I was the repository of the legend – nobody else seemed to know.

Doris Saunders told me after my article was published that it was well received and that the people were relieved that there was no monster at Traverspine!

The amazing features of the story were that no one ever saw a monster and the event must have occurred almost 100 years before. It had been almost 40 years since I was in Labrador. It would have been 10 years or more before that since Dr Paddon had used dog teams and Voisey had lived from a young man to an old man, maybe 50 years!

Part 4

Colour Pictures

Page numbers referred to in the text (C--.-) indicates the page where picture will be found.

Index of Coloured Pictures

34 Middle East
35 Miscellaneous scenery
36 Japan, Iceland, Prague
37 Family
38 Art
39 Art
40 Paintings
41 Australia
42 Australia
43 Australia
44 Churches
45 Buildings and People
46 People
47 People
48 People

Home and School – Kenya

1.1. Author's mother.

1.3. Our house at Tumutumu.

1.2. Munuhe, mother's gardener, and Priscilla, his daughter.

1.4. Telephoto view of Mt Kenya from our house.

1.5. Market stall beside Tumutumu hospital.

1.6. Prince of Wales School, Nairobi.

1.7. Two engine train leaving Karatina.

Mount Kenya

2.1. Mt Kenya from the west.

2.2. Mt Kenya from the Naro Moru trac

2.3. Camping on the moors amongst giant groundsell – Richard Carles by tent.

2.4. Curling pond, Lew Glacier and main peak Nelion, from east.

2.6. Nagenia trees and bamboo at 3000m on Mt Kenya.

2.5. Giant lobelia.

2.7. Wet weather on the Chogoria track (east side).

Kilimanjaro and Aberdares

3.1. Composite painting of trip up Mt Kilimanjaro.

3.2. 150m drop on Kururu Falls on the Aberdares.

3.3. Glaciers in the Kilimanjaro crater.

3.4. Moorlands at 3000m on the Aberdares with Mbogo-ini.

3.5. Ola Relling at 4300m on Kilimanjaro.

3.6. Caraluma (almost black flower) on Mt Kulal.

KENYA ANIMALS

4.1. Buffalo.

4.2. Rhinoceros – Pixie in Amboselli P

4.3. Chameleons – which change colour for camouflage.

4.4. Gerenuk.

4.5. Zorilla.

4.6. Grevy's zebra with narrow stripe Samburu Park.

4.7. Waterbuck.

STRATHPEFFER, SCOTLAND

5.1. My grandmother's cottage – Ardival.

5.2. Looking across to Ben Wyvis in winter.

5.3. Strathpeffer

5.4. Strathpeffer Square.

5.5. Golfing at Strathpeffer – 80 year old Uncle Kenneth driving.

6.1. Ruins of dry stone houses, Mingulay village.

6.2. Puffins on the western cliffs of Mingulay.

6.3. Cliffs and sea pinks.

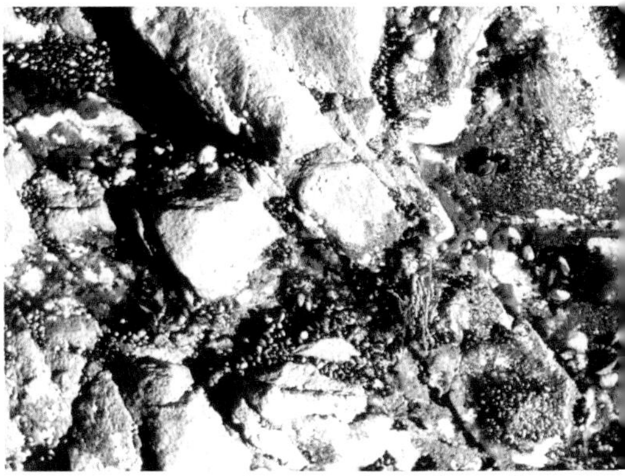
6.5. Close up of a rock pool.

6.4. Wildflowers.

6.6. Monach Islands (Heisker).

7.1. Mingulay Bay

7.2. Looking north from Mingulay towards Barra.

St Andrews and Abergeldie

8.1. Students wearing gowns
on the pier walk, St Andrews.

8.2. St Andrews from St Rule Tower – cas
ruins in the middles, west sands in the dista

[Left] 8.3. Kate Kennedy's coach and
shieldbearers beside the chapel
before the procession.

[Below] 8.4. Pittenweem harbour, Fife

[Left] 8.5. Deeside –
Abergeldie Castle and Mains

[Above] 8.6. Corndavon Moors
with grousebeaters.

[Left] 8.7. Donaldsons at Douglas Terra
Dundee

9.1. Peyto Park and Lake in the Rocky Mountains – marmot in foreground.

9.2. Labrador sunset (1959).

9.3. Lake Louise – March 1962.

10.1. North West River from the south.

10.2. Aids Dora Ford, Kathleen, and volu
teer Sally Fowler with children patient

10.3. Hopedale from the air.

10.4. Dr Paddon with Eskimos in Hebron B

[Above left] 10.5. Bunchberry flowers.

[Above] 10.6. Iceberg off Hebron, 1959.

[Left] 10.7. Beaver aircraft – JAT, at the Pond, Gander, Newfoundland.

11.1. Hebron – two weeks before it was evacuated in September 1959.
The large mission building was constructed in Europe and re-assembled in Hebron.

11.2. Nain fron the air looking north-east.

Maraval Trip

12.1. Maraval leaving NWR.

12.2. Patients beside Maraval at Makkovik.

12.4. Nain pier.

12.3. Indian tent, Davis Inlet.

[Left] 12.5. Dock at Black Island.

12.6. Medusa Bay, north of Nain.

[Left] 12.7. Looking north from Oka to Kiplagait Mountains

13.1. Beth and Heather Watt among trilliums, 1961.

13.2. Sandy Middleton making breakfast by the kombi, northern Ontario.

13.3. NWT border – 60° north.

13.4. Alexandra Falls – frozen – Hay River.

13.5. Louise Falls on Hay River.

13.6. Crossing the Mackenzie River on ice.

13.7. Fish drying and Indian tents, Fort Rae.

14.1. Yellowknife from the air looking north. Old Town with Yellowknife Bay beyond. Hospital with red roof by Frame Lake in the middle.

14.2. Close up (15cm) of ground cover at Yellowknife.

AROUND YELLOWKNIFE

15.1. Old town, Yellowknife.
Anderson Thompson's house in foreground.

15.2. The house in winter with plug in for car at the gate.

15.3. Labrador tea.

15.4. Frost on tree before freeze up.

.5. Red throated grebe beside nest.

15.6. Holding a 34kg gold brick.

15.7. Pouring a gold brick at Giant Mine.

16.1. Inuit tents at Arctic Sound with huskies – November 1961.

16.2. Tom Nanutak and his son with sealskin clothing.

16.3. Arctic Sound community with frozen seals

16.4. Clear Arctic winter day near Arctic Sound

North West Territories

17.1. Betty Lyall and ice porch at Spence Bay.

17.2. Wilberforce Falls – 50m high – half frozen.

7.3. Holman Island settlement – 70°N.

17.4. Holman Island Eskimos (Inuits).

17.5. Discovery Mine – minus 35°, February 1962.

18.1. Mt Sir James McBrien, Brintnell Lake.

18.2. Entrance to the First Canyon.

18.3. First Canyon (mountains 1900m, river 550m).

18.4. The "Gate", Third Canyon.

18.5. Hot springs.

18.6. Search planes at Dall Lake.

19.1. Matthews Range, NFD, with anthill.

19.3. Crater of Mr Kulal.

19.2. Samburu moving camp. NFD.

19.4. Bay on Lake Turkana (Rudolf).

19.5. El Molo Camp beside Lake Turkana.

[Right] 19.6. El Molo girls and decoration.

19.7. Flamingos on Lake Nakuru.

20.1. Lugard Falls.

20.4. Ruins at Gedi, near Malindi.

20.5. Landing sailfish (29kg).

[Left] 20.2. Flame tree and Kikuyu woman carrying firewood.

[Right] 20.6. Native cattle on a dusty road.

20.3. Fort Jesus, Mombasa.

20.7. Hornbill.

20.8. Kikuyu girls – 1958

ANTARCTICA – ROSS SEA TRIP

[Above left] 21.1. King Penguins and elephant seals on Macquarie Island.

[Above right] 21.2. Macquarie Island with royal penguins and elephant seals on the beach.

21.3. Watercolour of Borschgrevink's Hut (1899) and ruins of a Scott party hut (1911), Cape Adare.

21.4. Ross Ice Shelf.

5. Adelie penguins landing at Cape Adare.

21.6. Campbell Ice Tongue, with zodiac. Mt Melbourne is in the distance.

22.1. Shackleton's Hut 1907, looking across to Mt Lister (4000m).

22.2. Mt Erebus reflected in the sea near Cape Royds.

South Georgia

23.1. Salisbury Plain with about 100,000 king penguins.

23.2. Albatrosses on Albatross Island.

23.3. Shackleton's grave, Grytviken.

23.4. Grytviken – old whaling station.

23.5. Robin Bradshaw at Stanley, Falkland Islands – cathedral behind.

Antarctica and Tierra del Fuego

24.1. Gentoo penguins nesting on Cuverville Island

24.2. Jade icerberg.

24.3. Iceberg w[ith] blue stippling

[Left]
24.4. Lago Fognani, Tierra del Fuego.

[Right]
24.5. Stunted trees near Ushaia.

24.6. Patagonian geese.

24.7. Sunset with "solar pillar".

Asia – Dress

25.1. Northern Thailand hill tribe costumes.

25.4. Japanese lady musicians in kimonos.

25.2. Korean formal dresses.

25.5. Henna hand decoration for wedding, Pakistan.

25.3. Indian dancers.

26.1. Dilish and his Indian lunch.

26.2. Roadside vendor, Northern Pakistan

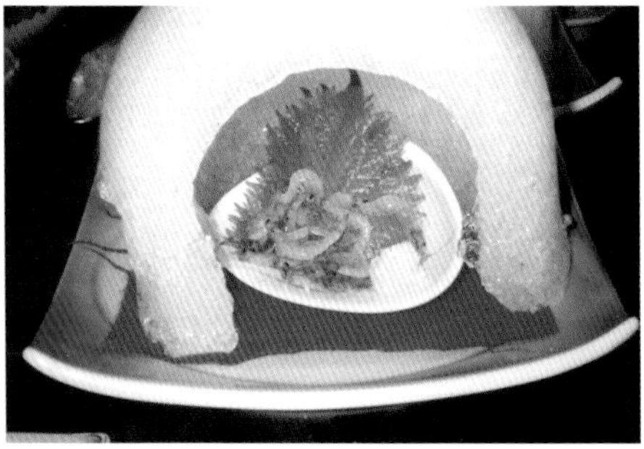

26.3. Japanese ice cave and shrimp.

26.4. Cooking beef on a hot stone.

26.5. Japanese sushi.

26.6. Reflections by Japanese tea house.

26.7. Great expectations – Montreal dessert.

Peru

27.1. Inca Terraces near Colca Canyon

27.2. Colca Canyon.

27.3. Inca gate and rainbow, Sansahuanman, Cusco.

27.4. On the altiplano going to Colca Canyon.

South America

28.1. Mist rising off Machu Pichu, Peru.

28.2. Machu Pichu.

28.2. Machu Pichu.

28.4. Iguassu Falls from the air.

LA PAZ, BOLIVIA

29.1. La Paz, highest city in the world.

29.2. Plaza and government buildings.

29.3. Indian street stall.

29.4. Street letter writer.

29.5. Valle des Lunes, with Carlos Riquelme from Chile.

Bolivia

30.1
Crossi
mount
near La
at 420(

30.2. Old door, Coroico.

30.3. Reed boat builder who built RA II for Thor Heyerdahl, Lake Titicaca.

30.5. Tiahuanaco – statues.

30.4. Tiahuanaco – ancient site.

Ecuador and Galapagos

31.1. Plaza Grande, old Quito.

[Right] 31.3. Otavalo Market – Indian with typical local hat.

[Left] 31.2. San Juan de Dios – oldest hospital in South America – watercolour of courtyard.

[Right] 31.4. Blue footed boobies, Galapagos.

[Above] 31.5. Iguanas, about 60-80cm.

[Left] 31.6. Tortoises, which are island-specific.

[Right] 31.7. Sea lion and crab.

CHILE AND ARGENTINA

32.1. Reflections – Torres del Paine (south Chile).

32.4. Guanacos.

32.2. Ice breaking off Perito Moreno Glac
south Argentina.

32.5. Old church at Mamiña, northern Chile.

32.3. Composite oil painting of trip f
Arica to Lake Chungara (northerr
Chile). Church designed by Eiffel

33.1. Palmyra, Syria.

33.2. Amphitheatre at Bosra, Syria.

33.3. Baalbeck, Lebanon.

33.4. Karnak Temple, Luxor, Egypt.

34.1. Amphitheathre and Forum, Jerrash, Jordan.

34.2. Troglodyte houses at Cappadocia, Turkey.

34.3. Ed Deir, Petra, Jordan.

34.4. Colourful rocks, Petra.

MISCELLANEOUS

1. Dingle Peak near Lake Hawea, NZ.

35.2. Blue mist, Mangawera, New Zealand.

3. Sand dunes in Namib Desert, Namibia, over 100m high. (watercolour)

35.4. Huge underground crystal (over 3m long).

5.5. Near Kinlochervie, northwest Scotland.

35.6. Fraser and his canal boat on a London canal.

35.7. Farmhouse at Molo, Kenya (1958)

Japan, Iceland, Prague

36.1. Horyu-Ji Temple, Nara, Japan. Oldest wooden building.

36.2. Todaiji Temple, Nara. Largest wood building – 48 m high.

[Right] 36.4. Iceland – pseudo craters beside Lake Myvatin.

[Left] 36.3. Iceland – fissure in the rocks.

36.5. Iceland – geothermal steam.

36.6. Charles Bridge, Prague.

36.7. Astronomical clock, Prague.

Family

37.1. Janet and twins, Stanley Park, Vancouver, 1964.

37.2. With Janet, Maryann and Ken, after receiving AM at Government House.

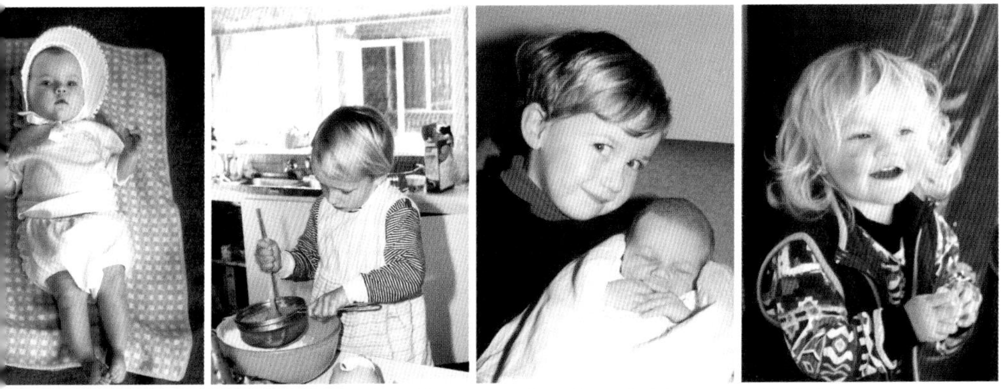

37.3-37.6. Children and grandchildren growing from babies to small children.

37.7. Curiosity – Fraser studying a Monstera.

37.9. With Janet at MD graduation, 1980.

37.8. Father and sons all playing for a Kew Hockey team.

Art

38.1. Monet's house at Giverny.

38.2. Sylvie Herbeau and rc
at Givernty

38.3. Stained glass ceiling of the NGV,
Melbourne (Leonard French).

38.4. Autumn colours through
the water wall, NGV.

38.5. Modesty – sculpture in Ballarat Gardens.

9.1. Terry Dalley painting by the Thames.

39.2. Rock in the Swat River, northern Pakistan.

39.3. Bow Lake, Canadian Rockies (watercolour)

39.4. Mt Kenya, north side (watercolour)

39.5. Portrait of the author by Sue Jarvis.

39.6. Mt Terror, Antarctica (acrylic).

39.7. Hamnøy, Lofoten Islands, Norway (oil).

Paintings

40.1. Mt Feathertop, Victorian Alps.

40.2. Reflections on a London can

40.3. Kings Canyon, Central Australia.

40.4. Chambers Gorge, Flinders Ranges, South Australia

40.5. Mt Sondor from Glen Helen, central Australia.

AUSTRALIA

41.1. Hills near Buchan, eastern Victoria.

41.2. Masuharo Katsumo supporting London Bridge, one year before it collapsed.

41.3. Twelve Apostles, western Victoria.

41.4. Remarkables, Kangaroo Island, South Australia

[Left] 41.5. Pinnacles, Western Australia.

[Above] 41.6. West Australian wildflowers – grevillia.

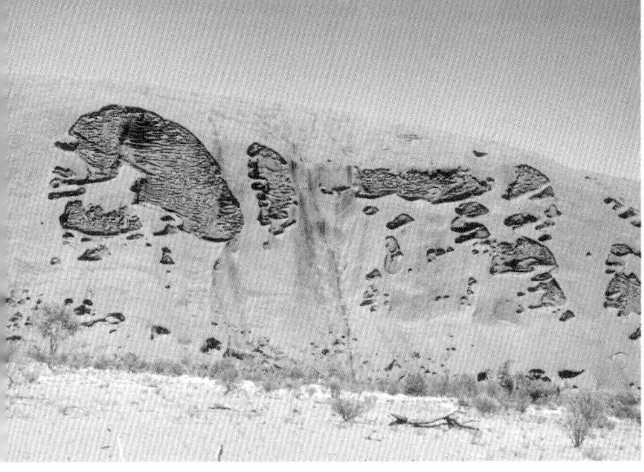

[Left] 41.7. Natural sculpture on Uluru (Ayers Rock).

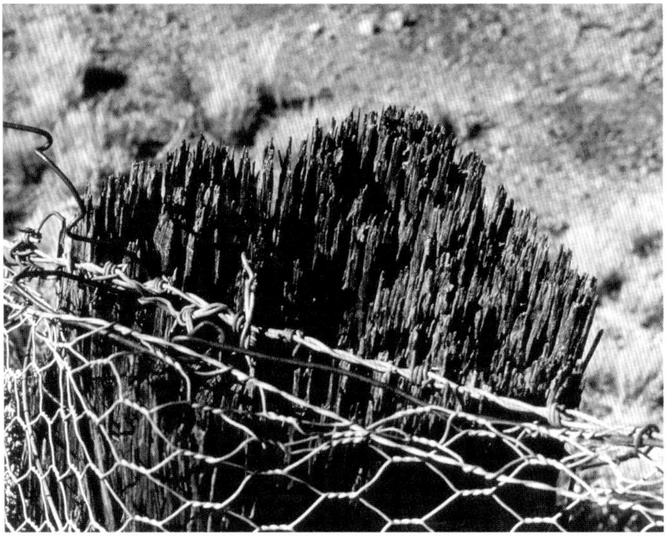
42.1. Old fence post near Broken Hill.

42.2. Stages of flowering and
formation of Monstera delici

42.3. Wattle in flower.

42.4. Echidna and baby.

42.5. Frilled dragon.

42.6. Tree ferns and eucalypts in Victorian hi

Australia

.1. Whisky Bay, Wilson's Promontory, Victoria.

43.2. Aboriginal art, Obiri Rocks, Kakadu National Park.

43.3. Road train, Northern Territory.

43.4. Devil's Marbles, Northern Territory.

43.5. Katherine Gorge, Northern Territory.

43.6. Cradle Mountain and Dove Lake, Tasmania

Religious Buildings

44.1. Amiens Cathedral, France (13th century).

44.2. Domes in Mohamed Ali Mosque in C

44.3. Baroque pilgrimage church, Weis, Bavaria (Zimmerman – 18th century).

44.4. St Basil's Cathedral, Moscow.

45.1. Golden Temple, Amritsar, Punjab, India.

45.2. Man selling head scarves at Golden Temple.

5.4. Sixteenth-generation gatekeeper, Ranakpur.

45.3. Jain Temple, Ranakpur, India. (Inset: interior.)

45.5. Colosseum, El Jem, Tunisia.

45.6. M. Souiden at Dougga Roman ruins, Tunisia.

PEOPLE

[Left] 46.1. Old man, Swat Valley, north Pakistan

[Right] 46.2. Gabra mother and baby, north Kenya.

46.3. Sikh tailor, near Simla, India.

46.4. Shoe shiner, Istanbu

46.5. Boatman, Lamu, Kenya.

46.6. Basuto village chief.

46.7. Crusader Castle caretaker, Jordan.

PEOPLE

1. Shopkeeper in Urgup, Turkey – antiques and musical instruments.

47.2. National costume Surubaya, Indonesia.

47.3. Australian Rules Football fanatic.

47.4. Selling local knit-wear near Cusco, Peru.

47.5. "Central Heating" – Kikuyu children with their fire in cold weather (1958).

47.6. A young Samburu with armbands and necklaces (1963)

People

[Left] 48.1. Old Eskimo (Inuit) woman with tattoos (1962).

[Right] 48.2. Haunting eyes, Bangladesh.

[Left] 48.3. "Ndeke", a Kikuyu in Kenya.

[Right] 48.4. Old lady spinning, Finland.

[Left] 48.5. Artist on Charles Bridge, Prague.

[Right] 48.6. Children by fake manhole, Bratislava, Slovakia.

Part 5

Canada

CHAPTER 16
MOVE TO CANADA

My final year was dominated by study relieved at weekends by playing hockey locally for Queens College, Dundee. Social life was minimal. I was determined to pass my final examinations because I wanted to get on with life and especially because I had arranged to go to Canada to intern. It would have been a disaster to fail but fortunately I passed.

Travelling by sea was still common in 1960. I crossed the Atlantic on one of the Empress liners which sailed from Greenock in Scotland to Montreal, taking nearly a week. The first views of Canada were in the St Lawrence estuary as we sailed towards Quebec. We stopped there for long enough to go ashore and walk up to Chateau Frontenac, a magnificent hotel, standing like a citadel on the cliff overlooking the mighty St Lawrence River.

A little to the west, outside the city wall, is the Heights of Abraham where General James Wolfe amassed his troops on 13th September 1759 and defeated the French General Montcalm in a crucial battle which lasted only an hour. Both generals died shortly afterwards. This victory for the British resulted in Quebec becoming British and later, part of Canada. But war is a strange business. So often the victors appear not always to fare so well. It was two centuries later that President de Gaulle of France shouted "Vive la France, Vive la Quebec" and began the resurgence of French Canadian feeling which led to some seeking independence from the rest of Canada. Long before, the Liberal party had recognized the importance of the French Canadians by alternately selecting an English and French speaking Canadian as their leader. De Gaulle's outburst made the rest realize that the French needed more recognition and led to Canada becoming an officially bilingual country. In the west, where the French influence was negligible, WAC Bennett, the Premier of BC at the time (1965) said that if British Columbia had to be bilingual Chinese ought to be the second language! He was recognizing the large Chinese influence in that province.

From Montreal I took the train to Toronto and on 200km southwest to London, Ontario. It was then a city of about 160,000 through which the Thames River ran. The tree lined streets with the gardens open at the front to the streets gave it a attractive ambience. Its situation between Lakes Huron and Ontario gave it a hot and very humid climate in summer. The fall, as the North Americans call autumn, was stunningly beautiful with the vivid colours of eastern Canada as the leaves changed to yellow, red and orange. They were particularly magnificent where the Thames ran past the Storybook Gardens, a children's park with nursery rhyme themes. The winter was cold, the trees were bare and the river froze. Spring hardly lasted two weeks. Suddenly the buds on the trees burst forth and summer had arrived again. I left before the intense heat and humidity returned.

Canada was different. It was a huge country. I had to get used to their accent, the fact that they drove on the right hand side of the road and that they had different terminology for many things.

My summer in Labrador had expanded my vision and gave me the idea that interning in Canada would be an interesting change and that my opportunities might be better than if I stayed in Scotland. This proved to be so as the rotating internship gave me a wider range of experience than I would have gained in a smaller centre in Britain.

Little did I realize what a significant year it was to be. I gained valuable medical experience, was exposed to a different culture and found a wife. My job as an intern was at Victoria Hospital on South Street. It was an 800 bed general hospital, with an attached Children's Hospital across the road. It served then as the major teaching hospital for the University of Western Ontario. This had a well regarded medical school and it proved to be a good place to do my internship. My colleagues, mostly locals, turned out to be convivial and good fun. One group of five interns decided to sing Christmas carols onto the dictating machines to entertain the stenographers – the only problem was that they weren't good singers! Several of these interns went on to reach eminence in various fields. One, Elli Dunn, became an anaesthetist in Sudbury.

Victor Yap, a Filipino ENT resident, kindly showed me around when I arrived and helped me by taking me to the station to collect my trunk which contained most of my worldly possessions – it is hard to believe after over 40 years how much one can accumulate. He also took me for a drive around London and the University of Western Ontario – a very attractive, spacious campus then with well designed, light sandstone buildings.

The room next door in the residents quarters was allocated to John Watt, an orthopaedic surgeon from Vancouver who was to become a lifelong friend. He did not live in as he had his wife, Mary, and two small children with him. I always enjoyed their hospitality and sometimes baby-sat Beth and Heather for them. (C13.1) John was a very practical, get on with the job person. He used to say "why take three hours to do an operation when you could do it in two and have the third hour at home?" I met many surgeons over the years who did not seem to share that philosophy. I often quoted John to them but maybe they did not want to go home early, in case they had to help with the children!

I was two weeks late in starting my first job because of the later finish of our term and having to sail across the Atlantic. The interns worked in groups of five. My colleagues were Ralph Redding from Lethbridge, Alberta who went on to become a respiratory physician in the United States, Marg Sonada from Edmonton, who became a psychiatrist, Kerry Ferguson and Jim Dixon who were locals. Kerry did Emergency Medicine and ended up in Toronto. He was the only local intern to invite me home for a meal although several others indicated their good intentions. When one is far from home the hospitality of John, Ralph, Kerry and their wives meant a great deal. I still keep in touch with John and Kerry.

I had become quite friendly with Ralph and Maureen Redding. She was a physiotherapist working at the hospital. Like me, they did not have many friends in London, having come from Alberta. I played tennis with him on a very cramped court behind the nurses home – it had less than two metres behind the baseline. On one occasion Ralph was serving to me and there was a ball lying on the service court. For some strange reason I thought the ball he was serving was going to hit it. It did! That is the only time I have ever seen a ball lying in the service court being hit by the served ball in over fifty years. One would think that the odds of this happening would be much greater. But then I calculated that 6,500 balls are needed to cover a service court making the odds quite low especially as balls are not often left lying in the area on the court where the service lands.

I found many differences when I began work. We all wore white uniforms – the tops buttoned up the side and on the shoulder. There was a whole new language to learn. They had different names for instruments – forceps were snaps and so on. "You're welcome" was a routine expression with which I was not familiar. It was not used so widely around the world then as it is now. They also began work earlier in the morning than in Britain.

I gained some excellent medical experience. I looked after a lady who had cancer of the breast. She was in hospital for several months because fluid used build up in her chest. When this happens the lungs are compressed and breathing becomes more difficult so we had to drain the fluid off once or twice a week. We used a technique where we inserted the needle into the chest and then put the other end of the attached tubing into a blood collecting bottle. At that time blood was collected in a bottle which had a low pressure vacuum. These bottles therefore sucked the fluid off more rapidly. This lady was always serene and grateful when we removed the fluid. I learnt from her how some patients with deep religious conviction can face imminent but slow death with tranquility.

I wonder whether the fear of death for many people results from not believing that there is anything after this life, and that death results in permanent and total extinction.

I also learnt about the cruelty of life – how malignant disease can develop at any age. I looked after a 20-year-old lady with rectal cancer and a 33-year-old with children who had malignant melanoma. Sadly, they died before they really had a chance to enjoy the fullness of life.

One afternoon I was called to see an old lady who I thought was dying of heart failure. I told the relatives that I thought she would be gone within hours. I called her doctor and he ordered some pethidine, a pain reliever. To my surprise she lived for three more days. So I learnt that it is hard to predict the time of death.

Our training took us through all the specialties, including paediatrics and obstetrics, and we gained good all round experience. I thought it was better than the British system where one usually did only a medical and a surgical job in the first year. I learnt a little of the basics during my two weeks in anaesthetics – enough I thought, with my interest as a student, for me to say when I went to Yellowknife later that I was interested in anaesthetics.

We had many good teachers but the one who made a great impact was Earl Plunkett, an endocrinologist. He had reviewed many patients in the local mental hospital and found a significant number had hypothyroidism – a deficiency of thyroid hormone which is very important in controlling metabolism. Too little thyroid hormone results in general slowing down and mental dullness and eventually these people may seem to be severely depressed. What a boon to have this treatable problem diagnosed and for all these people to be able to return to normal life. Subsequently, when I was in general practice I made this diagnosis in an unusual patient who presented with thick skin on the back of her heels. I gained more experience in the field in my later training. He also picked up a number of patients with the rare Klinefelter's Syndrome who have an aberration of their sex determining XY genes.

The chief medical resident had been brought up in British Guiana. He was a few years older than I was but coincidentally had been taught chemistry by the same teacher, Whiskers Watson, who taught me in Kenya. I might have done better in Higher School Certificate if he had stayed in British Guiana as he failed to teach us the full syllabus!

Where did the future lie? I had no notion of specializing. My university career had not been academically outstanding and I really doubted that I had the ability to specialize. So it was for general practice that I seemed destined. The possibility of returning to Labrador was considered. I had received a telegram from North West River in September- "could I come and help for two weeks in Labrador?" We did not have any leave until we completed our year in mid June apart from five days over Christmas or New Year. Always believing that the worst that can happen when asking for something is refusal I went to the Medical Director, Dr Kirk. He said I could go! So I went for 10 days and renewed some of my acquaintances there but I had to sacrifice my Christmas holidays.

After some consideration I had decided that I would go north but why not go somewhere else than Labrador and see another part of the country? I read Pierre Berton's *Mysterious North* with interest. Frobisher Bay in Baffin Island, named after Martin Frobisher, sounded interesting but it was a government job, so after some communication I decided not to go there. It would have been interesting travelling around Baffin Island visiting the Eskimo settlements. Berton described the great island with its eastern wall rising to 2600m. – a land of gorges and chasms where the mountains soared straight into the clouds, and rivers of solid ice poured through the valleys to the water's edge and so on. It all sounded very exciting and I regret never having seen it.

Frobisher was the first person to seek a short cut to China by the North West Passage in 1576. He found his way into the bay which he named after himself and discovered some dark ore there. This finding led to another expedition the next year to bring back more ore. During that trip he became better acquainted with the Eskimos and built an English style house for them as goodwill. Its remains were found by an American explorer, Hall, an incredible three hundred years later, in 1860. Frobisher wrote the first accounts of the hazards of the pack ice – "the force of the yce was so great, and likewise rased the side of the ships, that it was a pitiful site to behold, and caused the hearts of many to faint."

I then found two large books which were encyclopaedias of all the hospitals in Canada and USA. I looked up Yukon, North West Territories and Alaska and decided to apply to Juneau, Alaska but that required sitting American entrance examinations so I abandoned that idea. Yellowknife, a gold mining town, sounded possible. My next move was like a fisherman casting a fly into a river hoping to catch a fish! I wrote a letter addressed to "The Doctor, Yellowknife, N.W.T." saying that I was looking for a job as an assistant in July and asked if they needed one. The reply came that there were three doctors and one was leaving in June – they would like me to come. Now I only had to pass my licentiate for Medical Council of Canada examinations in May. So I was destined to do general practice in Yellowknife.

The Middletons were a Scottish family with whom I became great friends. They sometimes invited me to their home for Sunday dinner which was a nice change from the hospital food, especially as Mrs Middleton was excellent cook, having been a domestic science teacher. One wintery Sunday after working late I fell asleep after lunch in front of their fire. Some would regard that as bad manners but not Mrs. Middleton. She said to me when I awoke that to go to sleep like that was the greatest compliment I could pay them because it meant that I felt at home in their house! They had four boys. Sandy and Peter, both enthusiastic naturalists, were still at home. Mrs Middleton even tried to introduce me to an Australian physiotherapist, Janet Penfold, who happened to be working at the hospital, but we were already going out together! Some weeks later we became engaged. Her mother was

Canadian and she had come to visit relatives. She went home in March and I was to follow her to Melbourne for our wedding, when I finished my internship in June.

16.1. Mr and Mrs Middleton, Sandy and Peter Janet (February 1961).

Mrs Middleton was a remarkable woman. In later life her doctor thought she needed more to occupy her and suggested that she approach the film company which was making a film, "Agnes of God" near Guelph, where she was living. She auditioned and at the age of 80 was given the part of an old nun who had to die in the film. She told me that she had had plenty of practice dying before she perfected the part!

In February Janet and I bought our first Volswagen kombi for $1600. It was relatively new and increased our mobility. We went to Port Stanley on Lake Ontario and found the people, even little children, fishing through holes in the ice. They had little shelters to protect them from the wind. It was a very organized business.

We visited Toronto where Janet's relatives took us to see the Toronto Maple Leafs playing ice hockey against Boston Bruins in the National Hockey League at the famous Maple Leaf Gardens – pretty cold gardens. It was a fast and vigorous game. I had seen children playing around in London during the winter and also saw the Iodine Cup final between the doctors and the pharmacists in London played between 11 and 12 midnight – the only time that they could hire the rink.

In March Janet left for home after six months in London. Her parents decided that it was cheaper to pay for me to go to Australia after I finished my internship than for them all to come to Canada for a wedding. I went to Australia for a month for the wedding before going to Yellowknife.

The arrival of spring was very welcome. The squirrels were to be seen scampering around and up the trees, attractive little creatures with their bushy tails. The ice on the river melted and the trees rapidly became covered with the pale green leaves of spring. Flowers began to poke their way out of the ground. Trilliums, the provincial flower of Ontario were particularly unusual and pretty. Having a vehicle meant visits to Lake Huron and Niagara Falls became possible. The latter were spectacular, especially with the spring blossom on the trees and trilliums in the woods. Although they are not as high or as wide as Victoria Falls in Africa the Horseshoe and American falls were very impressive, especially when we went down an elevator to view the Canadian falls from behind.

On 13th June, with the kombi loaded with my worldly belongings, I left London with Sandy Middleton (16.1), a science student with a great interest in ornithology, as a companion for the trip across to Vancouver. It had been a good year.

Chapter 17

Trans-Canada by Volkswagen Kombi

The year in London over I now had to head to Yellowknife with a long side trip to Vancouver and Australia. I had ten days to reach Vancouver, over 5,000 km away with my companion, Sandy Middleton. We had to carry my trunk and extras that I had acquired during the year. We turned the middle seat in the kombi sideways and created two bunks to sleep on. (C13.2) The trip was a great adventure for both of us and we had planned the trip carefully. We had only one arranged stop, in Fort William. We headed west to Sarnia, across the St. Clair river into Michigan, north to the Mackinaw Strait which we crossed on a huge bridge and then on to Sault St Marie. My memories of Michigan are an abundance of spring flowers in the fields and the cluttering of the American landscape with huge roadside billboards.

I was happy to return to Canada to escape from these intrusions. We joined the Trans Canada Highway round the north side of Lake Superior. The days were long so we could drive late into the evening. We stopped near Wawa and the next morning we awoke to a enchanting view of low mist and in the distance a plume of smoke rising through it from a smelter.

The road was excellent as we travelled north and west, much of the way near Lake Superior, the largest lake in the world. The country was typical of the Canadian Shield which had been sculpted and smoothed by glaciers during the ice age. There were undulating hills, lakes and forests of pines, spruce, silver birches and other northern trees stretching to the horizon and beyond. We stopped for one break beside a beautiful sandy beach on the lakeside – the sky was clear and the lake a deep blue and very calm.

Later that evening we reached Port Arthur and Fort William, adjoining cities which were later amalgamated into Thunder Bay. Here we stayed with my mother's cousin and aging aunt who had come to Canada in 1906. I was the first relative she had seen since she arrived fifty four years before so we received a very warm welcome. Fort

William was the western terminal on Lake Superior from which the wheat from the Prairies was transported out through the Great Lakes waterway in summer. We visited one of the large grain elevators, went up Mt. Mackay, a flat topped hill south of the city where we had a grand view out over the fairly flat country to the west and the lake to the east. The factory where the famous Hurricane fighter 'planes were built during the war was pointed out.

The next evening we set out west, stopping briefly at Kakabeka Falls which had a good flow of golden brown water as it was spring-time. We drove on and on though the woods and lakes until we were near the Manitoba border before stopping for the night. The prairies soon began – an immense plain stretching on and on and on and on for 1600km. They must have been magnificent before white man came and destroyed the great herds of bison that used to roam freely over them. Now they are covered in wheat fields – hundreds of kilometres of them with only an occasional group of grain elevators by the rail-way surrounded by a few houses to break the monotonous monotony.

We reached Winnipeg, the capital of Manitoba, about midday. It was hot, 36°C. We drove around, past the Manitoba Parliament building with its dome and then visited a wildlife park where we had our lunch and saw a few bison munching the grass. They are great, huge beasts.

When we set out again for the west a headwind arose and after a short distance it was so strong that our flat fronted kombi could manage no more than 50kph.when the accelerator pedal was flat to the floorboards. We came to a wayside park so decided to give up and have a sleep as we had already driven for many hours. Two hours later we awakened, refreshed and fortunately the wind had died down so we set off across more flat, tedious prairie. Manitoba really is a flat dreary province to drive across but eventually we reached Saskatchewan where things improved – slightly. There were undulations and ponds in the hollows where there were masses of birds – a delight to Sandy as an ornithologist. I enjoyed them too as he taught me to recognize these water birds – plovers, sandpipers, spoonbills, waders of all sorts including the avocet with its cinnamon head and bill that turns upwards unlike most of the others which had straight bills, or down-ward curving ones like those of curlews and whimbrels. Towards the end of the day we were treated to a wonderful exhibition by a pintail duck faking a broken wing and making a lot of noise to distract us

17.1. Rockies coming into view in southern Alberta.

from its nearby nest and offspring. It was a fascinating display that went on until we moved away. Pintails are rather amusing to watch as they feed. They suddenly tip forward so that their pin tail, made up of two longer feathers, sticks straight up in the air. They can maintain this position for some time as they feed. It is even funnier when several are feeding at the same time and all these sticking up tails are most of what you see of the bird. We had driven across the Prairies for two long days.

Then we saw one of the most welcome sights of my life as we came over a rise in southern Alberta – the snow capped Rocky Mountains stretched out along the whole horizon.

What a relief, especially for someone, like myself, who was brought up looking out on mountains. I was reminded of the scene years later when I was crossing the pampas in southern Patagonia going to the Argentinian glaciers. We came to a place called Esperanza which means hope in Spanish. There were about half a dozen buildings and a gaucho arrived on his horse. It was only when I walked about 100 m along the road over a slight rise that I realized the place was appropriately named. There were the Andes stretching along the horizon.

The Rockies came closer and closer and eventually we reached them at Waterton Lakes National Park. There was a beautiful hotel situated beside a lake looking over to the mountains but that certainly was not in our budget.

In one part there was an enclosure with a few bison. It was good to see these being preserved but sad to think how few remained. In a dam nearby we heard a noise as a beaver slapped its tail on the water to warn its colleagues that there were strangers around. These remarkable animals are the engineers of the animal world. Their long front teeth are sharp enough to cut down sizable trees, at least 15 to 20cm thick. They fell them across streams thereby making dams These are packed in until the wall is complete. I was told that when these have been surveyed they are dead level. They then build their houses in the middle of the filling pond so that its entrance will be under water. They then can swim into the nest which is above water level. These feats of dam building are amazing but they can be a nuisance, especially where the beaver has been introduced because it can disrupt the normal balance of the particular environment.

We spent the night in the Park and next morning visited Red Rock Canyon where we walked up among its very striking reddish orange rocks.

We drove west into British Columbia, passing Frank's Slide where a great landslide occurred in the early part of the twentieth century. We turned north and followed the Columbia River on its way north. We passed Old Fort Steele, once a fort but now an interesting historic park with buildings from around the district concentrated there. From Radium Hot Springs the road passes through a narrow gap in the mountain, Sinclair Canyon, and goes on to join the Banff to Jasper road with the distinctive Mount Eisenhower opposite the junction.

The trip north from there is awesome, with great mountains on both sides of the road. We stayed at a camping ground at the foot of a big climb up to the Columbia Ice Fields where we went early the next morning. Travelers now zoom up and down these beautiful highways but at that time the road was just being built and we had to stop near the top because of road construction just short of the ice fields – an impressive site stretching away up to Mt. Columbia (3747m). This trip is very highly recommended in summer. There is only one problem – one can have a dose of visual indigestion from seeing endless views of magnificent mountains, many rising to over 3000 metres. On the way back towards Lake Louise we stopped at Peyto Park, surely one of the most beautiful, easily accessible sights in Canada. The road wound up the mountainside, the trees becoming steadily smaller until we almost reached the tree limit – trees only grow to a certain height on mountains. There we looked down on to Peyto Lake with its stunning, glacial green waters and then up the valley to a glacier and, in the other direction, away to row after row of mountain peaks. We had a wonderful walk up in the park where the mountain avens (Dryas) with their little white flowers close to the ground were in full bloom. We were entertained by a family of marmots near their burrow and filmed the two little ones having a boxing match. What fun they were having. (C9.1)

17.2. Lake Louise in April.

Bow Lake, further down the valley, is also worth a visit. (C39.3) Then on to Lake Louise which is one of the best known sights in Canada with its great hotel, built by the Canadian Pacific Railway, situated beside the lake and looking over it to the steep wall of rock surmounted by glaciers. There are beautiful walks along the shore amongst the trees. On another occasion I was there in April when it was covered with over a metre of snow – also scenic but very lonely on that visit. That was before it was developed for skiing.

Down a side road nearby one comes to Morraine Lake which is particularly beautiful when the row of peaks are reflected in still water.

We drove on to Golden arriving there about 5pm. The question was "Would we tackle the Big Bend that evening or wait until morning?" It did not become dark until about 11pm so there was time to go at least half way where the map showed some habitation.

The Big Bend was a 300km trip on a mostly unsealed road from Golden to Revelstoke, following the Columbia River to its most northerly point before it turns south on its long course back through the Arrow Lakes and the Coulee Dam in Washington, past Portland, Oregon to the sea. Most people avoided the Big Bend by putting their car on the train. A few years later the spectacular Rogers Pass road over the mountains was opened making the Big Bend redundant except to loggers. The final extinction came when the large Mica Dam was built and much of it was submerged. Our trip was therefore a historic one. We began from Golden at 5.30pm. Our first obstacle was the river itself. The water was high in spring and had risen over the road at one point for about fifty metres. We could see it emerging directly ahead. How deep was it? Could we get through or were we going to have to retrace our journey to the south? We stopped and prodded the road with a stick. We decided to proceed and fortunately it was only a few inches deep. With relief we emerged from the other end. It is a little nerve wracking to drive along in the edge of a huge river which was at least fifty metres wide flowing by fairly quickly. The drive then continued on and on and on through forests with tall trees on either side.

Empty stomachs finally told us it was time to eat so we pulled into one of the logging roads leading off to the side. We opened the door and whoosh! We were invaded by a cloud of mosquitoes. It took only seconds to decide that this was not the place for dinner! We closed the doors but not fast enough to prevent a multitude of mosquitoes from storming into the car. And so we drove on for another hour trying to eliminate the mosquitoes who wanted to feed on us! Pangs of hunger now drove us to stop up another side road. We had hoped that the mosquitoes might have settled in the evening, but no! It was still. There was no wind and they were as bad as ever. We were invaded again. So on we went. The map indicated that near the top of the bend there were cabins – we eventually came to them but they were in ruins. There was supposed to be a habitation and a store at the top of the bend but if there was it was up a side track and we did not want to drive any further than we had to. Driving was tiring, bend after bend, through tall trees all the way and the knowledge that we could be defeated by mosquitoes if we stopped in enclosed areas. There were some more cabins marked on the map so we lived on in hope that there might be some open space. But no, there were more derelict buildings. Hunger was giving way to fatigue but now at least we were heading south again. About 11pm we came to a widening on the road where it came out on to an embankment which dropped about 12 metres into the river. We stopped. When we opened the door there was a breeze and no mosquitoes – they do not like wind. We pulled over to the edge of the embankment and parked for the night. But we were so tired by then that we could not even be bothered to eat. We climbed into bed and slept. We were awoken early by a truck coming by. Fortunately there was room so that it did not push us over the edge. There was still a breeze so we had a good breakfast and then continued our lonely drive, not seeing another vehicle until we were nearing Revelstoke. And so ended an experience that can never now be repeated

17.3. One of the few views on the Big Bend.

but it is something to say we did the trip around the Big Bend of the Columbia River.

British Columbia! What a contrast to the two long days across the Prairies. Here there were mountains, forests, lakes – all so beautiful. It is certainly one of the scenic parts of the world.

In the afternoon we reached the Whites, old relatives of John Watts, who lived near Vernon in the Okanagan Valley. I have vivid memories of sitting under a weeping willow tree on the warm afternoon enjoying afternoon tea with scones and cake and being glad we could just sit in comfort for a few hours. It was a pleasure to stay in a house again and to have amenities like a bath as we had only had the kombi to live in for the last week.

The final day took us through the beautiful Okanagan Valley, beside Okanagan Lake which we crossed at Kelowna. The west side, around Westbank and Peachland, was a wonderful sight as it was blossom time for the fruit trees which are grown there. Further south we passed through dry, eroded country between Penticton and Princeton and then climbed back into the forests in Manning Provincial Park where we saw some bears and deer. One of the features of British Columbian roads which makes travelling more interesting are the frequent signs telling about points of interest like Copper Mountain and Okanagan Lake. These were usually beside rubbish bins surrounded by imaginative, decorated Garbage Gobblers. The road then descends through forest to join the Fraser River valley at Hope. Going west to the sea the Fraser Valley is wide, fertile and well farmed. To the south there were occasional views of the volcano, Mt. Baker, cloaked with snow. It was a popular skiing area.

And so we entered the outskirts of greater Vancouver, our destination being Mary Watt's parent's home on West 25th Avenue. We received a very "warrem" welcome and a fine cup of tea. Her father came from Tiree in the Outer Hebrides off the west coast of Scotland and still had his beautiful lilting accent.

What a wonderful trip we had just completed – to have crossed this huge country and seen so much – Great Lakes, Prairies, Rocky Mountains and now the sea on the west coast as well as bison, bears, deer, marmots, beavers and many, many birds.

Sandy was a most congenial companion. We were to meet again in Australia three years later. He did post graduate studies in ornithology (the influence of cormorants on the fishing industry) at Monash

University in Melbourne where he became one of the first PhD graduates at that, then, new university.

I left Sandy in Vancouver. He was going to fly home. Next day I flew to Australia to begin a new era of my life.

CHAPTER 18

AUSTRALIAN VISIT AND WEDDING – 1961

There was an air of excitement as I headed to the Australian winter – seeing Janet again after three months, getting married and seeing this great land which was new to me. I had learnt about Australia as a child because of my interest in geography. I knew about the Aborigines' incredible physiological tolerance to wide variations in daily temperature. I knew about the states because of the pre-Federation stamps in my father's collection.

It was to be a busy three weeks. It was also a challenging time. I hoped that I would get on with the family. Not to get on with one's in laws can cause disharmony and sometimes sadness. I also had to meet dozens of people who were coming to the wedding.

I remember driving in from Essendon Airport, down Mt Alexander Road, past the palm trees which struck me as unusual so far south, and into Melbourne. It was very different then. The ICI (now Orica) building was the tallest in town. Now it is overshadowed all round and one would find it hard to believe that it was Melbourne's first modern skyscraper in 1958. The family home in Kew was on the corner of Studley Avenue and Studley Park Road. It was an Edwardian house with a large garden around it and a spare block next door, an acre in all.

18.1. Janet's family home at 5 Studley Avenue, Kew. (Demolished 1971)

Janet's father spent much of his spare time looking after it. In the middle of winter the large leculia bush beside the front door provided some colour – pink- and some sweat fragrance. It is amazing how flowers take it in turns to decorate the gardens with colour through the seasons.

The house was sold and demolished in 1971 shortly after Janet's father died. A hospital was built in its place. A flowering gum was left standing at the front fence. Evidence of our presence there was an old rope tied to a branch which was part of a swing that remained there for many years.

Kew is a suburb about 5 to 7km east of the central city area. Its northern and western boundaries are formed by the Yarra River as it meanders through Melbourne. Adjacent to it are huge areas of magnificent parkland, much of it natural bush, which are remarkable being so near the middle of a big city.

Many large park and garden areas in the inner city area make Melbourne a most attractive place. The Botanical Gardens have a wonderful collection of about 50,000 plants intermingled with lawns and lakes, really billabongs (oxbows) formed when the Yarra was straightened out through the inner city area. Among the parklands are a collection of excellent sporting arenas such as the Melbourne Cricket Ground which holds 100,000 spectators and was the site of the Olympic Games in 1956. The tennis centre is one of the best in the world and hosts the Australian Championships, one of the Grand Slam tournaments. Much has changed since I first came in June 1961.

18.2. Dr. H. Boyd Penfold.

Janet's father, Boyd Penfold came to Australia from England when he was eight years old. He was tall, had a good head of hair and a kindly disposition.

Having lived through the Depression years he was careful and not wasteful. He was a fairly practical man who, in his youth, had helped to build a beach house for his father at Mornington, which he eventually owned. He became a doctor and in his early post-graduate years worked with his father doing research on tapeworm for which he obtained a Doctorate of Medicine. His main medical interest became haematology – he was the first "resuscitationist" in Melbourne. He and, later, Dr Dreverman used to give blood transfusions and resuscitate patients for surgeons before anaesthetists took over most of this role. He was the first person in Melbourne to do an exchange transfusion in a baby for Rh blood incompatibility even, I believe, before the famous paediatrician, Dr Kate Campbell. He preferred private practice away from the politics associated with public hospitals. His patients adored him, as I found out when I went to look after his practice the day after he died in 1971. They came from all over the state. He practiced in Collins St., the Harley Street of Melbourne. So I can say I practiced for one day in Collins St. – the ultimate in Melbourne! He was very supportive to me and our relationship was bonded by our interest in Medicine.

18.3. Dr W.J.Penfold in his laboratory at the Baker Research Institute (1930s).

His father, William James Penfold migrated to Australia in 1916 to become head of the Commonwealth Serum Laboratories, a post he held for 12 years before becoming the Director of the Baker Research Institute at the Alfred Hospital. Interestingly, in the latter post he facilitated the publication of the first book on anaesthesia in Australia by providing funds for its publication to Kaye, Orton and Renton, the authors from the Alfred Hospital. (1932) He wrote the foreword.

Janet's mother was born in New Zealand from where she derived her unusual name, Aotea, from the Maori aotearoa. The family moved back to Canada, from where her parents originated, when she was three. Business brought them to Melbourne just after she had completed school, topping her year in the province. She then did an Arts degree at Melbourne University where she met her future husband. She was an intelligent lady with a strong personality.

I had ten days then to become acquainted with Janet's friends and family friends before our wedding at Toorak Presbyterian Church on a wet July day. A couple of parties were held for me to meet people. It required a supreme effort but I managed to remember most of them by name when the event occurred. Young brains have better memories, something that regrettably declines with age.

None of my family was able to come. The closest we could find was the son of someone who had worked with them in 1928-9 at Tumutumu, Hamish Christie Johnston. It was nice to have him there with his now wife, Hilary, who was related to a great family friend of the Penfolds. They became a life long friends. Hamish is a Presbyterian minister who later, after church union, became Moderator of the

Uniting Church and subsequently, secretary of the Victorian Council of Churches. He worked diligently to try to bring the various churches and faiths to a better understanding of each other. At our wedding he read the telegrams.

18.4. Janet's family, including Campbell and Margaret and her cousin, Mary, at our wedding.

Our honeymoon was 'a get to know south eastern Australia trip'. We drove down to Sale and on to Buchan where we had an enjoyable visit to the Buchan Caves. These had most spectacular stalactites and stalagmites but the highlight was the "Blanket" about 5x4 feet and 2mm thick with beautiful wavey lines coloured by the minerals in the rock. It was an exceptionally rare piece. Years later someone touched and shattered it – a tragedy. Buchan is situated in the hilly country south of the Snowy mountains where the big hydroelectric development was being built. (C41.1)

We went on up that road and crossed the Snowy River, which still had a significant flow, at McKillop's Bridge. Since then the Snowy Mountains hydroelectric scheme has drawn most of its water off into dams. We stayed in Bombala to awaken to a cold and frosty morning, beautiful with the mist and early morning sun shining amongst it. The next night was spent at Jindabyne, the old town which now lies beneath Lake Jindabyne, one of the dams. We were heading west to cross over the mountains. There was snow at the top. We nearly made it over but became stuck about twenty metres from the highest point. Fortunately a landrover came along and pulled us over. Then down the winding gravel road – it still is – but some of the climb was steep and wet, especially up the Geehi Wall. Eventually we made it down into the Murray River Valley which we followed all the way to Renmark in South Australia passing Corowa, the venue of the first pre-Federation Convention, Swan Hill and Mildura. We arrived at Renmark at 1145 am on Saturday. I remember the time well because we drove up the Main Street and had a look at the river, which was large at that point, and then went back to town to find everything shut and the previously busy street almost deserted – only twenty minutes later. That was my introduction to midday closing on Saturday in Australia. I could hardly believe it as many today would find it hard to believe – things have changed so much. In those days pubs closed at 6pm. so people had to sink their drinks fast after work with the result that many left a little inebriated! It was called "the six o'clock swill."

The Barossa valley with its famous vineyards, started by German migrants, was next. These people apparently speak an old German which did not develop as it did in the homeland. In Adelaide we stayed with my Form 1 Maths teacher, Jim Duff, whom I regarded as the best teacher that I had ever had. He was a great gardener and was also an accomplished organist.

Our return journey took us to Keith, near the Victorian-South Australian border, to visit Janet's aunt and her husband who had been allocated a settlement farm in that rather flat, desolate area. They managed to make something of it and eventually sold out to wine producers as the land was found to be good for vineyards. We spent a night in Mt. Gambier where we visited the craters with their lakes. Blue Lake is particularly impressive when it is blue but it changes colour with the seasons.

We returned through Ballarat, a town that developed around the gold rush which began in 1853. Ballarat became prosperous and has many fine Victorian buildings. Years later Sovereign Hill was established. It is a re-creation of a gold mine, diggings and many old buildings which form a historical park, with the Gold Museum nearby. It is now a major tourist attraction. The road back to Melbourne was narrower, not the highway of today. The road crossed the one lane over the Djerriwarrh Bridge near Melton, a town which barely existed then. This bridge was built in the 1850s and is the only sandstone one of the type – most of the similar bridges were built of granite. I have painted several pictures of this bridge. On one occasion I told my secretary that I had stopped to paint the bridge on the way back from Ballarat. A few days later she told me that she had thought I had gone off the rocker (become a bit strange) stopping to paint the bridge – she thought I had actually applied paint to the bridge!

It had been an interesting trip and it gave me some idea about south eastern Australia. We had three days to pack up. We left many of our presents because we expected to return in a year or two – certainly not in four and a half as it turned out.

We planned to stop in New Zealand to visit my school friend, John Winter, who was studying in Dunedin. I was impressed by the steep hills there, the cold houses which were not centrally heated as in Canada and by the large number of old cars –1930s models – not so old really at that time. He took us up to Lake Hawea in the Southern Alps for two days. (C35.1) He had worked up there as a shepherd, carpenter's assistant and beekeeper before returning to university. He used to have a shack there but on this occasion we stayed with some of his friends. The views of the mountains standing over the lake with the sun shining on the snow capped peaks reflected on the intense blue water in the lake were stupendous. We stayed on a farm nearby and saw the unusual phenomenon of blue mist in the mountains at Mungawera in the early morning as the sun rose. (C35.2)

On the way back to Dunedin we passed Alexandra where we saw one of the last of the huge gold dredges which were used in mining. I think these are now historical. They were used in the Yukon following the Klondike gold rush in 1898 and I saw one at Maldon in Victoria many years ago but it was much smaller.

We had planned to have two days in Fiji but our flight from Auckland was cancelled so we had to spend a day there and only had one day in Fiji. We arrived in the early morning and flew across to Suva. That was interesting because we could see the relatively drier west side of the island with the sugar cane plantations and then the more densely forested, wetter east side. We had a few hours to wander round Suva and visit the market before taking a taxi for 5 pounds ($10) back to Nandi where we caught the flight back to Vancouver. We travelled round the south coast, visiting a typical Fijian village and Koru Levu Hotel, where we had dinner. It was a brief but fascinating visit. Years later I would return there to teach and to conduct the first post-graduate medical examinations to be held in the South Pacific.

Back in Vancouver we stocked up with tins of food, other useful items and car chains, of which you will hear more later. We then left on our long trip (2500km) north to Yellowknife and to a new, very different, unique phase of our life. It was like going to the Canadian equivalent of Siberia.

Chapter 19

Life in Yellowknife, N.W.T.

Yellowknife is an intriguing name. "Where is it?" I am frequently asked. It is 1100km north of Edmonton by air, half way between Hudson Bay and the Pacific coast on 62 1/2 degrees N on the bay on the north west side of Great Slave Lake, the fifth biggest lake in the world. It is in Canada's equivalent of Siberia. It is named after the Indian tribe who inhabited the area. (C14.1)

Yellowknife became the capital of the North West Territories in Canada when the administration was moved from Ottawa in the mid 1960s. It didn't exist as a town before gold was found there in1934 in that land of hundreds of lakes, rocks and stunted trees – stunted because they are only a 150km south of the tree line beyond which only a few small shrubs grow on what is called the "Barrens".

Not long before we went there the road from Peace River was opened – a long, often straight stretch of gravel highway which joined the northern end of the rolling Prairies at Peace River and Grimshaw to Yellowknife in the north. It wandered on and on and on, and on for hundreds of kilometres through the northern woods – Yellowknife is 1600km by road from Edmonton, the nearest big centre. There were occasional features to break the monotony. A sign telling us that we were entering the North West Territories was significant enough to justify a photo stop! (C13.3) We had reached sixty degrees north at last.

There are three impressive waterfalls near the road. They are magical in the cold winters when they became static, frozen pillars and sheets on mounds of ice. The Alexandra Falls on the Hay River were the biggest. (C13.4) Louise Falls, although not the highest were the most interesting because the middle section fell half the height on to a flat square section from which it flowed over three sides to reach the bottom. (C13.5) Further west we passed the Lady Evelyn Falls.

After leaving the last of the prairie farms north of Peace River there were very occasional small settlements such as High Level – a few cabins about half way – another, appropriately called Enterprise, which had a garage, and the third just after crossing the Mackenzie River. This was a "great barrier" to progress by road during freeze up and break up of the ice. In summer, this great river is a boatway to the Arctic, running from Great Slave Lake to the Arctic coast in north western Canada. It is too wide to economically bridge – why would one bother when for five months nature does it anyway with ice two metres thick which even the biggest trucks can cross. (C13.6) In summer there was a ferry and yet for six weeks in between, at breakup and freeze up, the road was not accessible to Yellowknife. During the period when crossing was not possible everything had to be air freighted in. Wardair, an airline established by Max Ward to service the north in the 1950s, later became an international airline. It had an old Bristol freighter aeroplane which was like a big frog that opened its mouth to ingest its load – the front opened and it could even swallow cars.

The last and biggest settlement was Fort Rae, 100km out of Yellowknife. It was inhabited mainly by Indians but there was a Roman Catholic mission with a school and also a store. I later had patients from there and paid it a couple of visits. In the late summer one would see racks of fish drying so that they could be kept for the winter. (C13.7) Berries were an important source of Vitamin C. We had two infants with scurvy at the end of the long winter as a result of its deficiency.

A hundred more kilometres to Yellowknife! It was dusty and we were a bit grubby so we stopped by a roadside pool for a wash and then proceeded on to our destination which was to be our home for the next 17 months. On arrival we found the doctors' office in the main street next to the cinema. Inez Running, a plump, wonderfully kind, reddish haired lady was the receptionist and kept the place in order. I think she was a bit shocked when I entered looking a bit scruffy and wearing shorts. She thought I was a patient and certainly found it unbelievable when I announced that I was not a patient but the new doctor! We became great friends. Later she taught Janet how to make bread and she helped me through a few tricky situations like putting temporary fillings in teeth.

Accommodation was our first priority on arriving in Yellowknife. We had to find somewhere to stay. Fortunately this turned out not to be a problem as somebody had gone out on holiday for a month and said we could have the use of their house. Marvel Barton worked at the hospital and her husband, Ray, worked as a printer with the local paper – News of the North. The Barton's house was a small, actually tiny, modest, well kept dwelling but very acceptable to us under the circumstances. It was about the size of two containers. We were amazed how people could be so generous to unknown strangers. One day they arrived back – almost a week before they were expected. What were we to do? George Case, the senior doctor, came to the rescue. He and his wife would go to Edmonton for a week and leave their daughter with us in their house. We had arranged for a house which was becoming available the next week. It belonged to John and Janet Anderson Thompson whose accent left no doubt about where they came from! They had retained their accent strongly as many Scots do! He had been in Yellowknife for years and had been invited to go out to Saskatoon for that winter to lecture at the University. Their house was a large one on a sizable block of land in the Old Town, down near Yellowknife Bay on Great Slave Lake. Further on, the Old Town spread on to Latham Island. Our neighbours were the McGoverns from Ireland with whom we crossed paths years later in Australia. Next to them were the Teeds, one of whose little boys fell into the Lake in freezing conditions and drowned. Next to them was the old store of Weaver and Devore who had been trading since the early days of Yellownife. Chuck McAvoy lived on the waterside behind us. He was a well known pilot who found many a lost plane all over the north but ultimately went the way of many bush pilots – he left on a trip never to return and no one has ever had any idea where he disappeared. The Anderson Thompsons' house was large and comfortable with an array of fine, potted plants which were treasures in such a harsh northern climate. (C15.1) There was a front lawn in summer but in winter the snow might pile up to nearly a metre high. (C15.2) Outside the front gate there was a power point where one plugged one's car in during the winter – essential if it was to continue functioning.

There was a knock on the door one night two months later. Les Mullins had come to ask us, strangers, if we could child-mind their four children for a week as they had an opportunity for the first time since they had a family to go "outside" for a holiday without them. Les was the mechanic at Ptarmigan Airways which he and Ken Stockall owned. They had a Cessna 185 in which I had recently flown with Ken on a trip north. We agreed and a few days later moved up to their little house near the skating arena to look after Pat (12 years), Maye and Faye (twins of 9 years) and June (6 years).

One thing went wrong after another. First Janet developed serious morning sickness, signaling the beginning of our family and, unbeknown to us, an even greater surprise eight months later. Then the temperature dropped to 40 degrees below zero – four days before I had planned to have my Volkswagen kombi winterized. Normally we had a battery warmer and oil heater installed to enable the car to start and a heater inside to take the chill off. At 35 degrees below zero the tyres freeze solid when standing so that when you start driving they thump as they go over the flattened part until they warm up! Changing gear, even with the thinnest grade oil, was like pushing the gear stick through a glue pot. I was in a predicament. It took three bursts of numbing activity to remove the battery because it was so cold. I then took it inside to warm up. Next day I reinstalled it and managed to start the engine. A trip to the old town to check on the house made me chillingly aware of another disaster. It was cold when I arrived – in fact 2°C below freezing and all those precious plants had frozen and subsequently died. It was our great misfortune that the heater gave up the ghost when we weren't there. And old John A. T. made us pay.

We had great fun with the children who remained lifelong friends. However one more problem arose – the parents didn't come back after their week away – we didn't hear anything from them and Janet was still sick. Another day and another, and another, and another, with no word – had they crashed? Then what would we do? There were no mobile phones, faxes or emails in those days. Eventually, after they had been away for two weeks, they appeared, much to everyone's joy and relief. They had had to go to Minnesota instead of Edmonton to get the new skis on the plane. We were now accomplished baby sitters and the experience proved useful as our own family increased in later years.

All good things come to an end – Anderson Thompsons came home early and we had nowhere to go. Fortunately there was a flat on the back of their house which we moved into but we had to share their bathroom, an awkward situation considering the problems that arose as a result of *their* heater breaking down.

What were we going to do? Max Macara solved our problem. He was wondering what to do after the War when he was invited to come to Yellowknife to start a much needed laundry. His occupation kept him in touch with everything going on in town. Did Max know of anyone with a house or apartment to rent? Yes.

He told me he was renovating a building in the Main Street which would have a laundromat downstairs and two apartments upstairs – one for him, and one for us. It would be ready in two weeks. Excellent.

Then he told us to furnish it from the Hudson Bay Store. Then a problem arose for me. He would not declare how much rent we should pay. I asked him twice and each time he said, "You decide." I then asked people how much they paid and came back to him with figures of $115 – $120 a month. His response was " I'll toss you for it" and proceeded to toss a coin. He told me that I won and it would be $115. Over 35 years later when we met again in Victoria, B.C., where he retired, I came to suspect that he had decided that I would win. He told me that he knew I hadn't much money, which was true, and that the people thought I was doing a good job for them so he didn't want to charge me much. What wonderful generosity. We lived there for the remainder of our time in Yellowknife. Another advantage was that we could have the free use of the laudromat – very useful when you have babies in nappies.

19.1. Max Macara with his laundry van.

Max was a wonderful character with a sense of humour. This was obvious from the signs on his laundry van. The first was "DON'T KILL YOUR WIVES. LET US DO THE DIRTY WORK!" and the second had "DRIVE CAREFULLY – BLOOD STAINS ARE HARD TO REMOVE!"

Ray Barton, our unknown first host, was an enthusiastic Conservative which was very unusual in that rather Liberal orientated community. He introduced me to Canadian politics. His joy was considerable in 1957 when John Dieffenbaker became the first Conservative Prime Minister since 1935 when Mackenzie King regained power to rule after the Depression.

Mackenzie King was the longest ruling Prime Minister in Canadian history – 22 years in all. He had socialist views and became deputy minister of Labour in 1900 at the age of 25. He wrote his personal manifesto before 1916 but it was too left wing for the Liberals of that time. However, when the CCF party formed in the Prairie provinces they were more left wing and Mackenzie King came into his own, took over the Liberal leadership in 1919 and moved their platform to the left to prevent the CCF, later NDP, from gaining too much influence. He became Prime Minister in 1921 and continued until he lost a vote of confidence and resigned in 1926.

Then one of the most mysterious turn-arounds in politics occurred. Canadian law at that time required that when a minister was appointed he had to go back to his electorate to have his election confirmed. The Conservatives had a slim majority of one or two seats. Mackenzie King waited. He knew that several ministers had been appointed but were still in the House. He asked those who had been appointed ministers to leave the House as they had to vacate their seats until their election was confirmed, called for a vote of no confidence, which he won, and forced another general election. He campaigned on the fact that the Conservatives had tried to run the country with an illegal government. He won the election with a large majority. He conveniently lost the next election in 1930 as the great depression was beginning, so that by 1935 the people wanted a change and re-elected him. He remained Prime Minister until 1948 following a remarkable career during which he introduced the old age pension. Mackenzie King's story was told by Bruce Hutchinson in his excellent biography, "The Incredible Canadian."

The Canadian Liberals introduced a policy when he retired of alternating English and French speaking leaders. Lester Pearson followed Dieffenbaker and in turn was followed by Pierre Trudeau, a brilliant young lawyer who was brought into Parliament a year before he became leader and Prime Minister.

Yellowknife in 1961 was a town of 3500 inhabitants. (C14.1) The Old Town was situated on the shores of Yellowknife Bay on Great Slave Lake and on Latham Island. Its lay-out was fairly haphazard as people just set up their shacks as they arrived about 1937-8. CON (Consolidated Mining and Smelting Co.) mine, the original gold mine started in 1937, lay to the south east and the New Town lay up the hill to the south from the Old Town. It was laid out in an orderly Canadian fashion with the wide main intersection at 50th Avenue and 50th Street. On one corner was Doug Finlayson's drugstore; opposite was the two storey Yellowknife hotel. Going south there was a Hudson Bay Company store with an empty block next door which belonged to Tom Doornbos. The picture theatre and the Doctors' office were opposite with Max Macara's laundromat building three doors away nearer the main intersection. 50th Street went west past the Elk's Hall, Wally Smith's, who ran the ambulance and was the undertaker, to the hospital which had an idyllic situation overlooking Frame Lake.

The airport and cemetery were out on the main highway to the south. The graves had to be dug in the summer because the ground froze, making digging nearly impossible, in winter. This meant that they had to guess how many people would die each year. The cemetery was beautifully situated on a hillside looking down on Jackfish Lake with spruce and pines and silver birches on the rocky hillsides.

Giant Yellowknife mine was at the end of a 7km winding road to the west. At that time it was one of the biggest gold producers in Canada. When we arrived it had a desolate appearance because the trees around had died back as a result of arsenic fumes released in the smelting process. It was good to see the recovery of the plants and the return of the birds once a process to remove the toxic fumes was put in place. I wonder what effect the fumes had on the humans?

Yellowknife, like many frontier towns, had many characters, some of whom had come there to escape their past. But even in Yellowknife that may not be possible. One man came into the hotel for a drink. The waitress took his order. The barman who was pouring the drinks had spent some time in the Dachau concentration camp. The American troops arrived just before he was due for extermination. When the girl pointed out who the drink was for he recognised him – he was one of the guards from Dachau. He took the man's drink over to him himself and then sat down opposite, looking him in the eye. The man took one sip and then realized who was opposite him. He left hurriedly never to be seen again.

Tom Doornbos was quite old, tall and slightly stooped. He wore a very old, well worn grey coat and a felt hat. In relation to other people in the town he was old because he had been there for twenty four years. He came in 1937 and worked as a water carrier with two buckets balanced on a pole over his shoulders. There was no regular water supply with pipes to the houses and shacks. Tom delivered water summer and winter – one received less in winter because some was always frozen to the bucket! He obviously made his way. He was a canny Dutchman who periodically returned to Holland where he obtained goods to sell on his return to pay for his trips. He invested in the mines and many suspected that he was wealthy but he never gave that impression. However, impressions can be deceptive. There were many stories of how he used to do things on the cheap – he was a scrounger. I picked him up near the airport once when he was returning from visiting the World Fair in Seattle. He told me that all he had to spend was $10 for entrance to the Fair! He had travelled about 6000kms!

In 1962 the Town Council introduced a bylaw which required people owning property in the town centre to build on it within two years or they would forfeit it. Tom had a very valuable block next to the Hudson Bay store and opposite our office. His response was to move a one room cabin up from the old town and dump it on the block. George Case, as Medical Officer of Health, put a notice on it saying that it was "unfit for human habitation." Some time later the Hudson Bay Company tried to buy it from him. They reached agreement on a price of $7000 – a fortune in those days for a block he had purchased for $200. Then Tom tried to push for more but the "Bay" was managed by a thrifty Scot who broke off negotiations and bought elsewhere. So Tom lost out on a good deal.

George McConnell was involved with mining exploration. He and his young wife Jane had come from Toronto. We became very good friends. Jane was a highly intelligent and well read person who was also very practical. She had a pilots license and had filled in at the hospital when they did not have a radiographer. Matthew arrived in May, two months before our firstborn arrived. They asked me to be godfather but after much thought I turned down the invitation because I thought we would end up in Australia which would be too far away to be of any practical use. Little did I know that a few years later they too would be in Australia, eventually living only 50km away from us. In fact, when Matt's child became sick in Melbourne and needed an operation, he asked the surgeon if I could give the anaesthetic because I was his godfather!

Jane and I had many great discussions – the longest went on for about twenty years. I put forward the view *that insects were superior to humans*. That riled her as she thought humans had superior brains and powers of thinking. I maintained that insects were superior because there were many more of them, they caused humans much more distress, sickness and even death than humans ever caused them. I gave examples of their skill as builders (eg. anthills), as work organizers, as survivors (eg. mosquitoes in the Arctic) and other superior features.

Finally, one summer in Australia when the flies had been particularly bad, Jane conceded. They were driving her crazy!

There were some very talented people in Yellowknife. Didi Woolgar, whose husband was a prospector, was a superb wild flower painter. She helped me to identify flowers which I had photographed such as Labrador tea. (C15.3) and grass of Parnasus (on the cover) She painted over three hundred flowers from the north in great detail. To ensure that the paintings were perfect she would pick up to eighty flowers so that she was always painting from a fresh one. They were all done to life size. I heard that years later she had tried to have them published but was unsuccessful in raising the necessary funding, even from the government. That was a tragic loss of a potential national treasure.

Bill McDonald lived on his own in a little house on Joliffe Island opposite the Old Town. He was a wonderful man, regarded as the most respected prospector in the country and a man with a photographic memory and an encyclopaedic knowledge of rocks, trees, animals and plants. Although he had dinner with us and I visited him on the island I would have liked to have had more time with him to learn from his fund of knowledge. He was a humble gentleman.

Andy Stewart-Hill was a South African friend. He had been in Yellowknife and then returned to South Africa and married Kelly. Coming from the same continent we became good friends on their return. Andy certainly entertained us with his stories and his antics – he could climb the wall in our passage like a spider by placing arms and legs on opposite walls. Their first baby was born there but died when only two days old – a great loss to them. Not long afterwards they moved out to British Columbia. Andy visited us in Australia – one of the hundred countries it was his ambition to visit. He succeeded.

Andy told us a very poignant story. After twenty years he decided to go back to Yellowknife for a visit. He walked out to the cemetery. Ahead of him was an old man walking more slowly. Eventually he caught up and began talking to him. He told Andy that many years ago he had had a young friend at the mine whose baby son had died. Since his friend left he had made this trip each year on the anniversary to tend the baby's grave. He was on his way there when they met. Only then did he realize that he was speaking to his friend. They had not recognized each other. We also visited the grave in 1985.

The Bromleys ran the hardware store. On one occasion I was told that they brought a horse to town making it a real one horse town! It did not stay for long. After we left, father and son Peter accompanied by the dentist, went on a canoe expedition up the Back River on the Barrens. They were looking for remains of Franklin's party, which had disappeared searching for the North West Passage in 1846-8 when disaster struck. Franklin, who had been Governor of Tasmania, went with the ships, Erebus and Terror, which James Ross had taken on the first visit to Antarctica a few years before. The Terror was captained by Captain Crozier who had been with Ross and who has a cape named after him in both the Antarctic and the Arctic. Some remains of Franklin's expedition had been found by some of the many searchers but still its ultimate fate was not known. The Yellowknife searcher's trip came to a tragic end when the two adults drowned leaving Peter alone. He was eventually found. Barb Bromley stayed in Yellowknife and helped to produce a book of old Yellowknife tales in 2000 to which I contributed a tale of 40 years before.

There were three doctors, George Case, Lloyd Powell and myself. Because we were on call every third night and every third weekend we had a day off during the week but were available if there was an operation or one of our patients was having a baby. Our work was not arduous. We went to the hospital for rounds in the morning. One of us would then see any outpatients and we might have an operation or an occasional barium meal to supervise. George Case had done a couple of years surgical training so could do a limited range of operating. We did emergency work but anything major was referred out to Edmonton which was our major referral centre.

We worked in our office in the main street from 2 to 5pm. The practice had contracts with the mines. A significant part of my work was doing pre-employment mine medical examinations. I had many interesting patients which I have discussed in my medical memoirs. (*Catalyst*, Brolga Publishing) We usually only had one or two calls a night to make and the visits were usually within one or two kilometres.

One of us flew to Discovery Mine, 110 km north of Yellowknife once a month to do a clinic. I went one time in winter when it was minus 36°C. (C17.5) We also serviced Taurcanis Mine about 300km away on the Barrens about once every three months. The plane landed on a frozen lake a little way from the mine. A caboose was sent to pick us up. This was like a little shed on a trailer, with a stove in it to keep us warm, drawn by a tractor.

I had several other trips north to collect patients or to do clinics when the government people were not available to do them and so saw much of the central Arctic.

19.2. Caboose at Taucanis Mine, NWT (March 1962).

The hospital was well situated about 300m from the town centre and looking out over Frame Lake. It had forty beds, one operating theatre and a delivery room. There was an x ray room and a small laboratory. Some of the nurses and other staff lived upstairs. Unfortunately, after we left, this hospital burnt down.

We acquired a canoe, which we kept out at the front of the hospital. We had many happy times paddling around Frame Lake when we were not busy in the summer.

Wildlife was a source of endless pleasure in the north. Sometimes we saw animals on the road including coyote and lynx on the road out. Around town bears sometimes came around the garbage tins. One wildlife officer had wolves which he was studying.

The ravens were one species that stayed around all year – large black birds which scavenged. They were a source of great entertainment. One day in winter we watched one on the cinema roof, which was covered with snow. The raven climbed to the top and then rolled down like a child rolling down a bank. It obviously enjoyed this activity as it went on up and down for some time.

On another occasion we watched a group of mischievous ravens teasing a dog. It had a dainty morsel when the ravens surrounded it. One would advance, the dog lifting its head threateningly as they were large birds. That raven would draw back but another would approach from the opposite direction. While the dog was distracted another raven would approach and so the action went on and on until the dog was driven crazy and left.

We came to enjoy bird watching. Snow buntings were small white

19.3. Ptarmigan in winter feathers.

birds whose arrival heralded spring. Ptarmigan were about the size of pigeons, but tended to be more like game birds in behaviour, often to be found on the ground. They had the wonderful adaptation to the Arctic of being able to change coats to suit the season – white in winter with feathery leggings for warmth, and speckled brown in the summer for camouflage.

Early summer brought the migrating birds north to nest. It was a wonderful time and armed with an excellent pair of binoculars which Sandy Middleton had given us for a wedding present we spent many happy hours out in the bush and by lakes.

Loons with their clean black and white stripes and chequered markings were one of my favorites. Grebes, with their long neck and duck-like appearance were of two types – the common grebe was smaller than the red throated one, which we filmed on several occasions. (C15.5) It was on a nest about two metres from the edge of a lake. I read that birds cannot count and therefore if two people go into a hide and one leaves the bird will think all is clear. My friend Jack McGovern came with me to act as a decoy. The red throated grebe left its nest, made of sticks and reeds, and swam down the lake. When Jack left, it returned and I was able to film it from a few feet away climbing on to its nest and settling there. The sound of the camera disturbed it and so it stood up and left the nest again. I had taken a wonderful segment of film. This was a very smart bird because it learnt the sound of my car. On subsequent visits when it heard my car coming over the crest of the hill it left its nest and swam down the lake!

A smaller common grebe nested just in front of the hospital on some reeds. I watched this from egg laying and for some time while the eggs were being incubated but unfortunately the chicks never hatched – something raided the nest and broke the eggs. Even on the lake the nest was vulnerable.

Out on the road to Fort Rae an eagle's nest was spotted on a rocky ledge on the side of a quarry. We went out to see it and were rewarded by a good view from 3 to 4 metres above it. By then the chick was already growing. It had been left a rabbit to eat. The nest was in a very secure position which would have been difficult to reach.

19.4. Eagles nest built on the side of a quarry.

The vegetation was interesting. As well as all the flowers, the ground cover was intriguing with lichens, mosses and other tiny plants. (C14.2)

Fishing was popular in the north where the lakes had large stocks of trout and carp. It was reported that a 14kg trout had been caught in one of the lakes. Jack McGovern and his with Moira were very keen fishers. I remember him telling me that once the mosquitoes were so thick that he could not see across the small lake where he was fishing. That was tough on Moira as the mosquitoes seemed to enjoy biting her and sucking her blood more than most – it must have been the Irish taste. She reacted badly to these bites.

My pilot friend Ken Stockall stopped at Barnstone Falls at the east end of Great Slave Lake on our way home one time. We had a very exciting half hour. He was successful. Mine got away after a wonderful battle as the fish rushed back and forth across the foot of the falls for about five minutes before, alas, it broke the line. Anyway, part of the excitement of fishing is the contest. I thought this one was probably over 2kg.

One day I canoed (with some motor power) with Bill Davidson, the Baptist pastor, up the Yellowknife River, where he caught some carp. We had to portage a couple of times past falls and eventually came to a deep cold lake. It was obviously very cold because the fish we caught did not even put up a fight. It

19.5. Ken Stockall catching a good sized trout at the Barnstone Falls, at the east end of Great Slave Lake.

took the hook and almost strolled up and into the boat – the most pathetic effort I have ever seen by a fish.

Most people have some idea that the climate in Siberia is unpleasantly cold because that is where the Soviets sent people to work camps for punishment. Yellowknife had a Siberian type climate. It is a long way from the sea and from anywhere for that matter. Temperatures reached -45°C while we were there – that meant that when we left our houses, which were rather warm, we experienced a temperature drop of nearly 70°C. The deep freeze was outside the back door – an arctic char we were given lay in the open until we were ready to eat it! At least the precipitation was low and we did not have a lot of wind to increase the wind chill factor.

There were some compensations. While the lakes were still freezing up there was still some moisture in the air which precipitated on branches forming exquisite patterns of fluted ice on one side if there was some wind blowing from the other. (C15.4) Even a burst pipe pumping water out could produce magnificent mounds of ice.

The *Aurora borealis* (Northern Lights) were spectacular, especially about September and October (back cover). Yellowknife was at the optimal position for seeing them, being about 22 degrees from the Magnetic Pole, which is the region of maximum intensity. We had these magnificent waves of green, yellow, red and purple billowing in the skies like sheets of coloured silk being blown in the wind. Some claim that they can hear them. They are one of the world's greatest natural sights.

The other magnificent site are the *Sun Dogs* (parahelia). This is a phenomenon caused by ice crystals in the air tilting in an unusual way so that they form a spectrum like the end of a rainbow near the horizon on either side of a low sun. They are far enough apart that a wide angle lens is needed to photograph them. On rare occasions a whole ring forms where the light in the sky changes intensity with the parahelia at the apex as well as at the horizon. We never saw this but I have seen a photograph taken near Yellowknife and paintings by Edward Wilson done when he went with Scott to the Antarctic. I thought this phenomenon was restricted to the higher latitudes but I have seen it once near Vancouver, B.C., once with very unusual weather conditions in Melbourne, Australia and once very faintly in Antwerp in Belgium.

Some sports were played in Yellowknife. There was a three team ice hockey competition, curling and badminton in winter and golf and tennis in summer. The golf course was unusual. The tees were wooden boxes with a central strip of plasterboard into which one could stick a tee. The "greens" were blackish oiled sand and the course was predominantly sand with some rock here and there. Stunted trees lined the fairways. On midsummer's night there was a tournament which began at midnight.

19.6. Yellowknife golf Course with sandy fairways and oiled sand 'blacks'.

We played badminton in the school hall. I had not played it before but found it a very enjoyable game apart from wrecking my tennis swing. A most memorable visit to Fort Rae was on a cold winter night when I went to play for the Yellowknife team which had some quite experienced and skilful players. The Fort Rae team was composed of a couple of priests, the storekeeper and some local Indians. They had little outside experience and we were very confident of an easy victory. But in sport, local home ground advantage often plays a part. It was like the occasion when the famous soccer team, Manchester United, were drawn to play a non-league club, Yeovil Town in the fourth round of the F.A. Cup in 1956. The first game at Yeovil was drawn because the press printed convincing, faked photographs showing the Yeovil ground sloped from side to side! The Manchester team was psyched out. So it happened in Fort Rae. The court was in the school with the desks arranged around the side of the room so that the court would just fit in. It was a two roomed school with a movable partition separating the rooms – this was pulled back. Our problem was that there was a fixed part of the partition which came down 30cm or so to carry the concertina folding partition. This was situated right over the net. Anyone who has played badminton knows that one often hits the shuttlecock high over the net – this was impossible so it made it technically difficult for our players. In addition, there wasn't any room at the side of the court so our style was definitely cramped! Surprise, surprise! We were soundly beaten. We generously invited Fort Rae for a return match at the Yellowknife School where the hall had wonderful, high ceilings. The result was obvious – sweet revenge!

The arrival of summer after nearly nine months of snow and ice was a welcome change. Life returned. Seeing buds on the trees caused enough excitement to induce me to take photographs of them! It warmed up sufficiently for people to swim in Frame Lake for two weeks in July. It reached 27°C for two days.

Our *baby* was expected on 30th July. On 16th July, two weeks before, I went home to find Janet busy cleaning the kitchen. I know now that this is common pre-delivery behaviour. Not long after we went to the hospital. We were in for a big surprise. Catherine was born but there remained a large lump. Could there be another. Twenty minutes later Maryann appeared, unexpectedly! They were the second pair of twins to be born at the hospital. They weighed 6 and 6 1/2 pounds and were very healthy. We were grateful, as Janet had been sick for most of the first three months. Even at six months no one suspected that she was having a baby. Her health had been good and her antenatal examinations had been rather cursory.

The evening before, I had been having coffee with my landlord, Max Macara. We had been discussing the world population explosion. You can imagine the reception I received when I told him we had twins! There were other consequences. An old Scottish lady, Margaret Fairfull, who worked at the school, had knitted our baby a beautiful, woolen shawl. She set to and made another one!

Others left food at the door to help when Janet came home. There was an advantage of not knowing beforehand. Had we known we were having twins there might have been pressure to have them delivered outside in Edmonton or Vancouver which would have been less convenient and would have been unnecessary. Our life certainly became busier but we were lucky to be living over the laundromat.

19.7. Margaret Fairfull and Janet with the twins wrapped in their shawls.

The twins became travelers from an early age. On warm evenings when they wouldn't settle we would take them for a drive around – this helped them to sleep. At two weeks of age they had a speedboat trip across a lake when we went to visit Con Hydro, where the power for Yellowknife was generated. It was an interesting visit. I learnt how the people there prevented the frost damaging their vegetables by keeping a sprinkler on all night. We fished for greyling at the falls nearby. It is a sleek very tasty fish.

We also took the twins out in our canoe in the top of their pram. It is a pity that children do not remember all these pleasant experiences.

I went out to Vancouver for a refresher course in anaesthesia in March. It was quite a trip but I learnt a lot and came to realize that I might benefit from some more training in a bigger centre. I turned down the offer of partnership when I was offered it after a year in Yellowknife. I wrote to Vancouver to see if I could get six months of anaesthesia. I thought I might also try to do some more medicine and possibly paediatrics after that and then I could return to general practice somewhere. My request for six months in anaesthesia was granted starting in January 1963. Our sojourn in Yellowknife ended and we left on 2nd December 1962 so that we could take the twins to see Janet's family in Australia before starting my next job in Vancouver. We left with many interesting memories.

I returned to Yellowknife twice in the next three years to do locums to earn money for our travels to Kenya and Australia respectively.

The third trip was a sentimental journey to see what it was like twenty three years later. We collected our luggage at the airport and were looking around when a lady asked if we were looking for transport?' Then she stopped and said to Janet, "I know you." She turned to me and I told her my name. She said "I know. You delivered my daughter – she is twenty three now."

Much had changed. The government had moved in, the population had increased to 16000, and a new hospital had been built. I went in to have a look and met one of the doctors. He did not know that there had ever been another hospital, let alone two more! John Anderson Thompson was still around as was his old red Land Rover. We wandered all over town and down to the old town – there were many new houses there. We visited the cemetery and saw several graves of people we knew – some had been my patients.

We met an old Chinese cook whom I had known and then we thought we would knock at the door of the Parker's house and see if they were still there. Helen was and gave us a great welcome. She was going to the airport to meet her husband, John, who had by then become Commissioner of the Territories. She took us with her and we renewed his acquaintance too. He presented me with a polar bear lapel badge, the insignia of the North West Territories.

It had been strange going back. It brought back so many memories but it had changed for ever. It was not a frontier town any more. It had already passed that stage when we were there although we now felt like old timers. It was the capital of the NWT.

We had a great surprise when we arrived back in Edmonton. The Mullins girls were there to meet us – the family we had child-minded for two weeks in 1961. What a reunion we had with them and Anne and Lloyd Powell, one of the doctors with whom I had worked in Yellowknife.

Chapter 20
The Miners

The men who work underground in mines have a hard, relentless life. Those who have shares in mining companies and sometimes reap large rewards probably never think of the men who undergo hardship to remove the ore from the ground, sometimes at great personal risk. It is a tough life.

I visited the gold mines in Yellowknife to have a look, both underground and through the mills. Giant Yellowknife was one of the deepest gold mines at the time. The temperature remained constant – about 15°C regardless of the outside temperature which in Yellowknife varied from 28°C in July to minus 45°C in the depths of winter. I also saw gold bricks being poured and was impressed by their weight when I tried to hold one – about 30kg, which was worth about $35000 at the time. (C15.6, C15.7)

I did not see the men actually blasting and digging but the descriptions I have read tell of how they have to dig, blast a little to loosen the rock and then shovel it into carts for conveying to the central shaft and thence to the surface. At the end of the day the miners emerge from the depths and take a shower before wending their weary way home or more often to a bunkhouse, where they may or may not have privacy. Eat, sleep and return to work day after day. It is not much wonder that when the time comes for a break they go to somewhere more civilized – a relative term, because it depends on how isolated the mine is how far they reach. Those from outlying mines might only reach Yellowknife where they would begin drinking. Maybe they would get no further before their money ran out. Then they would have to go back to work. Some, however, will go to the cities or even go back to their homes for a break.

These are strong, tough, hardy men. I used to do pre-employment medical checks on them when they came for employment at the mines around Yellowknife. We had contracts with the mines – Giant and Con (CM&S) in Yellowknife, Discovery (110 km out but still within the tree line) and Taurcanis further out on the "Barrens". In years gone by there were many small mines around Yellowknife but most of these had closed and many had disappeared by the time we went there. Some,

20.1. Main frame at defunct Ptarmigan Mine.

like Ptarmigan stood inactive.

For some time one medical problem perplexed me. Nearly all the men had elevated blood pressure when they came for their mine medical examinations. It seemed to relate to having a few drinks before coming for their pre-employment check up. I had always thought that alcohol had a vasodilating effect which should lower blood pressure. This did not seem to be the case. They would return next day without having had a drink beforehand and their blood pressure would be normal. Maybe apprehension about passing the test made them nervous and elevated their pressure. Eventually I realized that I could determine whether they had real hypertension by looking at the fundi in their eyes with an ophthalmoscope. High blood pressure causes characteristic changes which I did not see. Later I had a patient, who had been drinking heavily, who I found had high blood pressure and, more significantly, albumin in her urine, which usually suggests some kidney problem. I admitted her to hospital. She recovered three days later. Both abnormalities disappeared about the same time suggesting that alcohol can have adverse effects on blood pressure and the kidneys.

Sometimes these men came to see us for other medical problems. One such patient was Elmer Luomo, a big, strong man from Finland. Three weeks later he was dead. He had been working in Discovery mine when a large rock slipped and crushed him, smashing his spine in the process. Years later I found his grave on the hillside of Yellowknife cemetery. It was a beautiful resting place overlooking Jackfish Lake with pines and silver birches growing around it producing dark green and gold contrast in the fall. I often wondered about him – where was he from and what of his family? Why had he come to Canada? Maybe he came from the mining area around Rovaniemi in northern Finland. I will never know.

Shortly before I left Yellowknife another young man had an

incredible escape – at least we thought he had. Working in Giant Mine rock gave way in a vertical section, carrying him with it. By luck he ended up in a space with air and, miraculously, without any broken bones. His colleagues in mine rescue performed a heroic rescue, working up from below to release him. He had survived a most terrible episode. Then we realized that his kidneys were failing as a result of the damage to his muscles releasing myoglobin, which could collect and block the tubules in the kidneys and lead to kidney failure. We had to transfer him to Edmonton for treatment. It was at a time when dialysis was just coming in, but renal transplantation had not begun so his chances were not as good as they would be today. I left Yellowknife a few days later and never heard his final outcome.

Chapter 21
Flying in the Canadian North

Travelling by plane in Labrador introduced me to the pleasures of flying in small planes. It was a way to see this huge country. Yellowknife was the centre for flying to the central Arctic. Ken Stockall was 32 when I met him in Yellowknife not long after our arrival in August 1961.He was already a highly respected bush pilot, the only one with whom the northern Judicial Party, led by Judge Simmons, would travel.

He had flown with the Canadian Air Search and Rescue before settling in the north where he first flew with Wardair, then flew for Hank Koenen before joining up with Les Mullins, a mechanic, to form Ptarmigan Airways in March 1961.When we arrived they had recently taken delivery of MZZ, the first Cessna 185 (single engine) plane in the north.

My first big trip was with Ken to Cambridge Bay to pick up a sick baby. It was in late October.We were the first flight north after freeze up so we stopped at the small, primarily Eskimo (now called Inuit) settlement of Bathurst on the Arctic coast to deliver their mail.They had been isolated for five weeks during freeze up while the ice froze to a thickness on which we could land.

This was my first contact in the Arctic with Eskimos, a people I came to like and respect as wonderful patients. They were in their winter parkas with wolverine fur surrounding their faces. Being isolated our visit caused great interest and even little children came out to see us.

We were told that there was a sick man at a little Eskimo camp at Arctic Sound (C16.1) about 50km to the west.We flew in there to pick him up. It was an encampment with three caribou skin huts and about fifteen people. Nobody spoke English but we found the old man,Tom Nanutak (C.16.2), and took him to Cambridge Bay. He told the interpreter after we arrived there that he was wondering why he had been given the aeroplane ride as he had recovered from his illness. He had had a bout of gastroenteritis about two weeks before! I am sure he was amazed to be flying but it was an experience for him and gave me the chance to visit a very interesting and isolated place twice.

The days were becoming short and it was dark when we arrived. Cambridge Bay was a settlement on Victoria Island at 70°N, which had developed as a DEW (Distant Early Warning) line base to detect any Russian intrusion over the north.

We went to the nursing station to find that the baby we had come to collect had recovered. Our trip seemed to be developing into a "wild goose chase" until we received a request in the evening to go to Spence Bay, 500km east, where the Hudson Bay Company store manager had injured his back. So next morning we flew off to the east over the white, snow covered land and icing up sea, to Spence Bay, which is almost in the centre of the Canadian Arctic on 70°N. On the way we had an entertaining sight of a polar bear. He heard us coming and began to run. As we came closer he turned to look at this strange 'bird' that was intruding on his quiet existence – unknowing he came to the edge of the ice and crashed into the sea. He must have had a fright but polar bears are well insulated and are good swimmers so he came to no harm.

I had no idea at the time that Sir John Franklin's ships, attempting to find the North West Passage in 1845, had been crushed near King William Island, over which we flew, and that the prolific Arctic explorer, John Rae, who worked for the Hudson Bay Company, had found the channel named after him which joined the seas from east and west to form the North West Passage. We crossed it going to Spence Bay. He had charted hundreds of miles of the central Arctic Canadian coast (between 1846-54) during his remarkable time in Canada. He also was the first to obtain evidence in 1854 that the famous Franklin expedition had ended in disaster. Everybody had died from lead poisoning, scurvy or starvation. Many expeditions had already gone to look for them unsuccessfully. Because Rae indicated that the Eskimos had told him that some of Franklin's men had eaten parts of their dead companions, he was denigrated back in England, and did not receive the recognition he deserved. (McGoogan)

Spence Bay had a few scattered houses and the Hudson Bay store a little distance up the hill away from the edge of the frozen sea on which we landed. It was here that I first encountered an outer porch on the house, built out of ice blocks to provide extra protection in winter from the icy winds. (C17.1) It could be 40 to 50°C below zero.

Our patient turned out to be Ernie Lyall who had been born in northern Labrador and who spent his life in the Arctic. I had met his brother two years before at the hospital in North West River when I was working in Labrador. Ernie had not seen him for 32 years as he had lived his life in the far North. We took him back with us to Cambridge Bay where we spent the night before returning with Ernie to Yellowknife. We took Tom Nanutak home. We had a spectacular, clear, sunny day as we flew over the frozen sea and land to Arctic Sound – fantastic for photographs. (C16.4) I obtained an excellent one of Tom and his son wearing their sealskin clothes and mukluks (skin boots) (C16.2), a group photograph of all the inhabitants in front of one of the tents, their dogs lying in the snow in front of sledges and another of their seal supply lying frozen in the snow.(C16.3) In recent years some people have objected to this slaughter of seals but they fail to appreciate that the Eskimos only killed what they needed for food and clothing. It was all part of the balance of nature that had been going on for centuries.

This was a detour from the normal Cambridge Bay to Yellowknife flight route. I was very fortunate as it enabled me to see the 50m high Wilberforce Falls, which are not on the regular routes. It is a very interesting waterfall coming down in two streams. The eastern one falls part of the height and then turns a corner to complete the fall while the western one falls straight down in two steps. The only thing was that they were not falling much – they were almost frozen (C17.2). A frozen fall is a majestic sight as the water freezes from the top and also when it strikes the bottom – it is like stalactites and stalagmites in caves. These were structurally one of the most interesting waterfalls I have ever seen.

The treats were not over yet. We came across a herd of caribou on their migration across the "Barrens". It was not a huge herd, as the numbers have declined since the days described by writers such as Farley Mowat, who saw huge herds on their annual migration north and then south again in the fall. Our herd was being followed by a few watchful wolves just waiting for a weakling or a sick one to fall by the wayside. It is interesting to watch nature keeping the balance. It is easy to feel hostile towards the wolves but they are just doing their job and they do not kill wantonly.

Ernie became very excited when we reached the tree line about 160km north of Yellowknife because he had not seen a tree for eight years since he was last "outside". The tree line runs diagonally from the Mackenzie delta in the west to the south of Hudson Bay in the east. It is the northern limit of tree growth, the trees becoming more stunted as the line is approached. Beyond that there are only some very small shrubs and the tundra. It is somewhat similar to climbing a mountain with trees becoming smaller and more stunted as one ascends, eventually to come to grass and rock and then bare rock with only lichens growing on them.

We had the opportunity to entertain Ernie before he returned north. He had been born in Indian Harbour in Labrador in 1910. His mother was mostly Irish and his father of Scottish Hudson Bay Company descent. At the age of one the family moved to Port Burwell at the northern tip of Labrador. He was sent to school in Makkovik. His parents moved to Hebron. At 15 he was sent to school in St Johns which had a population at that time of 25000. After two years he was sent to Montreal to train with the Hudson Bay Company. He told us about a cheque made out to HBC – Here Before Christ! Soon after he was sent north but was shipwrecked on the way. He reached Wolstenholme, which does not seem to be on the map any more, and then reached his destination at Cape Smith by dog team. He moved around the eastern Arctic for several years but had been in Spence Bay, where he helped to set up the Hudson Bay Store, since 1949. He married an Eskimo called Nipisha and they had eleven children. I met Betty, an older daughter who obviously helped to care for the younger ones. She was an attractive girl and features in one of my photographs. (C17.1) I read later that he left the Hudson Bay Company in 1962 to work for the Government as an equipment mechanic and later became a J.P. and a game officer. In 1979 he wrote a book, *Arctic Man*, "to counteract all the baloney written by short term visitors"!

For one born almost on the Equator living in Yellowknife at 62 1/2 degrees north, with the days lasting only four hours in mid winter, was unusual. To go north of the Arctic Circle where it was dark continuously for a month in midwinter was intriguing. I went with Ken on a trip to Coppermine on Boxing Day. There was only a faint lightening of the sky – not even twilight – in the middle of the day. It is not surprising that depression can take its toll for people living in such places. It seems more surprising that people generally adapt to the cold and darkness as well as they do.

The first European to visit the area was Samuel Hearne. He worked for the Hudson Bay Company and was stationed at Prince of

Wales Fort near the Churchill River on Hudson Bay. He was asked to travel to find a river in the north-west which was reputed to be rich in minerals, particularly copper. He made two abortive trips which failed to reach their destination but he learnt a great deal about bushcraft, survival and the Indians during them. He left on the third trip on 7th December 1770 with some Indians, including women who were particularly strong for carrying loads or pulling sledges and useful for cooking and making clothes. On the previous trip he had not been allowed to take women which proved to be a great disadvantage. They trekked through the winter across the Barrens and finally came to the river about forty miles from the sea in early July. His Indians and some local Copper Indians attacked a nearby Eskimo camp and annihilated them. Hearne could not understand this cruel mentality and yet that was why some of the Indians made the trip. The inhabitants from another camp across the river escaped down river by canoe. There are no Indians that far north now.

They finally reached the sea at the mouth of the Coppermine River on 17th July, 1771. There were no mines as such at the river but after scouring the area one 2kg piece of copper was found. It took ten months to return. During the early part of the return trip the Indians were anxious to return to their wives who had been left some distance south. They were travelling lightly but Hearne had to carry his own load of 27kg. During the first three days they covered 160 km. Hearne could not risk being left behind although his feet were sore. They caught up with women after about 300km as they had started to move south. By then Hearne's feet were bleeding and painful but he was extremely tough and kept up. It was a massive trip as they covered over 3000 km each way in tough, cold conditions, pulling or carrying loads and often hungry. Maybe his nine years at sea in his adolescent years made him the incredibly tough fellow he became and prepared him for this extreme hardship.

Hearne was also remarkable because he had no experience of this country, its people, hunting or travelling in the winter before he began his first attempt. He was regarded as one of the most inexperienced Europeans ever to set off exploring in North America, and yet he succeeded. He mapped much of the country he traversed, until his equipment was broken, and became one of the most knowledgeable people ever to write about some of the northern and Chipewyan Indians, many of whom subsequently died in a smallpox epidemic. It is amazing that this disease which wiped out hundreds of people in different parts of the world was made extinct by vaccination.

One night a call came from Contoyto Lake, 400 km north, where there was a Department of Transport Radio Beacon. They had a sick Eskimo lady with abdominal pain. The government nurse, who usually arranged transport for indigenous people who were in need of treatment, was on leave. I was on call. It seemed from the message that we should pick this woman up. I phoned Ken who agreed to take me. We set off into the Arctic night, out over the frozen land, on over the tundra for over two hours. It was a clear, cold night with the stars shining in all their glory. Our destination was easy to locate because of the radio beacon. The landing was more tricky. The DOT men had laid out flares to mark a potential landing strip but when we came in we found that there were cross drifts 20–25cm high – not big but big enough to make an awkward landing for a small plane. Our first touch was bumpy so Ken took off again and circled for a second attempt – a bumpy landing but it was accomplished safely. I was left wondering what would have happened if the plane was damaged or a ski had broken during a rough landing – we would have been stuck there for a while. My faith in Ken as a pilot was well founded. He was, after all, regarded by many as the foremost pilot in the north, careful and with good judgement. We loaded our passenger on board. She still had pain but it did not seem critical. We arrived back in Yellowknife safely. To my chagrin, the following day I found out that this patient had done this before and had had surgery but no cause was found. So it seemed that we had taken unnecessary risks to bring her into Yellowknife as we did not find any significant cause. Maybe her husband had threatened her or a shaman had cast a spell on her. We will never know.

During our trips Ken had told me of the Nahanni Valley, which he said was spectacular. It was the "tropical valley" referred to in rumours of the past. There are hot springs there. Many weird stories circulated about this valley. It was even known as Headless Valley on account of the two Macleod brothers being found with their heads missing, three years after they had gone to explore it in 1905. Others had gone in never to return. One man was found in his cabin with a notice tacked on the door: "Dead man inside." He must have died of starvation. The most recent story was about five prospectors who were flown in one spring not long before we went to Yellowknife. There was some confusion about their retrieval at the end of the summer. Eventually one of the pilots, Chuck McAvoy, flew in to check. He only found two almost starved men. Two had decided to walk out and were never seen again and the third could stand the wait no longer. He tied a belt of dynamite around his waist and blew himself up. So it seemed that this was a haunted valley.

One day Ken invited me to join him on a trip into the Nahanni as he was going to stake a plot for a tourist cabin. He needed one other to share the petrol costs. Henry Busse was a 60-year-old photographer who had exhibited at an International exhibition. He had lived for 20 years in Yellowknife and I knew he would be interested. He welcomed the opportunity. The time for the trip was well chosen. The Fall (autumn) season north of 60° is short: within two to three weeks the leaves change through their brilliant autumnal colours, and then they are gone leaving the deciduous trees bare, except for a coating of snow, until spring returns in May. The first snow falls in September, so by the middle of the month the mountain tops of the Nahanni are white while the valleys are aglow with the silver birches and tamarac turning gold among the evergreen spruce.

We three met early on the morning of 12th September at the Ptarmigan dock where the Cessna 185, MZZ, was waiting. It was still on floats as most planes in the north are in summer. As winter comes these are changed for skis. There was a buzz in the air as we climbed aboard with our collection of cameras and films. Soon we were skimming across the water, then MZZ was airborne. We banked over the town. Not many people were about yet. We set our course to the west and followed the Yellowknife highway – our terrestrial link for nine months each year with the outside world and Edmonton, 1600km away. Our course changed to south west. We crossed the north west arm of Great Slave Lake, then White Beach Point with its glittering white sand. Soon we were again flying over stunted spruce trees and muskeg and many small lakes. It could be anywhere in thousands of square kilometres south of the tree line. But Ken knew all this country and even I recognized where we were when we crossed the highway coursing south to the ferry. The land rose as we flew across the Horn Mountains and further on, a wisp of mist marked the course of the mighty Mackenzie River, a barge waterway to the Arctic coast during the short summer.

Two and a half hours after we had left Yellowknife we circled over Fort Simpson. It was a settlement of about seven hundred inhabitants, mainly Indians. There was an experimental farm. The fields were golden and some of the crops had already been harvested. The growing season is very short but the growth of crops is very rapid due to the endless daylight. We landed on the Mackenzie River, a little downstream from its tributary, the Liard.

Albert Faille was an old prospector who for years and years had laboured up the Nahanni River each summer from Fort Simpson in his elusive quest for gold. He was still somewhere out there.

21.1. Ken Stockall refuelling MZZ at Fort Simpson. The small man is Henry Busse.

Having refueled and picked up our other passenger, the government surveyor, we took off again on a fine sunny day.

Soon mountains began to appear to the south. Our anticipation grew. The view compared to the one of the Rockies when they eventually appeared after our drive across the prairies. Eighty miles south we flew over the village of South Nahanni, situated at the confluence of the Nahanni and Liard Rivers. The little blue-roofed log church with a tower stood out as the most picturesque feature of the place. Nahanni Butte, a mountain that stands guard over the beginning of the Nahanni Valley, was on our right as we set our course westwards. The valley opened out for about 65km with the river dividing into many channels in a stretch called the Splits.

The mountains began to converge as we approached the entrance to the first canyon. Below were the hot springs where Gus Krause had lived for many years. He could stay there all winter because the hot water could be used to heat his cabin. He could grow potatoes with ease due to the warmth of the area around the springs. The water temperature ranged from 37 to 40°C.

We could take wonderful photographs from the plane because the window opened upwards in the Cessna and were kept open by the draft. (C18.2)

The First Canyon was stupendous, 16 to 20km in length, the sides deeply eroded, steep and angular, dropping from the mountain tops at nearly 2000m to the river, far below at 600m. (C18.3) This was fantastic. We were flying in the canyon taking photographs of these amazing cliffs. An open valley appeared and then the Second Canyon. It was beautiful with the fall colours of the trees, particularly the tamaracks, spread over the smoothly curved hills. It was not so grand and rugged as the First Canyon.

Our flight crossed "Headless Valley", where the Macleod brothers had been found headless in 1908.

The Third Canyon had a spectacular "Gate", a feature where the river made a U bend between towering, perpendicular limestone cliffs, about 200m high. (C18.4) It was a short segment where the river had broken through a narrow ridge which ran across the valley.

The canyons left me marvelling at the tremendous power of erosion as water carves its way through mountains to leave these fantastic formations.

21.2. Virginia Falls – 100m high.

What an incredible trip – so much variety to see. The next feature was the confluence of the brown water from the Flat River and the glacial green water of the Nahanni. The waters remained separate for more than a kilometre below the junction under Direction Mountain before they finally mixed.

The cliffs by the river became redder and soon the magnificent 100m high Virginia Falls appeared. They are a great sight, twice as high as Niagara Falls. The fall starts with a gradual decline before turning right to hurtle over the precipitous section which is divided by an island in the middle. We circled before we landed on a quiet stretch of the river above the falls.

Here we had lunch by one of Albert Faille's deserted boats. Each year he came to the bottom of the falls by motorboat, then man-handled his equipment up a steep path and, at the top, built another boat with planks in which to continue his journey. The National film board made a film of this hardy northerner on one of his trips.

After lunch we walked down a steep track to the foot of the falls. From the bottom there is an excellent view of the split falls tumbling down on either side of the central pillar. The river had carved a geological trench which exposed fossils in the lower third. These were ammenoids, spiral shell like molluscs.

It was a perfect day with only a few small clouds in the blue sky. As we pushed off shore it took a few seconds to start the engine. We began floating with the current. I was glad we were well above the falls. It would be awful to be unable to start the engine and get into the rapid current roaring towards the falls. It has never happened. The valley widened out into flat swampy land with the river coursing through it. We saw a black bear as it scampered out of sight into the trees. There were several moose wading about in the swamps. They have long legs adapted for that purpose. They are rather ungainly, quite large animals with huge antlers.

21.3. A large glacier feeding the valley into Brintnell Lake.

More hot springs appeared. These were beautifully structured – we visited them later. Rabbitkettle Lake, oval in shape, was surrounded by burnt out bush. There had been a big fire in the area. Soon we were heading into a gap in the mountains to Brintnell Lake, our final destination. It was a gem, glacial green water running in at the foot of Mt. Sir James McBrien which rose with sheer rock walls to the peak, nearly two kilometres in the air above it. (C18.1) The lake is at 850 m and the peak was 2800 m. We landed at a point, jutting out into the lake near the far end at surely one of the most stunningly beautiful camp sites in the world. Ken knew that. It was why he had come to stake it out.

21.4. Reflections on Brintnell Lake – the Cessna 185, MZZ and Mt Sir James McBrien

There were mountains to the right behind the campsite, then Mt. Sir James McBrien to the left before the valley curved further to the left, to the south, up into the mountains where it met a glacier creeping down the valley.

Across the lake we saw a grizzly bear. The camp site had moss and grass growing under scattered spruce trees. Bunch-berries, edible red berries which are preceded in summer by attractive little white flowers, were growing under the trees.

As I was standing on the shore a beaver came swimming along, oblivious to my presence. It came ashore within three metres of where I stood before it realized that I was something unusual and made a hurried departure. As it entered the water it gave a sharp slap of its tail to warn others of my presence and then dived to reappear further out in the lake. It had probably never seen a human before and may never have seen another.

21.5. Brintnell Lake.

The surveyor had been fishing and had caught a greyling, a sleek, delectable fish to eat. It is found throughout the northern lakes and rivers. While we had our dinner and talked, the moon rose over the mountains and lined the clouds with silver before disappearing behind them. It was so peaceful.

The next morning was perfect. The still lake reflected the mountains, the peaks bathed in splendour of the soft light produced by the rising sun. It was utter tranquility and beauty.

After breakfast Ken decided to do a circuit over the nearby mountains before setting out for home. We had to

21.6. Flying around the mountains near Brintnell Lake.

fly up to above 3,000 m to be above them. In the clear morning the peaks dominated the superb scenery. Small lakes nestled among the mountains like emeralds. A great glacier filled the valley and terminated where crevasses broke its even surface and large blocks of ice broke away to feed a mountain stream. Then cloud started to creep in from the south. We turned for home passing behind the peak of Mt. Sir James McBrien. It was an awesome view looking down the precipitous walls of the mountainside to the green lake and our camping site about 1800m below.

21.7. Looking down the side of Mt. Sir James McBrien on to Brintnell Lake 1800m below.

We landed at Rabbitkettle Lake, the nearest landing place for access to the hot springs about 5 km away. It too was tranquil, reflecting the mountains to the south. A grebe swam near the shore, occasionally diving and disappearing only to re-appear some distance away. A squirrel was collecting mushrooms for its winter store and drying them on a log.

The walk to the springs posed some difficulties. The first couple of kilometres were across country which had been ravaged by fire. Fallen trees lay everywhere. The natural process following a forest fire was occurring, small birch trees were growing to replace those which had been destroyed. Later, the evergreens, mostly spruce in this part, would gradually grow again. Our next obstacle was a deep cold river which was too wide to jump across. By good fortune we found two tree trunks, one fallen from each

21.8. Ken and the surveyor crossing the river on the way to the hot springs.

side, which met in the middle and formed a precarious bridge which we were able to cross.

The hot springs, through the ages, had built a light ochre-coloured mound about 15m high. On top was a still pool reflecting the surrounding mountains. The water trickled over one side forming a miniature waterfall which sparkled in the sunshine. The fall was a series of steps, from two to twenty centimetres high, which had formed very, very gradually over a long period as the minerals precipitated. (C18.5) Close by there were two smaller springs. At that time, in 1961, very few people would have had the privilege to have visited these springs. It was wonderful to view nature untouched.

Returning through the woods we saw several interesting plants including Lady's slipper, wild thyme and lupins. I learned that spruce gum could be used as chewing gum. At first, the taste is bitter and one has to spit the saliva out to get rid of that. Eventually it becomes almost tasteless. It is also used by the Indians in a purified state for repairing and waterproofing their canoes.

Taxi-ing the 'plane to take off we had to stop suddenly. A flock of ducks flew across our path. This can be dangerous it they are caught up in the propeller. We started again and were soon airborne, flying higher than on the way in. We flew over Virginia Falls, the Flat River junction and far below we saw a flock of snow geese. Then we were over the canyons and the "Gate", the lower hot springs, the Splits and down to South Nahanni where we stopped to re-fuel. I had wondered why Ken was reluctant to drop into the canyon for more photographs but found out that he was anxious about our fuel. The flight over the mountains had used more than planned. It is not good to run out of fuel in the mountains, so we were happy to be safely at South Nahanni. Here we met Gus Krause, the trapper who had spent his life in the area and at the first hot springs. As the sun was setting we arrived at Fort Simpson, where we spent the night.

Sunrise next morning was superb, pink, orange and yellow gradually merging into daylight as we took off for Yellowknife on our last lap of a most memorable trip – one of the best of my life.

It is no wonder the Nahanni valley became the first World Heritage Park. So many adjectives can be used to describe it – fantastic, beautiful, majestic, awesome, stupendous but also mysterious and ghostly. It is one of the most wonderful places that I have visited.

When we returned Henry Busse was disappointed that he had not taken his movie camera. He had several rolls of film lying in his studio. He would go back, he decided. I was very tempted to go to but I found that there had been some apprehension at home about me being away on this trip, especially with the twins so young. My friend Andy Hill told me years later that he too would have gone but could not afford it. They needed two others to share the cost. Two young fellows from Giant mine agreed to go but it was not until the second weekend after our return that they went. Three days later Ptarmigan float base phoned to ask if I knew their exact plans as they had not returned. They did not return. They never returned. Despite all Ken's skill and experience they had disappeared.

The greatest air search ever in Canada took place. I went out for two days on the search. Little did I think that I would see that magnificent and sinister country again and certainly not under these circumstances. We flew to Fort Simpson and then over to Dall Lake where we landed near a cache. It was one of those brilliant clear days with blue skies and more snow now as the season was advancing into winter. (C18.6) We went on into the Nahanni valley, over Rabbitkettle Lake and south down the valley beyond. Was it possible that they had trouble in a small circular valley off to the north side? It was occupied by a beautiful, small lake – an attractive place. They were not there. It would have been interesting place to visit if we had not more urgent business at hand. There were several other 'planes scouring the skies but there was no sign of MZZ. We returned to Yellowknife but the search went on.

There had been no news of them since they left Fort Simpson. We learned that it had been fine when they left but bad weather had come in rapidly from the south east that morning, across the mountains. The search went on for longer than any previous search, which was an indication of the esteem in which Ken was held by the pilots. It was a tragedy – Ken had five small children. He was so popular and highly regarded that people could not believe something could have happened to him. He once told me that several pilots had disappeared or crashed after flying a certain number hours in the north. He had done that time. The search was given up as winter was now settling in but we still did not know what had happened. That is always the worst aspect of a disaster – not knowing.

Next spring, as the snow was melting in the mountains a 'plane coming over from Watson Lake in British Columbia spotted the wreckage in a dead end valley. They must have been caught by the bad weather, entered the valley and in trying to turn to escape touched the wing tip and crashed. I lost two good friends, but the family and his wife, Anne, lost their breadwinner. The end of the story was that Anne married again to someone who accepted all the children. The eldest boy became a pilot.

I had some other flights with other pilots. One of the doctors went to Discovery Mine each month to do a clinic. It was 110km away. I went first on a day in February when it was 35°C below zero. (C17.5) I remember the occasion well as I have a wonderful photograph of the mine with snow covered trees around it. The next time was in summer when we flew by float 'plane and landed on the lake nearby. On that occasion I played tennis as they had a court there. One striking feature was the number of children who had eye problems.

On one occasion I had the idea that it would be interesting to drive out there in winter. The road crosses the lakes which have ice 2m thick in winter and between lakes they bulldoze roads– not usually very far as there are so many lakes. We made it for 60km when Janet persuaded me to turn back. Trucks travel for miles into the tundra in winter on such trails.

Taurcanis Mine was 320km out on the Barrens. We had a clinic there about every three months. I went once in winter. It was quite an experience. First we ran into a "white out". In winter the land is all white but features are recognizable. In a "white out" everything is white and nothing at all is recognizable. It is an unpleasant and rather scary feeling not knowing where you are sailing through the sky. At least there were no mountains in the area to crash into. They did not have a guiding beacon to the mine. Eventually visibility returned. We landed on a frozen lake which makes a flat landing place in winter. It was some distance from the mine. A "caboose" was waiting for us. This is basically a cabin on skis which is dragged by a tractor. (19.2) The nice thing about it was that it had a stove inside to keep us warm.

Our pilot that day was Jimmy McAvoy, whose brother Chuck lived behind us and was famous for finding lost 'planes. Jimmy was a less reliable pilot. On this occasion he did not bother to cover the engine to keep it warm. So after we were finished we returned to the 'plane to find that he had to warm the engine with a blow torch before he could start it – an unnecessary delay. Anyway we returned safely home.

My last trip was to do clinics in Coppermine and Holman Island because the government people who usually did these visits were not available. It must have been September, as the first signs of freeze up were occurring in the north. These were rings of ice forming around the grass and reeds in the ponds. I had been to Coppermine before on Boxing Day when it was dark. This time it was still bleak with overcast skies. Crossing the coast presented an uninviting brown and grey image with cold breakers washing the shore. We landed at Coppermine and saw the patients. I also saw a musk ox skull – it was a pity I did not see the live animals. There was a small herd further east. I also met an Australian nurse, Catherine Ross, from Mudgee in New South Wales. That was a surprising place to find an Aussie, but then why was I there?

Next stop was Holman Island (70°N) on the west side of Victoria Island. (C17.3) We were well beyond the tree line so the view was rather desolate. The settlement was inhabited by Eskimos, Hudson Bay Company staff, the Anglican and Catholic clergy. The Hudson Bay Company manager had worked across the north. He had a television set which received some programs. This was remarkable because 1962 was early days for television and the nearest relay station would have been over 1500km away. His second idiosyncrasy was that he played golf on the ice with red golf balls with the Anglican clergyman! So the latter had an additional function in the community. The young HBC assistant also had points worthy of comment. He had been born and brought up in Nyasaland (now Malawi), was educated in Scotland and played the bagpipes, much to the amusement of the Eskimos. So we had television, bagpipes and golf in this very isolated community at the end of the world.

The end of the world is certainly what it felt like to me when I climbed the hill behind the settlement and looked north. I can remember thinking, as I gazed out on the view over the hills along the coast, "it goes on and on and on, and on to the North Pole and there is nobody in between!" It was a strange feeling. On the walk I was also intrigued with the lichens which were yellow and black. To think that they survived those harsh winters and had probably been growing there, ever so slowly, for maybe a century or more.

There were other interesting sights at Holman Island. The Eskimos had parkas with magnificent, wide furs around the head pieces. (C17.4) They had seal skins pegged out being cured, before turning them into clothing or patterned rugs. I was lucky enough to obtain one of the rugs in Yellowknife depicting an Eskimo hunting walrus from a kayak. They also made soap stone carvings and I obtained some intricate little ones with an igloo and a man fishing beside it.

Some years later, when we were clearing out my in-laws house, we found a stonecut picture which had been given to Dr Penfold by a grateful patient. I noticed a Holman Island co-operative stamp in one corner. What a treasure I had accidentally found which could easily have been lost!

Flying was an exciting and probably the only practical way to see the North.

Chapter 22

The Long Road to Yellowknife

It is a long way to Yellowknife – 1600km by road from Edmonton and 2500 km. from Vancouver. We made the latter journey three times and once we went via Calgary and Edmonton, in our Volkswagen kombi. I have mentioned the first trip north to Yellowknife in an earlier chapter – through the grand Fraser Canyon with the road hanging on the cliff and a railway and the river below us.

22.1. Fraser Canyon with railway on the other side.

We were amused at a stop to find toilets marked "Pointers" and "Setters". The journey passed the arid area around Cache Creek, then the ranching country around Clinton going on to Quesnel followed by the forests of northern B.C. with Prince George in their midst. Dawson Creek was a hub where we met the road from Edmonton and the end of the Prairies joining the start of the Alaska Highway.

Our route took us through the Peace River country, past Grimshaw and eventually to Enterprise. It was an apt name and said something about the people who settled there. It had a service station at the junction of the road to Hay River, a settlement on the south side of the lake, and the Yellowknife Highway which turned west heading for the Mackenzie River crossing.

I remember reading a book called *Worst Journeys* in which many well known people described their life's worst journey. When I finished it I thought that I could have written the whole book myself. Maybe you will be shivering by the time you finish this chapter!

Our trip out in March was one of them – challenging, demanding and at times risky. I had decided to go to Vancouver for a refresher course in anaesthesia for General Practitioners. We had four days to get there, a week there and a week to return. I took our Volkswagen kombi, an eight seater minibus, for service at the garage. The fan belt was a bit worn and I was advised to have it renewed. When a new fan belt is fitted to a Volkswagen it tends to stretch a little and requires an adjustment to tighten it after 200 to 300km. It is usually a simple manoeuvre to remove a nut, take out two washers and put them outside the part holding the fan belt. We set off happily down the highway and passed Fort Rae when suddenly the car lost power and stopped. I realized what was wrong but then the problems began. The nut had been done up with a power driven spanner and I could not undo it.

A truck stopped. "You have a frozen gas line," the driver said and gave me some antifreeze to pour into the gas (petrol). Magic! The car started and off we went. Sixty kilometres further and we began to lose power again. By then we had our lights on as it was becoming late and the days were still short. I stopped to let the engine idle because I figured that if there was no stress on the fan belt it would generate electricity and replenish the battery. The engine stalled. Another truck came by and stopped. "Your gas line is probably frozen," he said and gave me more antifreeze. Magic again. The engine started. It was nonsense about the gas line freezing because in the kombi the petrol tank is immediately above the engine and therefore kept warm unlike the VW beetle where the petrol tank is in the front and the engine in the back. We crept on, stopping for a while when the lights dimmed. Finally we reached the Mackenzie crossing. There was a store nearby but it was already closed. We thought we might sleep there but after a while I decided to press on to Enterprise where there was a garage, another 130km on. All went well with our stop-start regime until we stalled about 35km short of our target. There was nothing for it but to climb into the back and try to sleep on the bed we had rigged up by removing the middle seat.

After an hour, about 11pm, the cold began to get to me so I tried to start the kombi again. Three cheers! It started. We crept slowly on and finally could see lights in the distance, but it turned out to be further than we thought. When we reached the garage/café at Enterprise it was past midnight and everything was closed up and deserted. Janet was six months pregnant, wrapped in a fur coat in her sleeping bag but still it was very cold – 24°C below zero! I was cold too. If one remained absolutely still it did not seem so cold. The worst part was being woken at 6am by someone arriving and hooting their horn. Once awake we really felt the cold but the café did not open until 8.30am. We were glad when we could go inside and warm up, but were very frustrated when we tried to get the mechanic to undo our stiff nut and recharge the battery. "I am in the middle of doing an urgent engine change over" he told me and did not have time. Frustration was rising and by 2pm we had managed to persuade him that he could fix our problem without much delay in his job.

22.2. Mackenzie Highway in March.

Now we were half a day behind. We set off down the dreary, lonely road. They had not sealed the road because the expansion and contraction of the tar in the extreme conditions would just break it up.

We passed the Alexandra and Louise Falls. It was amazing to see the mighty Hay River stopped in its track with the cascading falls frozen. We reached the cabins at High Level that night.

The next day was uneventful and we reached Chetwynd in northern British Columbia. The fun began again the next morning. It was Saturday and we had to be in Vancouver, about 1300km away by Sunday evening. Not long after starting we reached a sign which read "DO NOT PROCEED WITHOUT CHAINS OR SNOW-TYRES". I had bought chains in Vancouver before we went north but had not used them as we managed on the snow even without snow tyres. So out came the chains from under the back seat. You wouldn't believe it but they were Beetle chains which were too small for our wheels! Now we had a dilemma. To go on without chains or snow tyres through miles and miles of deserted forest or should we go the long way round by Edmonton and Calgary – an extra days drive which would make us a day late for the course? We went on. At our next stop we had a soft tyre so we pumped it up and continued. At our next refueling it was down a little again so we pumped it up and proceeded. Then we had 130km through forest (and B.C. forests are thick) without any habitation or signs of human life. Finally, in the evening, we reached Quesnel and were glad to find a motel and have a good warm sleep. Our problems were nearly over but not quite. I took the kombi down-town to have the now very soft tyre fixed. They checked the wrong one first. We eventually reached Vancouver in time.

The week in Vancouver was spectacular – the sun shone every day and the snow-covered mountains on the north shore were a magnificent sight. People say that it is one of the most beautiful cities in the world on a good day. We had a good week and it is not surprising that we later decided to return. However, it is often dull, grey and depressing during the winter.

The course proved very useful. I learnt many practical things, although I wondered about some of the content of the lectures – later I found out what they were talking about. I realized that this was no refresher course for me. It was learning some of the basics which I had not picked up in my two weeks training during my internship. I realized then that I needed some more training.

Our return journey was much less adventurous although we passed some spectacular scenery in southern British Columbia and going through the mountains. We went east through the Rockies and visited Lake Louise when it was covered with over a metre of snow. (C9.3) The view across the frozen lake in front of the hotel to the mountain behind was breathtaking. In those days skiing had not become a craze. We went through Calgary, then a city of 200000, and on up to Edmonton. Here I met some relatives for the only time and visited the hospitals and some of the doctors to whom we referred patients. I bumped into Arthur Tulloch who had been with me as an orderly at East Fortune, the sanatorium near Edinburgh where I had worked as a student. He subsequently became an anaesthetist and I met him again at conferences.

The long drive north began across northern prairie to Peace River, Grimshaw and then hundreds of kilometres to Enterprise. We reached the Mackenzie River before break up so crossed on the ice road. (C13.6) We arrived back in Yellowknife rejuvenated and I knew much more about anaesthetics.

Our last trip out was when we left Yellowknife in December 1962. The ice on the Mackenzie River was not yet firm so we drove our kombi into the Bristol freighter. The nose of these large cargo planes opens providing access for even large vehicles. (22.3)

We flew across the ice-covered Great Slave Lake, the seventh biggest lake in the world, to Hay River. The road joined the Yellowknife highway at Enterprise from whence we proceeded down

22.3. The Volkswagen being driven into the Bristol Freighter owned by Wardair.

the now familiar road to Vancouver – Enterprise, High Level, Grimshaw, Chetwynd, Dawson Creek, Prince George, Quesnel, Clinton, Cache Creek, through the Fraser Canyon with its highway and two railways – amazing feats of engineering – to Hope, aptly named as it was only 160km from Vancouver. This time we had two additional passengers, our twins so I was glad that we had an uneventful journey. They slept side by side in the top of their pram in the back.

From Vancouver we flew to Australia for a short summer holiday before I started work at the Vancouver General Hospital. Janet's parents wanted to see their first grandchildren.

CHAPTER 23

LIFE IN VANCOUVER

We went to Vancouver so that I could gain some more experience in anaesthesia and, I hoped, medicine before going back to country general practice where Janet, who is a physiotherapist, was going to work with me. Unlike today, when resident medical staff in hospitals are paid a salary commensurate with the hours worked and recognising their qualifications, ours were meagre. We were making a significant financial sacrifice and received only $200 per month – a quarter to a sixth of what I was paid in Yellowknife. Half of it went on our apartment rental so economy was the order of the day – lots of spaghetti and meatloaves on our $10 a week food budget and frugal shopping. We did not even buy a newspaper regularly.

23.1. Our home in Vancouver at 1151 West 12th Avenue. (Since demolished.)

We lived in a flat three blocks from Vancouver General Hospital where I worked most of the time.

The twins were babies, then toddlers. We had a double pram for them and later had them in reins so they would not run away. They were contented and good children most of the time. The constancy was hard for Janet. When one is young and away at work most of the time, it is easy not to appreciate just how stressful it is for a mother to care constantly for two infants. Fortunately Janet was able to get a part time physiotherapy job at the Canadian Arthritis Rehabilitation Centre two evenings a week when I could look after the girls. This gave her a change from home and the twins. She also took a night course in history at a school two blocks away. In the summer she took the opportunity to go to a family camp in the Okanagan where there were people who could look after the children and give her a break.

I had an uncle and two cousins in Vancouver who were very good to us. Uncle Will had left home before the First World War when still a teenager. He never told me his life story. I used to wonder what all he had done. He lived in Alberta for many years. He returned home to Strathpeffer in Scotland twice – once during each war – on both occasions he arrived without warning to see his parents.

We felt quite at home in Vancouver with relatives and friends. One week we stayed at the Watts, friends that we made in London, Ontario, so that Janet could look after their three children while Mary was in hospital having the fourth.

We met up with one long-time family friend from Kenya. He happened to live over the fence behind Mary Watt's parents. One day he phoned me to say that he was getting married at the registry office and that he would like me to come to the ceremony. I said that I would try to get the time off as it was to be at 2pm on a Friday afternoon. I made provisional arrangements. Nearer the time he phoned again. "Was I going to be there?" I said that I would confirm that I could get time off which I did. The Registry office was conveniently near the hospital. I arrived a little before two o'clock to attend an unusual wedding. My friend was there with his bride, three other girls and one other fellow. As we walked in I found out why he was so concerned about my attendance – he wanted me to be his witness! Following the ceremony I discovered that the other man was one of the fellows who lived in his house with him. He had gone home at lunch time to pick something up and found my friend changing into his suit. On enquiring what he was doing, my friend told him he was going to get married and he was welcome if he would like to come. Nobody in the house knew of the wedding. There was no reception. The bride and groom had a photograph taken as a record of this important event. It was all so simple compared to most weddings that I have attended and yet the marriage has lasted over forty years, unlike so many nowadays, even where expense has not been spared.

His father was one of the early civil engineers in Kenya. He was a very interesting man from whom I learnt that November was the best month for seeing shooting stars or meteorites in the Kenya skies. Unfortunately our friend lost all his father's historic journals in a fire.

Friends and friends of friends came to visit. Jim Allen, who had been my friend when I first went to school, was one of them. I had lived for one term with his family. He was a brilliant man who had become a historian and was well versed in Arab and eastern culture. Later he returned to Kenya where, among other things, he established the museum at Lamu, an island settlement on the northern Kenya coast. I never saw him again. He died relatively young.

Another friend of a friend who stayed with us gave us a gold fish. I thought it was a ridiculous present but after some time I derived great interest from this apparently indestructible creature. The rest of the family were away at a family camp in the Okanagan in the summer for two weeks. I forgot to feed the fish and came home one day to find it looking like it was ready to take its last gasp. It lived in a round bowl about 20cm in diameter which sat on our mantlepiece. I poured fish food into the bowl with the vague hope that it would survive. I sat down and a few minutes later there was an almighty splash and crash – the fish had revived and leapt out of the bowl on to the floor. I thought " that's it, poor fish" and threw it back in the bowl. It survived.

One day I was looking at this goldfish and thought it must be a rather uninteresting life swimming round and round and round this bowl. I decided to fill the bath and let it have a decent swim. I did so and poured it into the bath. I was amazed at what happened. It did not go for a swim up and down but just swam round and round in the same circumference as the bowl. So my efforts were wasted but I learnt something interesting about confined goldfish – they lead a really boring life unless, of course, they can see the human activity around them! Years later I used this story in a debate to destroy my opponent by telling the story and then saying he was like my goldfish going round and round in small circles not saying anything worthwhile!

Another time I tried to anaesthetize a goldfish to remove a growth.

We put in long hours and often worked six days a week. When we worked at night we were on duty from 8pm to 8am for a week finishing on Friday morning so that we had a long weekend! Today that would be a joke as working hours are restricted. On these occasions we often set off in our kombi to discover parts of British Columbia. There was so much to see – the Okanagan, the great fruit growing area in central B.C. with rolling hills and wide valleys and Okanagan lake; up the coast to Brittania Beach and Squamish past towering cliffs and tall waterfalls; across southern B.C. through the dry country around Osoyoos, past a house built like a small castle out of empty embalming fluid bottles on the side of a lake (the owner had been an embalming fluid salesman) to the mountainous lake country around Nelson where Janet had relatives. Another time we took a narrow road from Kamloops to Mt. Robson Park. At times we could only drive at 30kph.

Now there is a super-highway through the same route. It was thirty years before I could walk up the Mt Robson track, which I did with my son Fraser. There was so much magnificent scenery dominated by mountains and lakes. We either camped or slept in our bus on our trips.

One weekend we went south, through Seattle to Mt Rainier in Washington State. It is a volcano but unfortunately it was covered in cloud when we arrived and we nearly turned back for home, but I was tired so we found a campsite beside a river and spent the night there. About 2am we were awoken by three racoons who were scavenging around. They are quite distinctive little animals with black and white stripes across their faces. It was moonlight and the cloud was breaking up so we had glimpses of the mountain. In the morning the sky was clear, the sun was shining and we had the most magnificent views of this majestic mountain covered with snow.

23.2. Mt. Rainier almost engulfed in cloud.

How lucky we had stayed. Mountains are usually more grand if they are partly covered when one first sees them and then gradually clear to all their majesty, especially if the sun is shining on them. Squirrels were in abundance and we also saw some deer.

Vancouver Island has much of interest. The ferry trip across between the islands with the mountains on the coast was scenic. The capital of British Columbia is Victoria which is beautiful, especially in spring with all the blossom and flowers. Situated on the south end of Vancouver Island it spreads along the coast. A highlight nearby was the Butchart Gardens, situated in an old quarry with many sections portraying different flowers and trees. We crossed the island, through forests with massive trees so characteristic of B.C., to Long Beach and Tofino. We camped by the beach with great rollers crashing in from the Pacific creating spray and leaving logs, interesting pieces of driftwood, seaweed and other things on the beach. It was almost deserted when we visited and there were very few buildings – a peaceful change from the city apart from the wind blowing, waves crashing on to the

23.3. Mt Rainier the next morning in sunshine.

beach and sea gulls and other birds squawking and shrieking!

The parks and gardens of Vancouver were particularly attractive. The climate is ideal for wonderful displays of flowers – azaleas and rhododendrons in spring were abundant providing a mass of colour. Queen Elizabeth Park was created in an old quarry and had a wonderful display of flowers in spring and summer. Stanley Park was a favorite place, particularly the little zoo area with penguins, polar and other bears, seals etc.

We had an interesting experience one time at the zoo when Janet, the twins and I were looking at the penguins in their "dinner suits"! (C37.1) The man standing next to us was telling his friend all about the penguins. I joined the conversation. He was a whaler who was based in South Georgia in the South Atlantic. He had brought two pairs, Macaronis and Rockhopper penguins, back for this zoo. Unfortunately one of each had died but of opposite sexes. He was observing that the Macaroni, which was normally a more placid variety, had become much more aggressive like its new companion, the remaining Rockhopper. They kept each other company but did not reproduce. I found all this very interesting. A more amazing coincidence occurred a year later while we were watching the seals at the same place. We met the same whaling skipper again! Meanwhile he had made another trip to the Antarctic waters. Not long after that whaling was banned in an attempt to allow these great mammals to regenerate and avoid extinction.

When I was free I played hockey on Saturdays during the winter with a team called Grasshoppers. I have no idea where the name came from. One day I discovered that the fellow playing next to me was Brian Lowry who had played against me in Belfast some years before when we were students.

Occasionally we went to the pictures. I remember seeing *The Pink Panther* with Peter Sellers. It was a funny film but it intrigued me that the audience was divided and laughed at different things. There was evidently a completely different sense of humour in the two groups, one Canadian and one British. Jokes are not always transferable. On other occasions we would receive complimentary tickets through the hospital for concerts. It was my first exposure to a full orchestra. Claudio Arrau, the vigorous Chilean pianist, was one of the performers we heard.

After three months my boss, Dr Graves, asked if I would like to stay on the anaesthesia training programme. That was a surprise but after some consideration I accepted to continue for a while still thinking I might return to general practice. I also told him that I wanted to take my family to Kenya to see my parents and told him that we might eventually move to Australia. I had some wonderful opportunities in the next couple of years, twice going to the small Childrens Hospital for two months, doing six months in a medical job, doing research with a cardiologist, Al Cox, and some cardiac anaesthesia. In addition we went to Kenya (next chapter), after a month in Yellowknife earning the fare. There was a good teaching programme for anaesthetists.

The time spent with Al Cox became very significant in my later professional life because he stimulated my interest in teaching and gave me some good training in research. As a consequence of my work at the Childrens Hospital I attended a paediatric anaesthetic meeting at the Hospital for Sick Children in Toronto. I was very impressed with the place and managed to obtain an appointment there for six months from July 1965.

And so, in June 1965, a very pleasant two and a half years came to an end and it was not without some sadness that we left Vancouver. It is a beautiful place surrounded by magnificent mountains and by the sea.

23.4. Vancouver from Kitsalano beach with Mt Seymour behind.

I had only two weeks off to make the journey. We had two weeks to cross the country again to Toronto, then the business centre of Canada. We went east to Nelson and then down into Idaho and Montana where we spent a night in Glacier National Park, another beautiful part of the Rockies. Our twins were almost three and it was here that they first walked for about 3 km.

The journey took us back into Canada to visit friends in Medicine Hat. About twenty miles past Swift Current , Saskatchewan, just outside a little town called Herbert, disaster struck. Our engine seized up. We wasted time there as we had to buy another car to proceed to

23.5. Janet and the twins in Glacier National Park.

Toronto where I arrived three days late. Years later I found out that a Canadian classmate of mine in Dundee, Otto Goertz, was practicing in Herbert, Saskatchewan. It would have been an amazing coincidence if I had found that out at the time.

Toronto in 1960 was a run down city. By 1965 they had built an impressive new City Hall designed by a Finn. Now it was becoming one of the magnificent cities of the world.

I had a great learning experience for six months at the Hospital for Sick Children in Toronto, which was one of the top paediatric centres in the world. While I was there I had some involvement in Intensive Care and was asked to give a talk on ventilation of children after heart surgery. This paper was eventually published in the Canadian Anaesthetist's Society Journal. Years later I found out that it was the first one published on the subject. The direction of my life had now changed to becoming a paediatric anaesthetist.

23.6. Toronto City Hall.

So, at the end of 1965 we decided it was time to move to Australia and for Janet to return to be nearer her family in Melbourne. The twins were then 3 1/2 years old and ready for kindergarten.

Chapter 24

The Winds of Change in Kenya – 1963

My family in Kenya had not met my wife, Janet, or our 14 month old twin daughters, Catherine and Maryann, so we went for nearly three months to visit them. After a month in Yellowknife doing a locum we travelled by New York where we met my university friend, Lachlan McKenzie, at the airport. It was possible to do that during transit in those days. Then we went on to Dublin to visit my Uncle Fraser. He was regarded as the black sheep of the family as he did not conform to their ways but he actually achieved greatness as a horseman. He ran away to the first war and was already in the trenches in France when they found out that he was only 16. When he retired from the Scots Greys, a cavalry regiment, he was invited by Colonel Dudgeon to train horses and teach riding at his stables near Dublin. He trained at least one horse for the Royal Family. During this visit we saw him in action teaching someone from Argentina. He was a very impressive instructor. He also gave the twins their first ride on a horse.

We hired a car at the airport and as we were driving off we passed a man standing waiting for transport. As we had room in the car we offered him a lift to the city which he accepted. During our conversation I found out that he was Egyptian, that he had been at a course at Columbia University in USA for six weeks and that he had studied at Trinity College, and hence his visit to Dublin to see some of his friends. Having been at Trinity College, I asked if he could guide us to the college library to see the Book of Kells, a very famous early manuscript. He did so. The beautiful cal-

24.1. Fraser Macmaster with Janet and the twins on horseback.

ligraphy and decoration have given these Gospels, written in 700-800AD, the reputation of being possibly the most beautiful manuscript in the world. It was magnificent. We then dropped our companion at his hotel, the once famous Hibernian Hotel which has now gone. We accepted his invitation for coffee, not suspecting a surprise when I asked him what he did. He was the Egyptian President's private secretary who dealt with his correspondence in English and French! I was amazed and even more so when he invited us to visit Cairo, an offer we were unable to accept at the time.

After our visit we went on to Belfast to visit Eileen Lockhart, an old friend from Kenya, where her husband had spent many years as headmaster of an African Secondary school near my home. Before that he had been headmaster at a similar school in the Gold Coast which later became Ghana. Both these schools produced people who went on to become leaders in their respective countries. He was much admired in Ghana. When they returned some years later the newspaper headlines read "The Lockharts are back". He was a funny man. I remember him asking me when I was a boy what were those little white things in my head? Self-consciously one immediately thinks of dandruff, or worse, lice but he was simply referring to my teeth!

After a few days in Scotland we went to Switzerland. This was unplanned but we had found out by chance, when we went to confirm our onward flights, that our plan to visit Athens on the way to Kenya was impossible. South African Airways, on which we were due to travel, were no longer allowed to land in Nairobi because of the recently introduced Apartheid policy.

We changed our plans and flew to Zurich for two days. We hired a car and drove out through Zug, Altdorf where William Tell had lived, over the Susten Pass to Interlaken and the nearby village of Wilderswil, where we spent the night in a magnificent 250-year-old Gasthof. It was a memorable place to stay as from our balcony we could look out and see three of the great mountains of the Swiss Alps – Eiger, Munch and Jungfrau, all in a row. The other memory was that we asked for boiled eggs for our twins for breakfast. Our bill for the night was the amount plus two eggs! The next day we went on to Grindelwald. It was all so neat and clean and different to anywhere that I had been previously. In Zurich I was impressed by the clock with the biggest clock face in Europe and by some frescoes with pale and delicate colours which we came across. It was a wonderful two days.

There was much joy and celebration in the family when we arrived in Kenya. This time we were not going to Tumutumu, but Nanyuki, 70km further on at the foot of Mt Kenya on the north-west side.

Nanyuki is directly on the Equator so the length of days does not vary much. Another feature of this location is that water goes directly down the plug-hole and does not rotate clockwise or anticlockwise as it does further away from the Equator! Talking of plug-holes, one amusing incident for the girls was to find a frog in the bath. It had come up through the plug hole as the water drained directly through a short pipe to the garden.

My parents lived in a stone house near the Cottage Hospital. There was a single room stone building in the grounds where my father saw his private patients. We stayed in a timber slab guest house. The garden had plots of magnificent, tall dahlias and canna lilies which made a glorious show of colour. There were some very large gum trees (eucalypts). These are native to Australia. I sometimes wonder whether the greatest mark Australia has made on the world was the export of its eucalypts – they are all over tropical and temperate parts forming an important part of the landscape in places as far apart as Uruguay, California, South Africa and Kenya. In addition the black wattle had been imported to Kenya, largely for use as firewood, especially for the steam engines on the railways.

My father had a General Practice but was also the doctor for the government district hospital and the honorary doctor for the Mt Kenya Safari Club. This is a luxurious place higher on the slopes looking up to Mt Kenya (C2.1) with beautiful gardens, ponds and lawns sweeping across the hillside to the bungalows and the forest beyond. There was an animal orphanage but peacocks, geese, ducks and a wide variety of bird life were to be seen wandering in the gardens.

During our stay in Nanyuki I helped my father with his practice. I stood in for him for two weeks when he returned to Scotland to see his failing mother – she was 94 and died soon after. I gave an anaesthetic with chloroform, as there was not much choice and it happened to be an appropriate drug to turn the baby in the uterus so that it was in the best position for delivery. It is the only time I have used this old drug, which was introduced as an anaesthetic by Sir James Young Simpson in Edinburgh in 1847.

Kenya, being on the Equator, does not have winter and summer – it has wet and dry seasons. It is supposed to rain in March – April and in October. Sometimes the rains fail leading to drought which nowadays is the cause of great hardship and famine. That year the October rains began shortly after we arrived and went on and on until we left after Christmas. This was rather unfortunate as it made the roads worse, especially the less major gravel ones. It also meant that when we went to game parks there were fewer animals near the game lodges and their viewing areas because the concentration of game was dispersed as water was available everywhere. Despite that we saw plenty of animals in the parks we visited – Samburu in the north, Nairobi, Tsavo on the way to the coast and Amboselli on the border with Tanzania at the foot of Africa's highest mountain, Kilimanjaro. One of the fascinating features of visiting parks in different parts of the country, particularly Samburu in the north, is the different characteristics of some of the animals. The lions up there do not have the great manes of the ones in some of the southern parks, the giraffe have much more angular markings (reticulated) compared to the more common one; the Grevy's zebra has much narrower black and white bands than the common zebra giving the Grevy's a grey appearance in the distance. (C4.6) The gerenuk which was common in Samburu is an antelope with a long neck. (C4.4) It can stand on its hind legs to reach higher up on the trees for leaves to feed off. It is a very graceful animal. There used to be so much game but the increasing population has encroached on land and poaching has been a big problem, especially of elephant and rhino. The latter's horns are considered to be aphrodisiac and are used in Chinese medicines. They fetch a high price in the east. Their survival reached such a dangerous point that it was decided to cut off the horns so that the animals would not be killed by poachers.

When we were children we often used to see herds of Thompson's gazelles and impala on the plains traveling to Nanuyki. They made a beautiful sight. Tommies were a small antelope with a distinctive black stripe along the side. Even in those early post war years concern was raised about the preservation of the game. Controlled licenced shooting was permissible, as this prevented overpopulation which could lead to food shortage for the animals.

Nairobi National Park was the first one to be established. It was only 20 to 30 minutes drive from the city and one could see a great variety of animals there – lions, impala, wildebeest, eland, Thompson and Grants gazelles, buffalo, ostriches, and many, many more. In Tsavo West we saw hippopotamus, rather closer than intended – they can be dangerous.

24.2. My brother's fishing boat, Johari.

We had some time at the coast at the old town of Malindi – the first European to visit was the Portuguese sailor, Vasco da Gama, on his trip to India in 1498. My brother had a deep sea fishing business there. He had built a beautiful fishing boat, Johari, and was well known in fishing circles as he and his wife, Barbara, had several Kenya and African records for marlin and sailfish on light tackle.

He took us out fishing one day and Janet and I both caught sail-fish.(C20.5) His house was situated on an idyllic spot beside the beach at a corner where there was a coral ridge. Somehow they managed to develop an attractive garden with succulents and plants such as bougainvillea. The beaches at Malindi went for miles, smooth white sand gradually sloping into the sea. Not far out were beautiful coral reefs with their magnificent accompanying fish in so many brilliant colours.

A few miles down the road was the enigmatic place called Gedi, which was thought to be at least four or five hundred years old. It was a complete settlement which has some fine ruins. (C20.4) The mystery was why had it suddenly failed – was it failure of the water supply, disease or maybe a tsunami? It was found in the bush in the 1940s, was excavated and cleared and is now a National Park. It is still surrounded by thick bush which would not take long to overrun it again if it was not kept clear.

Mombasa is a very old port which has been a trading centre for centuries with sailors arriving in their dhows from Arabia and the east. Fort Jesus is an impressive fort (C20.3) built beside the sea by the Portuguese over four centuries ago. It has been used as a fort, a prison and now a museum. In it are displayed pieces of china from as far back as the Ming Dynasty in China showing the extent of trade along the east African coast centuries ago.

Mombasa was where the railway line began in 1898, to open up communication to Lake Victoria and Uganda. There is a railway museum with the grand old steam engines, Garretts, that used to pull the trains up and down the lines. The highest station, Timbaroa, was nearly 3000m above sea level.

Travelling was quite challenging especially on wet, muddy roads. We had the use of a Morris Minor station wagon which was a good little car, but we did have a few problems which added to my fund of stories of bad journeys.

We left Malindi one morning and had a puncture about 50km down the road. No problem! – we changed the wheel. About 15km further on we had another puncture. This was a problem as now I had no spare. I had noticed a petrol station about 1 1/2 km back so I had to roll one wheel back to it. The puncture was quickly repaired and I returned, sweating a bit, as it is always hot at the coast. Fortunately we didn't have another puncture before Mombasa where we had the second puncture repaired. We drove on and reached McKinnon Road before nightfall. When we stopped there we realized that one tyre was soft so had it changed and repaired. Eventually we discovered that the slow punctures were due to a stick which had spliced through the tyre and was nipping the tube. There were no further problems once the stick was removed.

At one point there had been torrential rain and the road was flooded. There was a great spirit of cooperation, with people helping each other push their cars, trucks and buses through the water. Janet, barefoot, helped but acquired several leeches on her legs for her efforts!

Our next problem was more serious. We were on the way from Nairobi to Nanyuki going down a hill just past Fort Hall, now called Maranga. We approached a bend before a bridge over the Mathioya River, which at that point was about 15 metres wide. I put my foot on the break preparatory to changing gear – nothing happened! My breaks had failed. This was a nerve-wracking situation requiring a rapid response. I rapidly changed down and down through the gears to slow our progress. Then – horror! – a sign "GIVE WAY TO ONCOMING TRAFFIC". There was a car coming at the other end and then another. We were getting closer and closer to the bridge – it was only one way. Would the cars get across before we reached the bridge? We were getting closer. What should I do? Go into the river 5-7m below – very dangerous? I could run into the pillar at the end of the bridge and smash in the front of the car – not desirable either. The second car was on the bridge. I would have to make a decision soon. Maybe swing on to the bridge and crash the car. By great good luck as I started to veer on to the bridge the other car was almost over and swung away just enough to avoid us and let us on to the bridge. What a relief. We still had about 100km to go until we reached home.

You may wonder why we did not call for a tow truck. Well, that wasn't really an option in the circumstances. I knew the road well, there was relatively little traffic in those days, I knew that I could slow the car by changing down to low gear but there were still three critical bridges to cross. I decided to continue. The next bridge was at the bottom of a big hill with a right turn on to it. It crossed Kenya's biggest river, the Tana, and was 15 to 20 metres above the water. We crept down the hill, came round the last corner. No oncoming traffic and there was a bank to run on to if the worst came to the worst. We were lucky because a herd of goats was crossing the one way bridge in the same direction as we were going so we followed them slowly.

The next bridge was now two-way so it was not a problem. The final one was at the bottom of a long winding hill just past Nyeri and we could see any traffic coming down the other side. I had cycled this road ten years before and thought I remembered it well. A car was coming down the other way but I judged it would have crossed the bridge by the time we reached it. We were approaching and I could see their lights as it was now dusk. Another problem suddenly became apparent. I had remembered the bridge in the wrong place. It was nearer us and the other car was approaching. We arrived almost simultaneously but I was able to slow down enough to let it cross just before we reached the bridge. Years later I realized why I had made the mistake. The bridge in the next valley was in the position where I thought this one was. Then it was uphill and only about 30km until we reached my sister's place. My brother in law, Bob Polhill, was managing a farm at Naro Moru at the time having recently been dispossessed of his farm at the Kinangop in a resettlement scheme. What a relief it was to arrive safely. On investigation the next day we found that the little copper tube carrying the brake fluid was severed. It had been a challenging trip.

We went to Amboseli National Park, beautifully situated on the plains at the foot of snow-capped Kilimanjaro. The rains were on, the roads were wet and not sealed. It was sticky going and up one hill I wondered if we would make it. We were behind a truck which was chugging very slowly up the hill. We were losing momentum. The road was sticky and if we had to stop it might be difficult to get going again. Somehow we just made it without getting stuck or sliding into the ditch.

When we finally arrived at the camp we took everything out of the car. The weather cleared in the late afternoon so we decided to go in search of game. As I have mentioned, the animals were scattered far and wide because water was available everywhere. We took a game scout to guide us. Arriving where the track crossed a swampy place with water up to the tracks we debated how to go on. He said the track was firm and we would be all right if we kept a certain line as that would keep us out of the rut. Unfortunately his advice was incorrect and we went into the rut. Part of the fan in the engine was under water which made it lift up and forward while it was rotating so that it cut a neat slice into the bottom of the radiator tank. The water leaked out. We pushed and heaved. Fortunately it was a small car. When we reached dry land again we checked the radiator. The tank was empty. It was several miles back to camp. Some ingenuity was needed. I stuffed my handkerchief into the hole but then we had nothing with which to fill the tank – I had emptied the car completely – not even a mug had been left. Then I had a brain wave! I took my shoe off and used it to carry the water and pour it into the radiator. Luckily I was not wearing sandals! And so we made it back to camp where the tank was soldered the next morning. The game was disappointing except for seeing one fine rhino called "Pixie." (C4.2)

Two major world events occurred while we were in Kenya. President John F Kennedy was assassinated in Dallas, Texas on 22nd November. The news stunned the world. It is interesting that the American clairvoyant, Mary Deare, had foreseen this event and tried to prevent it but had not been able to communicate her message to the President.

Less than three weeks later, on 12th December, Kenya became independent. Uhuru had arrived. It was an apprehensive time for the settlers. Would the occasion be marred by untoward events? There was much singing, dancing and celebrating. Fortunately the celebrations went off peacefully.

Britain had ruled the country for just over sixty years – all during my mother's lifetime. Great progress was made in that time – railways, roads and cities had grown up and large tracts of land had become profitable farms, but much was now to change.

The Kenya we were brought up in was a peaceful country where one could travel or walk anywhere in safety and without fear. World War II changed that – the British won the war but lost a great deal, including its Empire. Much changed when Kenya became independent. Many farmers were bought out by the British government and the land turned over to the Africans. Individual land ownership was a priority. Many successful and well managed farms were divided up into small units – 7 to 14 acre lots, which was not enough to make them financially profitable. In some areas trees planted as wind breaks were cut for hut building or firewood, leaving the country exposed to the vagaries of wind, which blew away the top soil. Some farmers were able to carry on – for a while. For many years Kenya continued to thrive especially due to its tourist industry which relied on the wildlife and National Parks.

Africans who had been students at St. Andrews University in Scotland with me now took on important positions such as Governor of the Bank of Kenya (Duncan Ndegwa), in the Foreign Office (Khamis Jeneby), professors at the University of Nairobi, founded in the late 1950s (Mohamed Hyder and B.Ogot), and Minister of Health (Dr. Wayaki).

Soon after witnessing this turning point in Kenya's history it was time to return to my next job in Vancouver – six months of medical residency. We travelled via the Cocos Islands on a Viscount, a plane in which the seats faced backwards, to Perth and Melbourne where we had a short visit with Janet's family before crossing the Pacific again to Vancouver.

Kenya was still a wonderful country with so much variety and beauty. Since then the population has increased by as much as 4% a year. Efforts to introduce birth control were thwarted for a long time by fear of tribal dominance by the other side if they did not follow the principles. Overpopulation followed. Nairobi grew into a huge city, unemployment increased and with it crime. The countryside also became increasingly populated and cultivation encroached into previously forested areas. The land was farmed more intensely on smaller and smaller, and hence uneconomical, areas. The amount of livestock decreased for many years, which was fortunate as it reduced the overgrazing, which was a problem. Droughts have affected large areas of the country leading to famine. It is still a magnificent country with its mountains, plains, coast and grand vistas, but it is not what it was.

AIDS has created further problems. The older generation, grandparents, are being left to look after their grandchildren as many of the parents die from this terrible scourge.

Vaccination eliminated smallpox, the disease that wiped out many of the population shortly before the Europeans arrived to find large, empty tracts of land. But other diseases have proved more difficult to control, and Man cannot control the weather, so natural disasters occur.

Greed and corruption have led to the loss of vital funding which would have helped the country maintain a better infrastructure and standard of living for more of its population. It seems unlikely that the country will return to what it was like in the "good old days" for a long time, if ever. Unfortunately it is not alone. Many countries suffer from the same problems, but since recent elections there seems to be some hope that Kenya will improve again. If corruption and greed can be reduced, it has a chance.

Part 6

Australia and Beyond

Chapter 25

My Professional Life as an Anaesthetist

After a short spell in General Practice I undertook post graduate training which led to me becoming a paediatric anaesthetist. When I qualified as a doctor I just expected to be a country General Practitioner. I had no inkling that I was setting out on an incredible life which would take me all over the world. Now, when I look back on it I wonder how I managed to do so much.

What is an anaesthetist or, as they are referred to in some parts of the world, an anesthesiologist? They are medically qualified doctors who have done postgraduate training, the duration of which has extended over the years and varies in different countries. In the 1960s in Australia it was two years minimum after a year of general training but this has steadily increased until now it is five years after at least two years basic medical and surgical training. The reasons for the extension are increased information, more complex surgery, the need to do some intensive care training and shorter working hours. The length of training varies in other countries between three and six years.

The work involves pre-operative assessment where the anaesthetist meets the patient and finds out if there are any health factors or drug treatment which may influence the choice and conduct of anaesthesia. The anaesthetist is then responsible for the patient's care and keeping them alive while the surgeon operates, keeping the patient pain-free (and unconscious during general anaesthesia), giving fluids or blood when necessary and monitoring the patient to ensure his/her well being. In the post-operative period anaesthetists are often involved in ensuring that pain and vomiting are minimised. Many are involved in intensive care and pain management. In some countries these are gradually becoming specialties in their own right. Intensive care units were often started by anaesthetists as an extension of postoperative care. They took their practical skills from the operating theatre to intensive care but now anaesthetists often work in intensive care units during their training to gain experience with the technical skills and the management and resuscitation of very sick patients.

Before I left Toronto I was advised to do another year of adult anaesthesia when I came to Melbourne because my training already had a paediatric anaesthesia bias. Consequently, I spent a year at the Royal Melbourne Hospital where I virtually completed my training, only having to pass my examinations during 1967.

I then moved to the Royal Children's Hospital in Melbourne where I have worked ever since.

25.1. The front of the Royal Children's Hospital in 1995.

My first appointment there was as the first Medical Officer to Intensive Care, gained on the basis of my experience and the paper that I had written in Toronto on ventilation of children after heart surgery. I was later approached to take up positions at the then new Monash University in Melbourne, in Vancouver and Toronto. Fortunately I stayed put as unforeseen opportunities developed. I went on to become specialist anaesthetist / perfusionist (looking after cardiopulmonary bypass for open heart surgery) and then in 1974, following the untimely death at the age of 43 of our Director, John Stocks, I became Director of Anaesthesia. I held that position for 26 years until shortly before I retired from full time work in 2000. During that time we had trained about 500 anaesthetists of whom about a hundred came from forty countries around the world.

I was fortunate to live through some exciting developments. Paediatric Intensive Care was in its infancy when I began. Putting a tube through the patient's nose into the trachea (windpipe) which allowed us to control the airway and assist breathing with a ventilator, if necessary, helped to keep some patients alive who previously would not have survived. The introduction of PVC (polyvinyl chloride) tubes, which did not cause any tissue reaction, meant that these tubes could be left in place for days or weeks.

Intensive pre- and post-operative care enabled surgeons to perform increasingly complex operations with a good chance of survival. Intravenous fluids and parenteral nutrition (providing calories intravenously) also contributed. An appreciation of the importance of keeping babies temperatures normal was another key factor.

When I started they could not do corrective heart surgery on babies less than 10kg because of the technical difficulty. They undertook operations to tide them over until they grew large enough to perform corrective surgery. In 1970 a new technique was developed in Japan which allowed the surgeon to operate on a still heart after the baby had been cooled to 18°C. At this temperature it was safe to stop the circulation for about an hour, long enough to do the operation. It was amazing to see a heart starting to beat as it was re-warmed and eventually return to normal function, beating regularly when normal body temperature was regained. One great thrill for me was meeting one of our early deep hypothermia patients 34 years later. He had led a relatively normal life.

The survival of premature infants improved, especially the small ones, when we learnt that the application of positive end expiratory pressure to the airways (PEEP) in early life could keep the airways open so that oxygen reached the lungs enabling them to live. Before that, lack of a substance called surfactant in the lungs of these tiny babies led to collapse of the alveoli, where gas exchange takes place, hypoxia and, in severe cases, death. PEEP extended the work of neonatologists significantly and gave additional challenges to anaesthetists in handling tinier patients. These included maintaining body temperature, because premature infants lose heat more easily, and ensuring adequate blood glucose and haemoglobin because the body stores of glucose and iron are less in prematures. Sometimes complications arose when these babies survived, mainly neurological, that interfered with normal development especially in the very low birth weight infants. These have decreased as medical and nursing skill in looking after them has increased. Unfortunately babies, particularly those less than 26 weeks gestation at birth, often still develop significant neurological and gut problems. One of the great ethical dilemmas in more affluent countries is whether babies born before this age should be treated at great expense, when the chances of significant complications are likely, when these will result in a poor quality of life for the patient and a burden on the family.

Accidental drug overdosage became a problem in small children in Australia after the tricyclic antidepressant drugs were added to the Pharmaceutical Benefit list in 1970. I undertook research into safety packaging and the management of the cardiovascular complications for which I eventually gained my Doctorate of Medicine from Melbourne University in 1980. (C37.9) This important research was responsible for rapid decline in accidental antidepressant overdosage in children when the government accepted our suggestion that these drugs should be safety packaged and ensured that this happened. This is the reason why some categories of drugs that are dangerous to children, are foil wrapped or otherwise safety packaged.

25.2. A group at Department of Electrical Engineering, Monash University – K.Ng, George Ellis (visiting from Brunei), Professor Douglas Lampard, Bill Brown.

I was involved in research in these areas and many others. Our department developed research associations with other departments within and outside the hospital.

One particularly fruitful one was with the Monash University Department of Electrical Engineering, headed by Professor Douglas Lampard. He was interested in physiological applications of electronics. We collaborated in research with his, then novel (1971), computer controlled systems related to anaesthesia, hypothermia and muscle relaxants. He was a brilliant man. His other interests were chemistry, making perfume and playing ukelele in Noel Cass' Jazz band, which was a social group that played once a fortnight for fun and for special functions. Noel and I were privileged to be a research associates in that department for several years. Noel gave me great support and encouragement during my early years in Melbourne and eventually was deputy director of our department for twelve very congenial years.

25.3. Dr. Noel Cass – leading anaesthetist, jazz pianist, sailor and skier.

Other outside collaborators included Richard Oppenheim at the Pharmacy College, Bert Hoveling and Keith Phillips at the Applied Chemistry Department at the Royal Melbourne Institute of Technology, and Melbourne University and the College of Surgeons

Anatomy departments. All these participated in projects that provided great interest and new information and ideas.

I became involved in teaching within the hospital and outside soon after completing my final examinations. This became a lifelong interest. I established a half day per week teaching programme for anaesthetic trainees in the hospital. My progressive involvement in anaesthesia at state, national and, eventually, at international levels, came mainly through my interest in teaching.

In 1970 I became Education Officer for the Faculty of Anaesthetists in Victoria for five years, followed by State Chairman of the Regional Committee, examiner in pharmacology, member of the Peer Review and Continuing Education Committees at their inception.

For the Australian Society of Anaesthetists I was convener of its Scientific Program Committee of for over 20 years concluding with overseeing the program for the World Congress of Anaesthesiologists in Sydney in 1996. In all, I organized nearly forty anaesthetic meetings and congresses.

In 1984 I was elected to the Education Committee of the World Federation of Societies of Anaesthesiologists and became chairman from 1987-1992. It was an exciting time during which we greatly expanded its educational role by sending teachers from twenty five countries to fifty countries in four years. I was involved with the WFSA for 20 years, eventually becoming President from 2000-2004. I travelled and taught in about seventy countries. I was able to this because we could have six months paid long service leave after fifteen years service, which I used in increments for these trips. These activities were all in addition to my work in the hospital, so I was very busy for many years. In 1997 I was made a member of the Order of Australia (AM) for my teaching and research work nationally and internationally. (C37.2)

Teaching others how to teach and present their work became a special interest especially among the overseas people who came to work with us. I also taught many of them how to set up teaching programmes so that they could go home and contribute to teaching and training in their own countries. Nearly all of them went home and many went on to contribute to anaesthesia as teachers or organisers in their hospitals and Societies and some even became members of WFSA committees.

I managed to build up a very good team of anaesthetists in our department, many of whom took responsibility for some aspect of the department. I always believed that the best way to administer was to delegate responsibility to people who could be relied upon. The individuals then feel more a part of the organization and if they have a share of the clinical work which they enjoy, a happy and cohesive department can result. It also enabled me to carry out the various duties I had as department Director, Director of Theatre Services for nearly twenty years, and Divisional Director for the Division of Specialist Services in the hospital for 17 years. These positions all became increasingly demanding as the financial responsibility increased, especially during periods of economic depression. Some of these caused marked restriction in funding.

I ensured that I spent at least half my time doing clinical anaesthesia in the operating theatre so that I would retain my credibility as a teacher. Too often administration takes people away from their clinical work.

I always enjoyed my clinical work. Until I became Director of Anaesthesia I was involved in cardiac anaesthesia and in intensive care as well as some involvement in other areas and covering much supervisory call out of hours. After that my main areas of involvement became ENT and airway problems, burns, neurosurgery and, latterly, some eye and dental operating lists where many of the difficult medical problems are managed.

My interests in photography and teaching people how to do practical things led to me making several films and many videos for teaching purposes with the Photography Department, which expanded into the Educational Resource Centre in the Hospital in 1981. One of these won first prize at the Canadian Anaesthetists Society annual meeting in 1985. Many of them had the sound-track translated into other languages such as Spanish, Japanese, Arabic and others. Anaesthetists are usually visual learners so that good diagrams and illustrations are useful when teaching them. An example is shown.

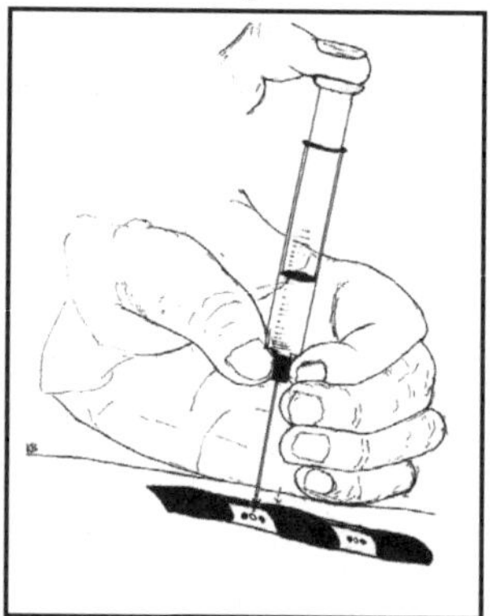

25.4. The hand positions when doing an intercostal nerve block between ribs.

I was also involved with publication as a member of the Editorial Board of Anaesthesia and Intensive Care for 23 years from its inception and as an author of two books, including Anaesthesia for Children, and over a hundred papers and chapters for other books. Close rapport with colleagues in other departments around the hospital is evident in my publications as thirty six of them co-authored papers with me.

One of the great features of the Royal Childrens Hospital has been the long service so many people have given. I have been there 38 years. Some even reached 50 years. The photographs show groups of anaesthetic technicians, nurses and surgeons, who worked with me for thirty or more years, while in another the three nurses, the surgeon, and the author had a total of 150 years service.

I worked out that when Geoff Klug retired as neurosurgeon that I had worked with him for about 6,000 hours.

25.5. A group of anaesthetic and animal laboratory technicians with the author. (From left: Ron Laird, Taffy Evans, Franz Mayer, Bernie Jahnkalns, and sitting KB, George Cauchi,) gave about 200 years service in total.

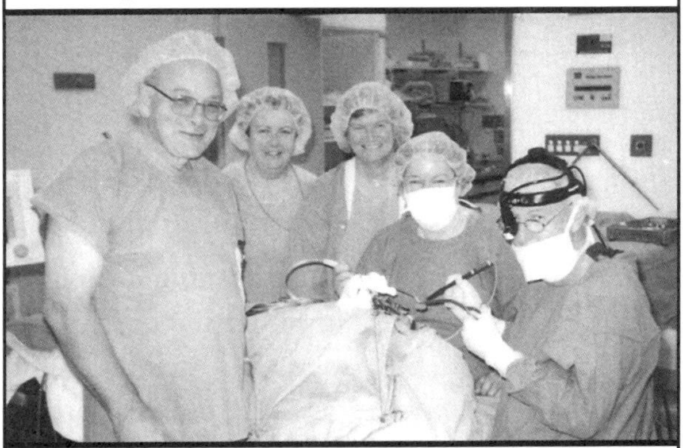

25.6. Warner Mooney (ENT surgeon), Claire Collins, Pam Crouch, Anne Bryan and the author had 150 years service to RCH.

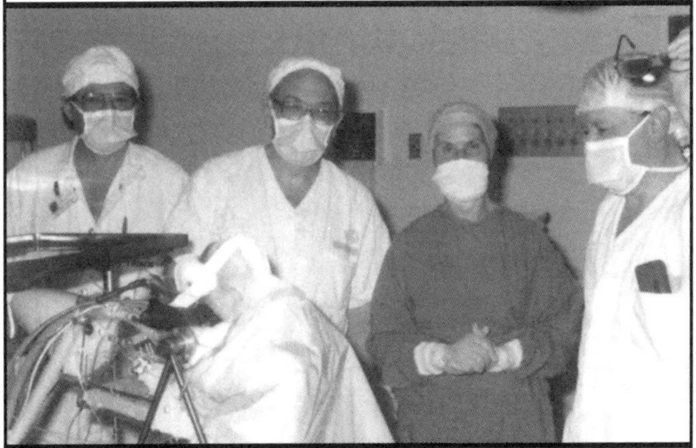

25.7. Geoff Klug, Hilda, KB, and Ron Laird at conclusion of neurosurgery.

25.8. A group of retiring doctors: Kester Brown (Anaesthetist), Justin Kelly (Surgeon), Henry Ekert (Haematology/Oncology), Julian Keogh (Burn Surgeon); sitting – John MacNamara (Paediatrician), Ian Hopkins (Neurologist).

The group with him, his scrub nurse, Hilda Jagermanis and Ron Laird (chief anaesthetic technician) all had over 30 years service.

The group of the author's contemporary doctors also all spent over 35 years at the hospital and each achieved eminence in his field.

The world is unfortunately changing and such loyalty to an institution is becoming rare.

This is but a summary of my very full professional medical life as a paediatric anaesthetist. My medical memoirs constitute another book entitled *Catalyst*, which provides much more detail of my professional activities, clinical interests and research, the evolving history of anaesthesia in the past forty years and various other medical developments which have taken place in that time. It also includes sections on teaching, training, organizing congresses, administration, and many photographs.

Chapter 26

Melbourne, Our Family and Holidays

When I was young I never expected to live in a large city for most of my life. I was a country boy. Melbourne has had a population of 3 1/2 to 4 million but is a very livable city. It is an attractive city with plenty of parks and gardens including the magnificent Botanical Gardens, Fitzroy, Treasury and Exhibition Gardens, 350 hectare Royal Park, which the Childrens Hospital looks over, the massive Yarra Bend Park and many others, all within 10km of where we live. The south side of the city spreads around the northern shores of Port Philip Bay so some suburbs have beaches. The Yarra River meanders through the city, entering from the north-east. There are bicycle and walking tracks beside it for 40km. It is also popular for canoeing and rowing and so provides many forms of pleasant relaxation.

Melbourne grew rapidly, especially in response to the gold rush, with the result that there are many fine Victorian buildings and houses, many of which have fortunately, so far, been retained. The ICI, now Orica building was the first skyscraper to appear in 1956, standing in solitary spendour.

Now the skyline, like all modern cities, is strewn with skyscrapers which rise to much higher levels.

Melbourne has a comprehensive cover of the Arts with fine Australian and International art galleries, a Concert Hall and a magnificent Theatre for opera and ballet, as well as many other fine, older theatre complexes. There are fine museums. The Royal Exhibition Building, where the first Australian Parliament met in 1900, has recently been added to the World Heritage list.

The Victoria Market is by far the largest of the markets scattered through the city. It is a place where one finds people from all over the world selling and buying a huge array of goods. Many Italians and Greeks migrated to Australia after the Second World War, followed by people from many other nationalities who have all added to the food and culture of the country. An artist, Sue Jervis, painted a representative of each nationality in the suburb of Dandenong for the Millenium.

There are 146 people in the picture indicating what an incredibly multicultural society they have. The painting (270x180cm) hangs in the Dandenong City Hall.

It is a big sporting centre dominated by the Melbourne Cricket Ground where cricket and Australian Rules Football are played regularly. It has a seating capacity of almost 100,000 and was the venue for the 1956 Olympic Games.

The Australian Open tennis championships were played at Kooyong, a large club where we play, until it moved to the very fine Tennis Centre nearer the city. The centre court now holds 15000 people.

Hockey was prominent in our family. I played for Kew for many years. Kew hockey club had its centenary dinner in 2004, which was attended by over 300 people including seven of our team that won the C grade Grand Final in 1968 – 36 years ago. I finally retired when I was about 54, having played the last two seasons in a team with my sons, Fraser and Ken, and on one occasion Kester as well. (C37.8)

Most other common sports are played in Australia. Horse racing is so important that there is a public holiday in the city on the first Tuesday in November for the Melbourne Cup. It is a big race with 24 horses running 3200m. I only once went to the races in 1970. The Melbourne cup was won in 1969 by a horse called Rainlover, but the event had been overshadowed by the scratching of the favorite, Big Phalou, because it had been doped. The day I went was the first time since the incident that the two horses were running against each other. During the week before all the other entrants withdrew from the race. It became a two-horse race. It was close all the way with Big Phalou leading until almost the end when Rainlover overtook to win by a head. It was an exciting and unique occasion.

Australian Rules football is something like a cross between rugby and Gaelic football. It has eighteen players a side distributed the length of the ground, which is oval. Goals (6 points) are scored between two tall posts and a behind (1 point) when the ball passes between a tall and short outer post. It is a high scoring game which adds to the interest and excitement. It is followed fanatically by hundreds of thousands of people through the winter, mainly in the southern Australian states, who discuss it endlessly. (C47.3) The misdemeanors of star players who have to be judged at a tribunal, rather than being sent off the ground immediately as they are in other sports, are frequently given prime news time. This seems inappropriate, and promotes bad conduct to children. The idea is that suspension weakens the team for following games. However, someone else plays in their place.

The climate in Melbourne is described as Mediterranean but it is very variable. People often say that all four seasons can occur in one day. In summer it can be hot when the wind comes across the desert from the north – sometimes over 40°C. If the wind then changes to the south west bringing cold air (there is nothing between here and the Antarctic) the temperature can drop suddenly and noticeably – sometimes 10-15°C in an hour or two.

Overall, I have enjoyed living and working in Melbourne. The people are generally friendly. It has been a good place to bring up a family, although it is a little less safe now than when they were children. We have five children, twin girls, Catherine and Maryann, and three boys spread over eleven years in age.

26.1. Our family in 1976.

When we were young, families with four or five children were not uncommon. Attitudes have changed. The world is overpopulated and the costs of bringing up and educating children have become a bigger factor. Women work more in regular employment rather than staying home to look after the children all the time and they tend to have their families later. The overall result is that families in Australia are generally becoming smaller.

Now we have several grandchildren. It is a delight to watch a baby grow into a toddler and then a child (C37.1 and 37.3-7), to see each step as they develop their individuality and skills. There can be turbulent times, such as adolescence and beyond when they are trying to find their way in the world. Ours had their ups and downs but we were largely spared the difficulties and sadness that many families face. We have all been fortunate that they have had a devoted and understanding mother. Our children have given us immense pleasure and now we are enjoying watching their children developing.

During the first year after coming to Australia we lived in part of Janet's parent's home in Kew. (18.1) Fraser (C37.7) was born while we were there. When I went to work at the Royal Childrens Hospital in 1967 we were allocated a hospital house across the street which was convenient as I was frequently on call for both the more complex anaesthetics and for intensive care.

After living in Parkville near the hospital for a year we moved to 183 Barkers Road, Kew and were living there when Kester was born in 1969. Ken, our youngest, was born in 1973 after we had moved to our present home. It is 10km from the Royal Children's Hospital in a pleasant suburb bounded on its north and west by the meandering Yarra River. It is in a dead-end street so there is relatively little traffic. When we arrived all the houses had been built in the late 1920s when the land was subdivided, forty years after the surrounding area was settled. It has a good sized block and has made a wonderful home. Since then, half the houses in the street have been replaced with more modern, extravagant homes. The most interesting feature of our house is the lounge room which has a fireplace in the centre of a curved window on the corner of the house. This unusual feature existed in three other houses in the area, including one across the road which was a mirror image of ours. It has since been pulled down to make way for a grander building. As the children grew bigger space became short again so we added rooms upstairs. Then the children began to move out.

One of the beautiful features of our garden has been a magnolia which grows in front of the house and is covered each September with magnificent white blossom. The back garden had several fruit trees including a large fig which had a cubby house in it. This was a source of much pleasure. Eventually it began to become uneven and fell into disrepair. Only the three support beams remained. One day I removed these and sometime later we awoke one morning to find the three main trunks had fallen apart and the tree had collapsed. We left the roots and the tree grew again. There were other fruit trees in the garden – a walnut which died, plums, grapefruit which produces two crops per year, lemons, mandarin, apricot, fejoia, loquat, crab apple and monstera deliciosa, which produces its strange fruit from time to time. (C42.2) It is covered with dark green hexagons and only when these are beginning to fall off is the fruit ready to eat.

The back yard had room to play games and hit a ball. Many a ball had to be bowled, especially to Kester. His seventh birthday was a unique occasion. The boys all decided to play hockey although the visitors had not played before. The consequence was that four continued to play and became part of Kew's under-8 team which I coached. Three of them had state under-13 trials, two eventually played for Kew firsts and one became a coach, went to England and played an important part in organizing the hockey at the Manchester Commonwealth Games. His sister also played for Kew Juniors – the first girl to play junior hockey before a girls league started. She eventually captained her school team.

Janet stayed at home most of the time when they were small and watched over their early development. It is said that the first seven years is the most important in developing their character. The care she has given them all is obvious as she now has five devoted, grown up children. It was not easy bringing up five children, especially during the years when finances were tight. She read to them frequently whereas I tended to tell them stories, often from my childhood and youth. I was often too tired to read in the evening but I could manage the stories. Old Jalopy, about my ride home from school in the ancient model T Ford, which I have recounted elsewhere, was one of their favorites. I always tried to set aside time for them, particularly to play games or take them to sport. Babies grow so fast, through the toddler stage to kindergarten and school. It is important to try to have time with them through each stage – there is no going back and it is sad to miss out.

The eleven year spread between our oldest and youngest meant that we had children around for a long time – 25 years of continuous schooling – but this was an advantage as there was only one year when we had three at secondary school at the same time, making the fees manageable. They all spent at least part of their primary schooling at the local state schools which were generally good because of the area where we lived. We live in what must be one of the most densely schooled areas anywhere. There are nine private and four primary schools within three kilometers, and a kindergarten very close by.

In 1976 we bought a block of land near the beach at Mt. Martha, on the east side of Port Philip Bay. It is 70 km from our home in Kew. The block was densely covered with ti tree, a straggly Australian native that grows in coastal areas. It was so dense that we had to cut our way into the block, which was a back one of four on a subdivided acre block. Eventually we had enough cleared to build a log cabin. The outside structure was built for us but we did all the internal lining with wood veneer boards, each room in a different wood – teak, cypress, walnut, cherry, ash and dao. We built in the cupboards and the kitchen but we had the plumbing and electricity put in for us. It was a great family project for about two years. Fraser, who was in grade 4, was allowed three days off school to help the builders as they laid the foundations and placed the floor joists. It was very satisfying to build such a house ourselves, especially as I had no previous experience in that sort of work. It took two summers to complete and build the verandah. It has been wonderful to have a house near the beach whenever we wanted, but we always spent Christmas holidays with various members of the family. It is an easy house to run with plenty of accommodation. There is a pass through from the kitchen which has an added advantage that anyone working there is not cut off from the table conversation. The main room is not square but has an area at one end for a table tennis table which has been much used.

Our piano tuner, an elderly Mr Lawson Clarke, who started training as a piano maker and tuner before the first World War at the age of fourteen, found us a good piano at a moderate price. Despite failing sight he used to come and tune it each summer as long as he was able. He enjoyed the day out to the beach and used to regale us with many tales of the early days. There were five piano makers in Australia then, but none are left. His mother came to Australia by sailing ship. His grandfather, Thomas Spendlove, came out to teach bricklaying and built most of the old church steeples in inner Melbourne. His visits were always interesting. Among other things he also told us about the cyclone that struck Melbourne in 1914 and the fact that his uncle brought out the first steam car, a Stanley, to Melbourne in 1910.

It is a great advantage to be able to walk in a few minutes to a beautiful sandy beach with orange, ochre and black rocky outcrops on the cliff at the end. The fact that we have to descend 190 steps to reach it keeps many people away, so that it is never crowded. Birdrock beach, so named because there is a large rock at low tide where sea gulls congregate, was the place where Matthew Flinders landed when he was exploring Port Philip Bay. The littoral views vary from peaceful, reflective seas, sandy beaches and cliffs to wild, windswept scenes with breaking waves, cold if it blowing from the south-west..

Australia is a huge country and one has to travel great distances to visit some of the interesting places. I will introduce some of these in the accounts of our holidays to them.

In 1976 we went to Broken Hill in western New South Wales. It is a town with mainly lead, silver and zinc mines. We travelled to Swan Hill, a town on the Murray River which had a Pioneer Village. Such places are of great historical interest, especially in a country with a short history since European settlement. The problem is receiving enough visitors to keep them viable. We certainly enjoyed our visit before heading north-west up the Murray River valley to Mildura, the main town in north western Victoria. This was in a thriving fruit growing district which has since suffered as a result of importation of cheaper oranges from countries such as Brazil. It seems ridiculous to have to import fruit that are grown plentifully here, especially as people's jobs suffer as a result. Such are the effects of modern trade practices. Mildura has a small art gallery with some quite good paintings, including some by well known British painters of the nineteenth century such as Lord Leighton. To the west is Lake Victoria which was the source of some excitement about that time. Aboriginal relics dating back 40000 years were found indicating that Australia had been settled for a long time.

Our journey then took us north through increasingly dry country typical of the Australian outback. The typical bush at one stretch was made more attractive by the native pines. Eventually we reached Broken Hill, a fairly typical major mining town. It has a reasonably sized hospital. A most interesting place to visit was Pro Hart's gallery. He is a well known painter with a distinctive, rather naïve style. He had one painting of the arrival of James Cook in 1770 which covered three sides of the room. Upstairs he had paintings by many well known artists. The problem was that the balcony where these were hung was very narrow so that one could not stand back to view them.

A few miles west was the prior settlement of Silverton. A few stone buildings remained including the hospital where we were able to look at the admission book – an interesting piece of medical history. That night we camped in the bush. We followed a track across a dry river bed until we found a suitable, peaceful spot. At 4.30am I awoke to flashing lights. When I poked my head out of the tent to see who it was, I found that it was Thor with his flashlight – thunder and lightning with a storm approaching. I didn't want to become stranded on the wrong side of the river should a flash flood occur so we quickly broke camp and drove off to the main road. We watched this great thunderstorm as we drove slowly back to Broken Hill. By the time we arrived water was running in the streets – down the middle as that was the way they were structured. Then we saw an amazing sight. A large red-roofed building had a double rainbow arching over it. The intensity of the colour in the sky – dark blue to purple- changed to become darker at each rainbow.

Beyond Silverton the road dropped down a small escarpment and the flat, red earth landscape beyond stretched away to infinity. I took one of my favorite photographs there – the top of an old fence post. (C42.1)

The Old Fencepost

In the outback beyond Broken Hill
Is the older settlement of Silverton,
Where the road descends until
It reaches the wide, flat plain
That to the horizon goes on and on
Looking all the way the same.
As the road goes winding down
There is an old fencepost,
Weathered spikes upon its crown,
Looking like a ghost.
Attached were many types of wire
With a background of reddish sand
Where an old owner did conspire
To mark the boundary of his land.

And now the old fencepost stands deserted
By chance it was photographed and inserted
Into the annals of the land.

The Flinders Ranges, north of Adelaide are wonderful to visit for camping, hiking, painting and photography. Wilpena Pound is a big sandstone bowl surrounded by quartzite hills. It has only one entry where the river emerges. The highest point is St Mary's Peak (1200m). There are some excellent walks in the area. It was here that all the children, including Ken, who was nine, out-walked Janet and me for the first time. This rugged country has many beautiful spots such as Warren Gorge, Brachina Gorge, Chambers Gorge and the hills going north to the old copper mining town of Blinman. Recent rain in that dry country in the centre of Australia had a magical effect – it brought the flowers out. One whole hillside near a rampart called the Wall of China was covered in bright red wild hops and Sturt desert peas. It was a stunning show. We traveled north east about 40km to Chambers Gorge where I painted the beautiful scene with its red, orange and mauve rocks and a couple of gum trees with their white bark. (C40.4)

The next place we visited was Blinman, which had been a copper mine back in the 1850s. We arrived there on a very wet evening having travelled along muddy roads. Camping did not seem to be the most enjoyable way to spend the night under the circumstances so we inquired at the pub about accommodation. They said we could have the cottage for $2 each a night. A bargain, or was it a realistic price for what we found! It provided a roof, beds with mattresses, a fireplace, no doors but we had access to showers and firewood. It was a very old cottage but it sufficed to give us cover and we were warm enough in our sleeping bags with the fire. Next morning was beautiful and sunny. We drove on west to Brachina Gorge where I painted. This had to be done quickly as the family soon became bored at these painting stops. I am grateful that they tolerated them because I have some wonderful memories of the holiday and some of them have provided material for larger paintings.

The Flinders ranges were well worth the visit as were places like Burra, Quorn and the Clare valley with its vineyards on the way. There were also birds and animals, mainly wallabies and euros which are a heavy-set type of kangaroo.

It was a long drive to the Warrumbungles in central New South Wales. We stopped for a night in Narrandera on the Murrumbidgee River. Little did we know that some years later my nephew and then my sister and her husband would settle there.

The Warrumbungle National Park includes volcanic hills which stand out from the flat plains. There are some remarkable formations of hard rock forming spires and a dyke left exposed after the softer volcanic ash eroded away. The most striking is the famous Breadknife which is a tall, very narrow vertical layer of hard rock standing out of the hillside. The valley is lightly treed with open ground where many kangaroos and wallabies can be seen. There are wonderful walks in the hills. On one of these we came across a frilled dragon on the path. It is a small, fierce looking animal, especially when it raised its frill as a defence. It stands about 20cm high. (C42.5)

The skies are usually clear so Mt Stromlo, one of the hills, was selected as the site for an important astronomical observatory. Bill James, a friend of ours, made some of the large optical mirrors. He was the only big telescope lens and mirror maker in Australia.

One can take a diversion through this Park when travelling north to Brisbane from Melbourne by the inland route. The road comes out again at Coonabarabran. Our children were enthralled by the Dinosaur Park just outside the park boundary. Tyranosaurus Rex would growl if fed 20 cents!

From there we went on to Dubbo and the Western Plains Zoo which is the large animal park for Sydney's Taronga Zoo. It was well set up and one could drive around viewing large animals such as giraffe, rhinos etc.

In 1987 Janet, Ken and I flew to Darwin and drove south to Alice Springs, Ayres Rock, and back to Alice Springs where I attended a meeting. Darwin is hot and tropical. We saw coral growing in tanks – one of the few places in the world where this had been done successfully. In the Botanical gardens I had a strange experience. A couple was walking with their two year old running in front of them. I spoke to the child and the mother came up and said "Are you Kester Brown?" I was amazed but it turned out that she had worked at the Childrens Hospital in Melbourne and recognised my rather distinctive accent.

We went to Fogg dam which was built for a rice growing project. The only problem was that it attracted thousands of birds which ate the rice! It made a fine place to see many water birds.

Kakadu National Park is renowned as one of the places to visit in Australia. Having been brought up in Kenya where National Parks were places where one saw many different animals I was rather disappointed with Kakadu – we saw few animals. They had some wonderful frogs, some good places for water birds like herons and pelicans. We saw crocodiles on a boat trip on the South Alligator River. The only water buffalo that we saw was old Charlie who was used in films. These animals used to be abundant but they were a source of disease which affected Australian meat exports so they had been culled.

The most interesting features of Kakadu were the rock paintings. We saw several sites but those at Obiri Rocks were the most impressive. Our guide was a student working there for six months who had an academic interest in the subject and so was very enthusiastic about it. (C43.2)

Travelling south we saw the Emily Falls tumbling in steps over red rocks into a beautiful pool. Katherine Gorge is a series of gorges. The distance one can take a boat depends on the time of year. After the rains one can reach much further up the river. The red and orange rocks and cliffs are spectacular and make wonderful subjects for painting. There were also some Aboriginal rock paintings. (C43.5)

Mataranka Springs are hot pools further down the road. We had a pleasant swim in the clear water spoilt marginally by the smelly bats which inhabited the trees above. We stayed at a motel where there were more peacocks than I have ever seen anywhere else.

Anneas Gunn's grave was of interest because of the book his wife, Jeannie, wrote, *We of the Never Never.* It was about her time at the turn of the twentieth century out the in the bush when it was really isolated country. He died in 1903 at the age of 41. She lived until 1961.

The road runs for hundreds of kilometres, often straight for great distances. From time to time a road train would pass stirring up the dust with the drafts they create. These are huge trucks often pulling three trailers full of cattle. (C43.3)

Periodically there are enormous termite mounds scattered in the bush. These are amazing structures. The termites can also open and close vents to maintain a constant temperature in them.

The distances are so great, with few sites of interest or places to visit, that we went off a side road for five kilometres to Daly Waters Pub. It was in the middle of nowhere and yet there had been an Air Force camp around there during the war.

The Devil's Marbles are on the roadside – huge boulders in a large pile, some on top of others. I like painting rocks so I made a quick sketch of them. (C43.4)

Tennant Creek, a rather bleak but sizable outback town with a dam nearby was a night stop for us. Next stop was on to Alice Springs, the main city in Central Australia. We headed east past several scenic spots – Emily Gap, Corroberee Rock and Trefina Gorge, which was dry but can be a raging torrent in the wet season. It has some grand gums with white bark growing beside the river course, with a backdrop of red-brown cliffs.

The road ended at Ross River where we spent the night in a cabin. A rock with carvings nearby made one wonder how old this carving could be – it had probably been done a long before white man arrived. Camel rides were available. These animals had been brought to Australia from the middle-east, mainly Afghanistan, to provide transportation in the desert areas.

The following day we returned to Alice Springs and then proceeded west past more scenic spots – the John Flynn Memorial, Standley Chasm, where the sun shines in the bottom only for a short time around noon, and on to Ormiston Gorge and our final destination at Glen Helen beside the gorge of that name. It is spectacular country with the red rocks, red earth and a view of Mt. Sondor, away to the west. It turns blue as the sun drops in the west. It was a wonderful sight for painting. (C40.5)

We returned to the Alice and then headed south to Ayres Rock via a meteorite crater and Kings Canyon, which I think is the most magnificent of all the sites we visited. One can walk up the hill and skirt around the canyon where there are unusual rock formations, some like pancakes piled on each other. The track then enters a narrow gully where bromeliads, very ancient fern-like plants, are to be found. This leads to the top of the falls where great views of the two sides of the canyon appear. On the right the cliffs are creamy white with some black streaks down them while on the left they are deep brick red and look like soft cheese which has been sliced with a sharp knife. This majestic scene was enhanced while we were there by three girls, one on the south side and two on the north side, singing songs from the *Sound of Music* in German with the melodies echoing around the canyon. (C40.3)

Mt. Connor is another huge rock formation near the road but is overshadowed in size by Ayres Rock so it rarely receives a mention. It is flat topped with cliffs all around it, standing up above the flat countryside.

Ayres Rock, now called Uluru, is a very grand spectacle. The world's largest monolith is six kilometres around the base. It is a good climb to the top but can be dangerous if windy. Nowadays climbing it is discouraged. It has some intriguing formations around it if one looks carefully around the base. There are some indentations which look like giant carvings in the north side of the rock but they are natural erosions. (C41.7) The colour changes which occur, particularly in the evening when it turns from red to purple are something unforgetable.

Thirty kilometres west there is yet another huge outcrop of rocks – the Olgas. They are a mass of mountainous rocks stretching for several kilometres but more irregular than Uluru. These spectacles are some of the natural wonders of the world and well worth a visit.

We had a short holiday going up the coast north of Perth in Western Australia. It was shortly after rain when the wild-flowers were at their best. The West Australian wildflowers are unique, quite different to flowers one sees elsewhere in the world. (C41.6) The Pinnacles is an area where erosion has left hundreds of beautifully sculpted rock formations standing out of the surrounding sandstone (C41.5). Kalbari, further north on the coast has some exotic cliffs with intricate formations eroded in them in wonderfully varied colours of rock – white, yellow, ochre and brown. We also visited sites along the Murchison River, which runs through a gorge with brick red cliffs for several kilometres.

Tasmania is a compact, beautiful and interesting island which we have visited several times. It began with Penal settlements near Struan on the west coast, Maria Island north of Hobart and Port Arthur. The latter is preserved as a historical park. Maria Island is like a geologist's dream to cruise around because there are so many interesting rock formations to be seen, particularly on the north end. After the convicts left it was taken over by an Italian called Diego Bernacchi who spent several years as a merchant in England until he was advised to leave for health reasons. He established an active community on the island with several ventures including a vineyard. Many of the buildings still remain. His son, Louis, went to Melbourne to study astronomy, meteorology and magnetism at the Observatory. He was keenly interested in Arctic and Antarctic exploration and managed to gain a position on Borschgrevink's expedition to Antarctica in 1899, and later joined Scott's expedition (1902-4).

The Great Ocean Road in western Victoria has towering sandstone pillars called the Twelve Apostles (C41.3), great natural arches and gorges eroded into the cliffs. It is a wonderful spectacle to see huge waves approaching and crash on to those rocks. One can feel the enormous power of the water as they explode, sending spray high in the surrounding air – it is no wonder that it has sculpted these magnificent formations over the millenia. One of the most famous was called London Bridge, which collapsed a year after I photographed a Japanese friend, Masuharu Katsumo, framed to look as if he was trying to hold it up. (C41.2)

Australia has so many interesting places to visit including Cradle Mountain in Tasmania (C43.6) and Kangaroo Island (C41.4). These were but a few of them.

Children grow up quickly. I tried to spend time with them at their sport and on these holidays. However, the special times were when I took them overseas with me, alone or in pairs. I wanted all of them to visit Kenya, the country where I grew up, as I thought that would help them to understand some of my idiosyncrasies! Periodically I went to visit my mother and the rest of the family.

The first of these trips was in 1977 when I took the twins to Kenya and then to Europe. We spent part of the time in Kenya with my sister who lived at Malindi on the coast where we could swim and surf on the magnificent, long, white beaches with beautiful coral reefs offshore. We then had a special treat. Eustace, whom my mother had helped as a boy during the dangerous days of the Maumau, wanted to repay her kindness.

26.2. From Right – Eustace, Mother in front, Johnstone (Dresser), Catherine, KB, Epafara (Dresser-anaesthetist), Tumuthai (hospital gardener).

He took us to the Ark, a game lodge which is supposed to resemble Noah's Ark. It is situated in the forest at the foot of the Aberdare Mountains. Here we could watch the animals coming to drink and lick salt. It was here that I first saw the elusive bongo which lived deep in the forest on Mt. Kenya and the Aberdares. It is a beautiful, large, rufous antelope with fine white stripes on its side. There were also buffalo, elephants, bushbuck and many other animals.

I was watching some animals from the verandah, sitting next to an American. I asked if he was on holiday. "No," he said. "I am accompanying my wife who is writing an article for the National Geographic Magazine on sable antelope." That sounded interesting. It turned out that she was interesting. Her father had been Canadian envoy to China when the Revolution occurred. Many years later, when it was still a closed country, he was invited back by his friend Chou En Lai, one of the country's most powerful men. His daughter accompanied him and wrote a fascinating article on China in a 1971 National Geographic. I asked what he did. He worked in newspapers, he told me. After further discussion I asked what he actually did in newspapers. "I am Editor of the New York Times" he said. I was quite surprised! I later had a chat with his wife and when we parted company back at the lodge where we left our cars she said "If you are ever in New York look us up. If you can't remember the name buy a copy of the Times. It is on the front page". I did not make it to New York until many years later.

We then flew to Rome for a day just to give them a feel of that great city. The time was short and the day strenuous but we visited a few highlights – the Borghese Gallery, which has some fine sculptures, the Sistine chapel in the Vatican with the wonderful paintings by Michaelangelo, St. Peters with the magnificent piazza and all its grandeur. The Pieta was particularly sensitive but the overall feeling that I gained was of glorification of the Popes rather than God. The huge dome is outstanding. Next we went to the Forum, which gave us a sense of history, as did the Colosseum which was our final stop.

We spent a day in Munich visiting the art galleries and a museum. Cathy was particularly thrilled to see the works of Albrecht Dürer, as he was one of six artists she had studied for a school project. Maryann enjoyed the museum with musical instruments. Next we went to Starnberg and southern Bavaria where we saw the elaborately decorated Baroque church, Die Weis, built by the Zimmerman brothers in 1746-57 (C44.3), and King Ludwig's Neuschwanstein Castle. We proceeded to Ehrwald where we took a chair lift up into the mountains.

The lady on the seat in front of us was yodeling, adding to her 80-year-old mother's enjoyment of her first chairlift ride.

26.3. Malcolm Miller at the south door of Chartres, Cathedral in France, 1992.

Next to Britain and then their trip ended up in Paris, where I attended a conference while they found their way, at 15, to Versailles and other interesting places. We visited Chartres Cathedral where we heard fascinating lectures in English by Malcolm Miller. He confined his talks to specific topics rather than trying to cover the whole cathedral in one session. We heard him speak on the stories depicted on the west window and on the principles of gothic architecture. Fifteen years later I returned with Janet and heard him again speak on the apostles on the south door and how the statues gave an indication of how they died.

Fraser and Kester went to Kenya with me in 1979. We found that the cheapest way to go was via Athens so we had a couple of days there. Seeing the historic sites such as the Parthenon, the Olympic stadium and the Archaeological Museum with gold masks gave them an introduction to the antiquities and added interest to young Kester's subsequent study of Latin at school. The time in Kenya was fantastic because we had some days at the coast at Malindi with its magnificent beaches stretching for miles. Fishing, surfing, goggling and swimming as well as bargaining for carvings were all part of the holiday. It happened that my brother was looking after a private game farm for six months upcountry between Mt Kenya and the Aberdares. Seventeen thousand acres of the farm were set aside for wildlife. We saw so many animals – buffalo, white rhino, lion, cheetah, giraffe, zebra and many of the antelope family as we drove around the park. They had a baby orphan cheetah at the time. On a trip up the Aberdare Mountains we had to pause for an elephant on the road and saw a small animal which I had not seen before called a zorilla. (C4.5)

Our return trip was via Mauritius, where we had to spend a night at the airline's expense, as in those days they paid if the flight did not connect. We drove across to the main town, St. Louis and visited the ponds with the huge Victoria water-lilies with leaves measuring nearly a metre across.

We took Ken to Kenya when he was one year old, as Janet and I joined a family safari organized by my brother, Monty, who took safaris into the Northern Frontier. Ken stayed with my mother and Priscilla who had worked with my mother since I was a child. She was a wonderful person, the daughter of my mother's original gardener. (C1.2) I last saw her when she was over 70 and still working at the Nanyuki Cottage Hospital, where my father had worked when he was ultimately in General Practice.

Our trip was memorable. We travelled north from Nanyuki passing several prominent ranges of hills including the Matthews Range, to Marsabit, which we had visited in 1958. (C19.1) It was an old volcano standing out over the arid land with Paradise Lake in the crater. We had seen a huge elephant, Ahmed, there on the previous trip. Its tusks, weighing nearly 100 pounds each (45kg), can now be seen at the Nairobi Museum. Then we went on to the Kaisut desert. We camped by a waterhole frequented by the Gabra people with their camels but also by two types of sand grouse. One group came to water in the morning and the other in the evening. The landing area was small but each bird came in and had two or three gulps of water. As it took off the next bird was already landing. This well organized procession made human airports seem quite inefficient. This place sticks in my memory for several reasons, partly through paintings and photographs. One of these is a wonderful picture of a Gabra mother with her baby on her back. (C46.2) One painting shows an old man who came and sat under a tree opposite me while I was painting the scene. He just sat and stared so I painted him into the picture. Another painting shows the varying colour of the desert sands – white, yellow and light brown with the land cruiser tracks going into the distance. But best of all was a large mug of tea which I drank with relish on the hot afternoon. Never have I enjoyed a mug of sweetened tea so much. Tea is one of the most thirst quenching drinks when it is hot and one is feeling dehydrated. Further on we passed an oasis with palm trees and camels using the shade provided.

Out in the middle of the desert the tracks came to a divergence, one sign pointing to North Hor. We took the other route to Mt Kulal,

26.4. Ndeke making bread in a camp oven, on safari at Mt. Kulal.

which is another extinct volcano. We travelled up a rough track to high on the mountain where we had panoramic views across the desert and, to the west, down an escarpment to Lake Turkana. We camped on the edge of the forest which runs round the border of the crater. Ndege, my brother's cook for many years, soon had the fire going and had constructed his camp oven in which he baked bread.

We hiked up to the rim of the crater the next day and saw down into the forested bottom. (C19.3) Monty told us about a previous trip when they had explored the side entrance to the crater which allowed the river to flow out. Like so many places in Kenya there were animals such as Thompson's and Grant's gazelles, plenty of birds and many wild flowers, including one which had the closest that I have seen to a black flower- caraluma. (C3.6) After a couple of days in the balmy mountain air we descended into the Rift Valley and the shores of Lake Turkana, named after one of the local tribes. Another tribe living in that area are the El Molo whose numbers are now small. The photographs show their dwellings and some of the children. (C19.5, 6) In earlier days it was called Lake Rudolf by one of the early explorers, Count Teleki, who was Hungarian.

My brother, Monty, wrote a book called *Where Giants Trod* about the exploration of the Lake Rudolf region between 1880 and 1920. By a strange coincidence I was able to help him. I was visiting him when he had nearly completed it. I asked how it was progressing. He told me it was finished except for a chapter on an Italian explorer from Parma in Italy called Botega. He had written to the library there for information without response. It so happened that we had a surgeon from Parma working at the hospital in Melbourne and he had given me his address only two weeks before when he returned home. I had it in my pocket. I wrote to him and he replied, inviting Monty to visit him when he was next in Europe. He went the following year and found all the information he needed. He also found a statue and fountain near the railway station commemorating Botega. Unfortunately, it was not cared for and was in a mess so Monty wrote to the Mayor of Parma saying that it was a disgrace that the monument to a famous son of the city had been allowed to reach this state. Some time later when I was back in Melbourne I received a message from Michael, the surgeon, saying that the monument had been cleaned up!

We stopped by a charming little bay on the lake. The heat was intense. It was so hot that we ran into the water fully clothed to cool off. After we came out our clothes were dry in about 10 minutes. (C19.4) The next part of the trip was over very rough, rocky terrain. We went slowly and bumped around but eventually came to smoother tracks. Later in the trip as we were climbing back towards the Highlands there had been rain and the road was wet and every now and again we had to push the land cruisers out of the ditch. This was not uncommon in the wet weather in Kenya! It was a memorable trip with all the members of my brother's and sister's families.

When Ken was ten I was to be in Europe during his school holidays. His teacher thought a couple of extra weeks off school was justifiable on educational grounds. Various friends and connections agreed to look after him when I went to visit hospitals. He went to Versailles with the mother of a French anaesthetist, Sylvie Herbeau, who was working with us at the time. We were taken to dinner at Gare de Lyons in Paris by the great craniofacial surgeon, Paul Tessier, who had arranged for his anaesthetist's son to work with us. He had an eye to the future. It was the first time that I had eaten snails. The dining room was very luxurious with classical paintings decorating the walls and ceiling. Through the window we could watch the TGV pulling out of the station. Tessier had a funny sense of humour and was obviously a practical joker. He regaled me with the tale of how he had tried to transfer tigers from Indo-China to Central Africa where he hunted. He had someone organized to provide the tigers and another to fly them across. At the time the planes did not have the long range that they have now and would have had to refuel in the Sudan, then under British control. They would not allow the plane to land so the project had to be called off. What an elaborate practical joke just to plant tigers somewhere where they would not be expected. What he had not thought about was that they would probably have died of some African disease against which the animals would have had no immunity.

In Paris we went to the Louvre but Ken was more interested in the birds that were being sold outside than in the great Museum itself. I persuaded him to see just a few key paintings, so that he would not become bored. We saw the *Mona Lisa*, Gerricault's *Raft of the Medusa* which impressed him greatly, especially the way the picture was designed, Louis le Nain's *Peasant family* and the Rubens room of the life of Marie de Medici.

In Geneva we stayed at a vineyard with the parents of another lady who had worked with us, Corinne de Moerloose. While I was at the hospital he was taken riding by her father and then to pottery by her brother. A year later a parcel arrived for him with his dinosaur marked with his name and *Made in Switzerland* imprinted on the bottom!

In London we went to Hampton Court Palace where he surprised me again with his powers of observation. He noticed that a large painting was not exactly the same as a smaller preliminary version in the next room. The figure second on the left was a male in one and a female in the other. Otherwise they looked exactly the same. And I thought he was just rushing past becoming bored! In Scotland he had some time with my mother, who was then 87. He played shinty with some boys. In Edinburgh he dragged me to the top of Arthur's Seat, where one gains a panoramic view of the city and away across to the Fife coast and the Isle of May. His comment at the top was that I was always fittest when I was travelling which was probably true. It was a great educational experience for him.

When he was 16, I took him to Kenya and then on to Egypt, Tunisia and Jordan where we saw fantastic sights such as the Pyramids at Giza and Sachara in Egypt and the colosseum at El Jem in Tunisia (C45.5). In Jordan we saw the most wonderful variety in two days – we visited the Roman town of Jerrash (C34.1), the Dead Sea, Petra with the magnificent buildings carved out of the coloured cliffs (C34.3, 4) and finally the Crusader Castle ruins – Montreal – whose guardian is illustrated in C46.7. It is not surprising that he was bitten by the travel bug.

All these trips were very special times which I shared with individual members of the family. As well as the bonding which develops I gained other interests because we did things that interested them which I would not have done otherwise. Fraser travelled through

South America with me in 1988 and later, when he was living in UK, he took me to train museums and a trip through the London canals on the canal boat on which he lived. (C35.6) It was another perspective of that great city which few people see. Amazing features were crossing the A25 on a canal bridge and travelling under Islington through a tunnel over 800m long.

I also gained a better appreciation of architecture from him and from Janet, who had studied fine arts before leaving home in 1959. A few of the great buildings which I have seen are illustrated. (C44&45)

One of the greatest pleasures in my life has been to have this family with their varied interests, who all get on together and with whom I have enjoyed interesting times. To miss spending enough time with one's children can lead to a distancing of them from their parents, which can have sad consequences especially in their teenage years and early twenties. Fortunately we have a wonderful relationship with our family.

26.5. With my bother, Monty, and sister, Catherine, in London.

Continuing contact with one's family depends on where they settle. It is harder to see much of them if any are married and settled on the other side of the world, as I did. My sister eventually came to Australia too but does not live very close by. I see my brother, Monty, occasionally in London and sometimes if I manage to visit Kenya. Years ago we also met in Paris airport and, another time, in Los Angeles when we both were visiting North America at the same time. Once, we all happened to be in London at the same time where we had a rare photograph taken together.

Chapter 27
Travel

Some people love to travel, others don't. I traveled back and forth from Kenya to Britain out of necessity when my parents went on leave and when I eventually went to university. I also went to Salisbury (now Harare) to do my national service training. I enjoyed the side trips to Nyasaland (now Malawi) and Victoria Falls. Probably I was finally really bitten by the "travel bug" when I went to Labrador.

I was brought up to have a great interest in geography, exploration and the primitive people of the world. I remember reading about the amazing adaptability to climate of the Eskimos in the Arctic, the Aborigines in Australia and the Bushmen in the Kalahari, and of their carefully balanced, efficient lifestyles. I was also a great student of exploration because much of the world was still being or had only recently been explored.

I read about Livingstone, Morton, Speke, Grant, Bruce, Mungo Park and others who explored Africa, mostly in the nineteenth century. They were tough, resilient men who underwent incredible hardships. As an eight year old child I visited the source of the Nile and saw the plaque commemorating Speke's discovery on 28th July 1862, less than a century before. It was almost within my grandparents' lifetime, not really very long ago.

It is not much wonder that I wanted to see the places they explored and many more. I was destined to be a wanderer. My children are all travelers. I am not sure if this is inherited or because I took them all travelling.

Some people travel with their work, often rushing hither and thither on business but seeing little else. That is not much fun. Some travel purely for pleasure and some, like myself, manage to combine the two, which is a great advantage if there is time. I was fortunate to be able to do much of my travelling during my annual, sabbatical and long-service leaves, usually combining lecturing and teaching with some pleasure and sightseeing.

Travel has been important as a source of subjects for photographs and for painting. Any trip where I can obtain either or both of these makes it more worthwhile. On my two Antarctic trips I did about a hundred paintings and took many photographs. I rarely write a diary but these pictures fulfill the role of one and remind me of places I have visited and people I have met. I have enjoyed the beauty of mountains, waterfalls, deserts and all variety of scenery. Nature with its variety of plants, animals and birds is fascinating. The people and their culture, music, dancing and special costumes (C25.) are all interesting. There is often a cultural display at congresses where these are demonstrated. I have been very privileged to have seen many of these all over the world.

It is a pity that the unique local dress commonly seen less than 30 to 40 years ago in so many countries has been replaced increasingly with western style clothes. This has resulted from increased mobility of people, globalization, the impact of television and advertising. In addition television and film has brought these costumes into homes all over the world so that some of the excitement of seeing them in their natural setting is lost.

People wearing their local dress or performing some special activity can make interesting subjects for photographs, although attitudes differ about having their picture taken. Some are happy to oblige, others want to be paid while some refuse to be photographed. In fundamentalist Islamic areas one is not allowed to take pictures of women. In the Andes I was refused because the people believe that if they are photographed part of their spirit goes with it. For a long time, I took very few pictures of people but they can make wonderful subjects, if they agree, particularly if they are wearing local costumes. Latterly I have taken an interest in portraiture. A selection is included among the colour photographs. (C46, 47, 48)

Travel is not always easy and pleasant. It can be tedious, boring, tiring, frustrating, lonely and sometimes hazardous or downright dangerous. Waiting hours for the next flight or for a broken down plane to be fixed can induce many of these sentiments.

Antarctic and southern islands

My ninth birthday present from my parents was a book about the early British Arctic and Antarctic explorers. It introduced me to Frobisher, Ross, Franklin, Scott and Shackleton. I have read widely on these heroic journeys.

Shackleton's amazing journey from Elephant Island (28.4) to South Georgia on the James Caird, a small boat with only a canvas covering for protection, to get help for his men was brave and risky – their only hope. Many people are aware of this tale because of film and television screening about it but few will know how lucky the party was to reach their destination. They left Elephant Island the day before the sea froze, which would have prevented their departure. Exhausted, one night the six men rested. The spray from the breaking waves was no longer coming through the canvas. It was freezing and they suddenly realized that their boat was gradually sinking. They had to chip the ice off to save themselves. They reached the wrong side of South Georgia for the whaling stations where they could get help. The west cost was protected for long stretches by dangerous reefs of which they were unaware. This resulted in them having to stand off the island overnight until they found a way through the next day, a gap a little over 100 m wide, to reach King Haakon Bay. The delay must have been hard for the six exhausted men. To find the island in the huge ocean was the result of good navigation by Frank Worsley, in weather where opportunities to take sightings of the sun were infrequent. Finally, it was too hard to sail round to Stromness, on the other side of the island and only three of them were fit enough to try to cross the mountains for help. They had to climb up and down the ridge several times until they found a place where it was not a sheer drop on the other side. How would they descend? They decided to use their coiled rope as a toboggan and slide over the side. They dropped about 500m in 3 minutes. They were in the wrong valley for the whaling station at Stromness. The morning siren guided them to their destination. They made the trip over the mountains, which had never been done before, in 36 hours on the only two clear days that winter. These elements of luck, which enabled them to succeed, are rarely mentioned in accounts of their amazing journey.

Scott went on his first trip to Antarctica in 1902 on the Discovery, which is now part of the Discovery Museum in Dundee, Scotland. He had rejected a very good Scottish scientist Dr William Spiers Bruce, so a Scottish expedition led by Bruce on the Scotia went to the Weddell Sea side of the continent at the same time. It was a scientific success. He also mapped 240km of coastline of what he named Coats Land. Bruce was said to be a rather shy, dour man who was not a publicist and therefore received little acclaim for his outstanding work.

My interest has enticed me to make two trips to the Antarctic and those southern islands. It is a beautiful, serene, pristine and, at other times, a wild part of the world with the additional interest of wildlife – millions of penguins and seals, whales and others.

In 1997 I went from Hobart via Macquarie Island (C21.1&2) to Cape Adare and the Ross Sea region which was the approach taken by Scott in 1902 and 1911, Shackleton in 1907 and Amundsen in 1911 when they were attempting to reach the South Pole. Scott's expeditions also had scientific components which resulted in some amazing but not so well known journeys.

One trip by Edward Wilson, the doctor, scientific leader and a brilliant artist, Bowers and Cherry-Garrard was to Cape Crozier to collect emperor penguin eggs in August because they laid their eggs earlier than the other species. They were exposed to temperatures of minus 70°F (- 64°C) on the way. At Cape Crozier they built a shelter of rocks and covered it with a canvas sheet. They placed their equipment in their tent. Both were blown away in a blizzard which lasted for two days during which they only had their sleeping bags to protect them. Later they recovered their tent. With considerable difficulty, having to crawl through a small hole in an ice wall, they obtained the eggs and made it back. Their sleeping bags weighed 12kg more on return due to frozen condensation. It was described as the worst journey in the world and is recorded in Cherry-Garrard's book of that name.

Another party, led by Campbell, for whom a huge ice tongue stretching several kilometres into the sea was named (C21.6), was

27.1. Scott Island

stranded on the coast for five months when ice prevented their ship from picking them up. They had to kill seals and penguins for food as otherwise they only had one biscuit per day, 1 cup of cocoa for five days per week, tea for the other two and a few raisins for special occasions. They had a near disaster when the vent to their ice cave blocked. There was not enough oxygen to keep the candles alight. This alerted them to the lack of oxygen just in time. Then in August, when light began to return, they had to trek down the west side of the Ross Sea and across the ice to safety.

27.2. Louis Bernacchi

Our trip took us to Macquarie island, round Scott Island (on 67°S and 180°) which has only been landed on five times, to Cape Adare where we visited Borchgrevink's hut, built in 1899 and now restored. (C21.3) His party, which included Louis Bernacchi from Melbourne, was the first to stay over winter in the Antarctic. The story of this rather unsatisfactory expedition is recounted by Bernacchi's granddaughter from his diaries and is summarized in the following poem.

Cape Adare, Antarctica

Out on Ridley Point at Cape Adare
A few lucky people come and stand and stare,
For there stands Borchgrevink's joint
Out on the windswept point.
It was the first hut where a party dismayed
In the Antarctic over winter stayed,
For Borchgrevink was at his best
When, to the hills for a while he strayed
And left his men at the hut to enjoy the rest
Of a few days without the Pest.

Borchgrevink came from Norway,
In Melbourne sometime he did stay,
Where Bernacchi, Louis by name
He employed to play his game –
The great Antarctic to survey
So others, later, could find their way

to come and look at the hut and more,
at Adelie penguins landing on the rocky shore,
exhausted, then rising to parade in a long line
across the shallow pond towards cliffs sublime
that form the point of Cape Adare;
A century later people came to stare
In wonder at Borchgrevink's wooden hut.
Adelie penguins in their dinner suits strut
And keeping up with the Jones,
They make their nests with stones,
By their constant, wicked labours
Stealing stones from their neighbours.

The hut was for long well aired
But now it has been repaired
So that when the gales of winter blow
There is no more entry of drifting snow.
Inside there is much to see,
a beautiful portrait of Marie
Looks down from the ceiling above
On Ellefsen, the cook, with love.
And on the shelf stands a bottle of chloroform,
Which would have helped through a surgical storm,
but there was no need for surgery
although Hansen passed through Purgatory
and lies forever at the top of Cape Adare
watching over Borchgrevink's lair.

Hansen's great desire was himself to see
The first Adelies arriving from the sea
In October eighteen ninety nine.
But only one arrived in time,
before his tranquil soul departed,
having to his companions said farewell
leaving them his sad tale to tell.
And then the penguins really started
Beginning as a slow trickle,
to reach an eruptive miracle ,
to arrive more and more

until they covered all the shore.
Before Nicolai Hansen expired
The wish he most desired
Was to be the first man to observe
Mother Nature's efforts to conserve
The Adelie.
These little penguins are still there
Watching Hansen's grave at Cape Adare.

In 1911 came Scott's men,
Victor Campbell and another five
But in a tent it was hard to survive.
Borchgrevink's hut was full of snow,
An aggrieved Adelie they came to know,
So a wooden hut they built
upon the sandy, windswept silt
on the beach at Ridley Point,
a cold and gale-swept joint.
They did not stand and stare
For to build their hut at Cape Adare,
and to do research, they were there.

Eleven months later the ship came by
To take them elsewhere to try.
Their hut they left
Slowly to become bereft
and as time elapsed
The walls collapsed
Leaving the porch still standing,
while the walls were disbanding.

Bernacchi was not happy with the poor leadership of Borschgrevink, who turned out to be a less able scientist than he made out. It was not long, however, until Bernacchi returned to Antarctica with Scott on his 1902 "Discovery" expedition.

Then we sailed south past Coulman, Franklin and Possession Islands, where our visits were made possible by the midnight sun, which gave a beautiful soft light throughout the night. Then on to Bird and Ross Islands, around which we spent several days and visited

Scott's 1911 hut at Cape Evans and Shackleton's 1907 hut at Cape Royds (C22.1), both in view of Mt. Erebus. It looked so close one felt it could be climbed in a day. I was surprised to find out that a group of Scott's party took nearly two weeks to climb it and return. Reflected in the calm sea, it was a breath-taking sight. (C22.2) This nearly 4000m volcano still has steam clouds floating above it. We visited all these huts in company of one of the New Zealand Hut Preservation Trust members who enabled us to gain access. Finding hay stacked alongside Scott's hut showed how things are preserved in the cold. They have repaired the huts, which still have contents that were left all those years ago.

At the north east of Ross Island is Mt. Terror which overlooks the massive Ross Ice Shelf (C21.4). The part I photographed is probably part of one of the massive chunks that have since broken off and floated away, one being grounded off Cape Crozier where it seemed to cut off the feeding Emperor Penguins from the ones which stayed at the nests. It must have caused disastrous starvation of many birds. Recently one has caused significant obstruction to the Ross Sea preventing some of the ice from leaving McMurdo Sound.

We were fortunate on this trip to have exceptionally good weather to enjoy the pristine beauty of it all. I expected everything to be covered with snow and ice, but we saw plenty of places where the rock was bare even though it was cold enough to freeze the water in my paint box. Seeing seals, penguins – mainly Adelies (C21.5), skuas and whales all added to the interest of the trip.

On the return trip we hit a 12-force storm which prevented us from landing at Campbell Island but we picked up four scientists, including Jenny Scott, who has spent years working on several of the sub-Antarctic islands including Macquarie, Heard, Campbell and South Georgia. We landed on another of the group, Enderby Island, where we saw yellow eyed penguins, Hooker sea lions and albatrosses which were nesting. It was interesting to see these gigantic birds taking off and landing on their defined landing strip. They need this runway to gain speed for take-off into the wind.

The urge to see the other side of Antarctica came in 2001 so just after I finished working full time, I went to the South American side. I had been told that there was even more variety of wild-life over there.

We sailed from Ushuaia on Tierra del Fuego to the Falkland

Islands and on to South Georgia where we made several very interesting landings including Fortuna Bay where Shackleton came off the mountains; the whaling station at Grytviken (C23.4), where Shackleton is buried (C23.3); Salisbury plain with 100,000 king penguins (C23.1) and Albatross Island where we watched the albatrosses courting. (C23.2) South Georgia is a rugged, amazing island with so much interesting wildlife. We then went south past several islands including Elephant Island, where Shackleton left his men when he went to find help. I sketched it as we sailed past. Deception Island is a volcano which erupted not long ago. There is a gap which allowed us to enter the crater where there are hot springs. Some of the passengers swam despite the bitterly cold evening they were exposed to when they emerged.

We visited colonies of different varieties of penguins – Chinstrap, Gentoo and Macaroni. The chin strap penguins (illustrated) seemed to be deep in conversation either discussing what we were or maybe, what were we doing!

27.3. Chinstrap penguins. "What did you say?"

We saw Gentoo penguins at Cuverville Island with their young on their stone nests, stained red by their droppings, set against the backdrop of an iceberg (C24.1). Gentoos demonstrated their art created by squirting out their excreta in white lines.

We sailed past some magnificent icebergs including a very rare, dark one (C24.2) and one with blue hatched lines in it (C24.3), to the Antarctic Peninsula. We entered the famous Lemaire Channel where we saw leopard seals lying on ice flows.

27.4. Gentoo Art!

On the way back some of the passengers were complaining that we had not had a good storm. We hit a force 8 one for a couple of hours as we approached Cape Horn! There was great clattering of crockery and cutlery in the dining room and kitchen as the giant waves suddenly hit.

On the trip to South Georgia I shared a cabin with a most interesting man, Robin Bradshaw (C23.5), who had been a bank manger in various places around the world including Nairobi, Kinsasha and Kathmandu. As a young man he had travelled by scooter from London across to South Africa. He told me of a time he broke down and had to wait 24 days before a truck came by. It was already overloaded so he had to wait another four days until help came. He has visited over a hundred countries. While in Kenya, he visited Nanyuki, where my brother lives. When I asked where he stayed it turned out that it was with my sister in law's mother! Another coincidence was finding someone at our table who had been at school with me in Kenya.

I spent four days in Tierra del Fuego walking in beautiful parks and mountains and visiting the anaesthetists. The first day I took the bus through the mountains, the southern end of the Andes, to Tolhuin, and then across the bleak, flat Patagonian pampas to Rio Grande, one of the bleakest places I have ever visited. The main streets were decorated with pipes bent into different patterns for each street and painted a variety of colours to try to brighten the place up. It seems that the great consolation for living there is that some of the best trout fishing in the world is only 50km away.

I made contact with the anaesthetists there, showed them some of my teaching videos with Spanish voice-over and had dinner with them. They don't receive many visitors! On my return journey I stopped for several hours at Tolhuin and walked several kilometres down to Lago Fognani where there were beautiful views across the lake to the mountains. (C24.4)

One day I visited the National park a few kilometres west of Ushuaia. As the wind dropped and the sun shone, I hiked across the soft grass with Patagonian geese feeding nearby beside a river with crystal clear water. (C24.6) I enjoyed a few peaceful hours to contemplate how fortunate I had been to enjoy so much beauty. Then it changed. The wind rose, there were rain showers and dark clouds gathered over the mountains. More ducks and geese wandered or swam by. A wonderful scene for photographing and painting presented, with a windswept tree in the foreground, white topped waves forming on the lake with the dark mountains in the distance. I was glad of my Alpaca jumper and parka to keep me warm.

Ushuaia has a backdrop of mountains and glaciers. The next day I walked up towards the main glacier alongside a stream. On an alternate path coming down I went through a grove of stunted, incredibly twisted trees.(C24.5) The final day I spent at the hospital to help with a difficult anaesthetic on a child needing a lung operation.

The trip had been a wonderful experience. I hope all the efforts to maintain the pristine beauty and wildlife of the Antarctic and the southern islands will be successful.

South America

South America is an interesting continent, especially if one speaks Spanish. I have been several times on extensive tours, mainly teaching but always being shown around as well. Recently someone asked me where to visit in South America. He was flying to Santiago. I suggested flying to Iquique, the gateway to the Atacama Desert, the driest place on earth. One can hire a car and drive to Pica, or to Mamiña at about 2000m in the Andean foothills. There is a little church in the square dating back to 1637. (C32.5) Nearby there are thermal pools. The desert can seem bleak but colours are enhanced because they can vary at different times of day. An alternative is to drive north to Arica near Chile's northern border with Peru. It has an iron church designed by Eiffel, of Eiffel Tower fame.

A trip to Parque Lauca takes one to Lake Chungara at 4600m near the Bolivian border, with views of volcanoes Pomerape and Parinacote rising over 6000 m. We were late arriving in the evening, so the tour people thought we had not come and did not book a four wheel drive for our trip. We decided to go anyway in our hire car – a Peugeot 205! Having been brought up driving in Kenya was good preparation for such a trip. It managed fine except for a short stretch near the small town of Putre where several people we met afterwards had experienced a similar problem. The cars just lose power. It is not just the altitude affecting the fuel mixture as the cars go perfectly well further on at higher altitude. We saw llamas, alpacas and guanacos grazing (C32.4), a cactarium and some other animals and birds. (C32.3)

One could go on to Peru, to Tacna and Arequipa which is surrounded by three large volcanoes. The old Spanish cathedral was damaged in an earthquake since I was there. I hired a car to go to Colca

Canyon, a six hour trip through interesting country including a stretch on the side of a crater at 5000 m. I paid US$120 (in 1994) for the car, a driver, a guide and a night in a little country hotel in Chuvay, two hours from the canyon – one of the best value for money trips I ever had! There was no electricity that night in Chuvay so the stars were brilliant – a memorable sight. The Colca River passes through a valley with Inca terraced hillsides (C27.1) into this amazing Canyon – 1200 m down to the river on one side and 3000m up the other side to the mountain tops (C27.2). Early in the morning one sees condors, huge birds with a wing span exceeding 3m, flying in the canyon. On the way back we visited friends of my guide who had lost their house in an earthquake – half the village was damaged. At Chuvay we went to the hot springs before setting out for Arequipa. On the way we had a stop to paint the stark, brown landscape. (C27.4)

There is a road from near Chuvay to Machu Pichu and Cusco but people commonly fly to Lima to get to Cusco, the old Inca capital. It is a fascinating area. Sacsayhuanman is an Inca site just out of Cusco where I was lucky to see the great hewn rocks built in the precise Inca style surrounded by a rainbow. (C27.3)

Machu Pichu is one of the most magical places I have ever been, especially if one can stay the night and visit it in peace after the train-borne tourists leave. (C28.1,2,3) It has a strange aura about it. It was an Inca city, maybe older, which disappeared into the jungle for centuries until the American archaeologist, Hiram Bingham, found it in 1911. The buildings and terraces are well preserved, although roofless. We stayed at Las Ruinas Hotel, beside the ruins. It rained in the night. The mist rising over the ruins in the morning gave a magical, timeless feel about the place. (C28.1)

La Paz in Bolivia can be reached by air or by train and boat or bus. It is 3500 m high, the highest inhabited city. (C29.1) The low oxygen tension at that altitude can make visitors short of breath. It is an interesting city, which flows down both sides of a valley, reaching beyond to the strange, spiky rocks filling Valle des Lunes. (C29.5) There are skyscrapers as well as the old Spanish buildings such as San Francisco church around which Indian artisans sell their wares. (C29.3) Up the hill on the north side is the Plaza with the Parliament, Government buildings and the Cathedral. (C29.2) In a side street we watched people dictating letters to a letter writer. (C29.4)

There are several interesting places nearby, especially Lake Titicaca and Tiahuanaco, another mysterious ancient site. At Lake Titicaca we visited the reed boat builder who built RA II for Thor Heyerdahl to sail across the Atlantic. (C30.3) Unfortunately, reed boats are almost a thing of the past as the people have given up making them in favour of the more durable wooden ones. There is another trip over the mountains (C30.1) and down 3000m on a winding mountain road for 80km to Coroico. On this road the traffic going down takes the outside when passing – quite terrifying when one looks out and sees a drop of 1000m close by. At the bottom we saw coca plants with the three veins on their leaf running in parallel. I took a photograph of an old door there. (C30.2)

The Galapagos Islands, famous because their unique flora and fauna on each island led Darwin to formulate his Theory of Evolution, can be reached via Guayaquil on the Ecuador coast. They are volcanic. The plants are adapted to suit the hot dry equatorial climate. The tortoises on each island were different, each having a unique design of carapace. (C31.6) There are few left and we saw the last of one species, Old George, in Santa Cruz. They had tried unsuccessfully to get him to mate with one from another island. The frigate birds with their red pouches which are blown up when mating, the boobies with their brilliant blue or red feet (C31.4) and flamingoes are among a wonderful variety of unique birds on the islands. The marine iguanas were smaller than I expected – masses of them clambering on rocks, black with touches of red form one of the ugliest sights I have seen in the animal kingdom. (C31.5) The sea lions on the beaches were tame. Some of the crabs were very colourful red and orange. (C31.7) They were intriguing islands to visit, each one different with so much unique flora and fauna.

Quito, which is 2800m, lies almost on the Equator. It is over 440 years old, having been built by the Spanish invaders. The old town has many fascinating buildings and streets. (C31.1) I was privileged to be taken to the original hospital built in 1575, San Juan de Dios by its last medical director, Dr. Cueva. (C31.2) It had functioned as a hospital for 400 years. Near Quito is the Equator monument with displays featuring dress and aspects of life from each region in Ecuador, Otavalo Market (C31.3) and some large volcanoes like Cotopaxi. The Amazon headwaters are accessible to the east from Quito.

An alternative trip would be to turn south and go to Argentina and Iguasu Falls, the biggest in the world. (C28.4) It is a spectacular sight which I also had the good fortune to see and photograph from a helicopter. This has now been banned because of noise pollution. The Pirana River first flows over the U shaped falls at the top but further down the canyon there are several stepped falls. It is situated where Argentina, Brazil and Paraguay meet.

Buenos Aires is a grand city, like an amalgam of Europe's great cities, particularly Paris and Rome. Among its attractions is an Opera house based on the Paris Opera and a Museo del Belles Artes with a good collection of Spanish and Argentinian art. One of my favorites is the large "soup kitchen" – "La sopa de los pobres" by Raynaldo Guidici (1884). There are many interesting places in Argentina, but the glaciers in the south were special to me and are worth visiting especially in spring. They can now be reached through Calafate. Perito Moreno Glacier is 60 square km, 4km across the bottom which is about 70 m high. As it moves about 2 m a day one can often see great blocks of ice breaking off. (C32.2) Every few years it blocks the flow of water from one arm to the main part of Lago Argentina. When the pressure builds up the whole end of the glacier breaks away with an almighty crash. There is also the even bigger Uppsala Glacier nearby (200sq.km), but we could not reach it because of icebergs which had broken off it into the lake.

Across the mountains in Chile is Torres del Paine Park, one of the most beautiful places I have ever visited. The day we went the wind was blowing and water was being whipped off the lakes. The next day was cold with rain and snow on higher parts. The third day was calm with fresh snow on the mountains which were reflected on the lakes, a most magnificent sight. (C32.1) There is a walk one can do around the mountains, which takes a week. On the west side is Lago Grey, which has a glacier spilling into it. The icebergs float towards the cabins where they ground about a hundred metres away. When we stopped for coffee on the way out the lady serving us told us that on a windy day people travelling on their own put rocks in their car-boot to prevent the car being blown over! Puenta Arenas is the nearest airport in Chile.

A visit to the beautiful lake country in central southern Chile, with magnificent volcanoes such as Osorno or Villarica is worthwhile. These can be reached via Puerto Montt, Osorno or Tacoma. There are flights from Australia and Europe to Santiago.

I have said nothing of Brazil, a vast country with much of interest, because I have travelled relatively little there apart from the Falls, Florianopolis with its 32 surf beaches, and around Sao Paolo.

I had many technical problems while lecturing in South America like the time when my lecture was being simultaneously translated into Spanish but I could clearly hear the translation because the translator's box was not enclosed. It is difficult to lecture in one language while hearing the translation!

Once I had to give a lecture at Las Condas in Santiago at 7pm. I had been taken up to the nearby snowfields, about an hour away, for the day. I was to return by collectivo – a multiple passenger share taxi. By the time it arrived at nearly 6pm I was becoming anxious about being late. I told the driver of my predicament. He told me we would be on time. We descended round the 33 numbered bends but the disaster struck. We got a puncture. He did not have a jack. A bus arrived which had one. When placed by the axle it was too big and they couldn't get it under. My anxiety increased. I was going to be late. Then someone suggested placing a rock in front of the wheel and driving on to it. It moved along in front of the wheel. Then a foolhardy fellow put his foot on the rock to stop it moving! The driver drove the car on to it and fortunately did not go over and crush the man's foot. What a risk he took. I was only five minutes late.

Europe

Europe has so much to offer in scenery, architecture and culture. One of our most memorable days was when we stayed in Versailles with Christian and Sylvie Herbeau. They had worked with us in 1984. She took us to Giverny, Monet's home where he painted many of his famous paintings such as the water lilies. It was June and the gardens were an exquisite array of colour.(C38.1&2) We then lunched at Manoir d'Anet, a 200-year-old restaurant across the road from a small castle. Next stop was Chartres with its magnificent cathedral, beautiful windows telling biblical stories, sculptured doors, one showing the apostles each with an indication of how they died. An Englishman, Malcolm Miller, can enhance the interest in a visit there with his lectures in English in which he just takes one aspect of this wonderful cathedral so that one can remember about it afterwards. (26.10) The day ended with dinner with my friend Claude St. Maurice, a well known paediatric anaesthetist, on the 58th floor of the Montparnasse tower overlooking Paris, which appeared like a model far below as the sun went down and the lights came on to illuminate the scene. It was a perfect day.

Iceland is regarded as part of Europe although it is a volcanic island away out in the North Atlantic. It is an interesting country with a very old "parliamentary" system. It is supplied with heat and power from geothermal sources (C36.5) and it has many interesting geological formations such as the fjords in the north west, pseudo-craters near Lake Myvatin, (C36.4) many waterfalls and occasional fissures across the country. (C36.3)

There are many interesting cities in Europe. One which is becoming increasingly popular amongst tourists is Prague. Charles Bridge is a foot bridge joining the two sides of the city. It is a hive of activity in summer with musicians, artists and artisans selling their goods (C36.6 and 48.5). In the city centre there is a wonderful astronomical clock. (C36.7)

Asia

Korea seemed to be one of those places on the edge of our world until we were invited to the thirtieth anniversary of Il Sin Hospital in Pusan. It was founded as an obstetric hospital by two Australian sisters, Helen and Cath Mackenzie. The occasion was magnificent especially as all nurses and lady doctors came in their gorgeous, traditional Korean dresses.(C25.2) Following this celebration I lectured at the university where I was presented with a plaque to commemorate this unusual occasion. I don't think many foreigners lectured there.

The next day, we travelled by tourist bus all the way up the east coast to Soraksan National Park with its towering, jagged mountains and bright autumn foliage on the trees. It was a most interesting trip because we saw the whole process of the rice harvest in one day. It was just beginning in the south and finishing in the north. Along the edge of the beach the sand was piled up and stones placed on top so that any disruption could easily be detected, such was the fear of intrusion from the north. Korea is a very beautiful, photogenic country and is justifiably called The Land of Morning Calm.

In Seoul we stayed with Horace and Dorothy Underwood. He was third generation in Korea. His grandfather had come as a missionary and established Yonsei University, now one of the most highly regarded in the country. Horace continued the family tradition of involvement in the University. He was an outstanding man, well respected in the community. He had acted as an interpreter between North and South Korea at the negotiations at the conclusion of the Korean War. I met him several times on my visits to Korea. On the occasion of the Asian Australasian Congress of Anaesthesiology in Seoul (1990) he gave the keynote address. It was a privilege to know him and learn something of that country from him.

27.6. Horace Underwood of Yonsei University, Korea, with the author in 2003.

Kyoto and Nara in Japan provide a window into their history and culture. The Royal Palace in Kyoto with its gardens coloured by azaleas in full bloom were beautiful. The philosophers walk with a tea house and ceremony, were tranquil and interesting. There are many temples, some with very precisely laid out gardens and rock placements. Nara, the old capital, has many old and famous temples. Many are made of wood. Some, such as the Horyu-Ji Temple date back as far as 607. (C36.1) Todaiji Temple is said to be the largest wooden building in the world, being 48m high. (C36.2)

My friend Dilip Pawar told me that India has everything – beaches, mountains, deserts, jungle, historic and famous buildings – the Taj Mahal reflected in the pool in front of it and bounded by two other impressive buildings not usually shown in the photographs. It is two hours by train from Delhi. Fatipur Sikri, 40km west of Agra, is a splendid site worth visiting. It was built as the Mogul emperor Akbar's capital, but was only used for a few years because of poor water supply. Some of the Indian temples date back thousands of years.

Travel in India is different. The traffic seems chaotic. But this is India and somehow it works. Dilip took me to Rajasthan, a destination many discerning travellers wish to visit, if they have not already been there. The name and its reputation ring bells. It is one of those exotic places with palaces surrounded by lakes, forts, marble temples and, in

Jaipur, famous brownish pink buildings and a magnificent palace which contains the museum.

Anything goes on the roads. Everything seems to have the right of way! Tolerance, patience and avoidance of collision are the keys to survival, supported by a cacophony of hooting by all the vehicles, which does not appear to be due to impatience as it is in many other countries. We were fortunate to have Dilish, an experienced driver, to guide us through this experience. He is pictured with his typical Indian lunch. (C26.1)

Who really dominates the right of way? The cows, which laze on the median strips and amble across the road when they feel like it. They may change their direction slightly as they cross to make way for a hooting driver but, always, they ultimately reign supreme: they are holy animals to the Hindus. What about pigs or dogs, some of whom look dead on the side of the road while they slumber? What about the donkeys, goats, camels or even elephants! Drivers avoid them all. Probably a collision with the latter would do more damage to the vehicle and may have unpleasant consequences.

Cars, scooters, motor bikes (which usually have riders without helmets and may be carrying two or three passengers), three wheel scooters used as cheap taxis, trucks, buses, carts drawn by horses, donkeys, camels and even sometimes pushed by humans, all compete with the masses of humans and animals on the roads.

Which side of the road do they drive on? One may well ask because traffic seems to go on both sides, at times in the same direction. They are supposed to travel on the left.

To an outsider it all looks chaotic, hopeless, even suicidal. But even amongst this mayhem people walk, cross four or five streams of traffic in the towns, while others pull their carts with produce ready to sell when they reach their destination.

There is so much on the roads in the towns that long term survival seems unlikely. The secret is that they all respect the other road users – no room for road rage here. They do not wish to harm anyone or any animal. Of course, the confusion causes the traffic to move slowly which helps, and in case the travellers do not know that they are surrounded, horns blare at them from all sides and your driver joins in.

Now we leave the city or town and hope for a more tranquil journey. It is not to be! It may be time to take a tranquilizer or a beta blocker – a drug that calms the heart and prevents the blood pressure going through the roof with fright.

The horn is going full blast, even when it seems to us that there is no reason to use it. It may be to warn someone that you are coming or to encourage an animal to keep out of the way. It may be in response to a sign on the back of trucks you are following – "Horn please" or "Blow horn" to let them know you are there. This is necessary because the truck may be in the middle of the road or even on the right side, looking for the best part to drive on. They need to make way for you if you want to pass. Sometimes the drivers are helpful, using the indicators to let you know whether or not it is safe to pass.

The horn blares again – this time at an approaching vehicle. I presume to let the driver know you are there in case he is having a snooze or a lapse in concentration. They don't move over much as you pass, preferring to hug the centre line. It was explained to me that this is the most stable part of the road, especially if the road has been widened. The surface can look uniform but apparently the edges are more likely to crack up.

If you aren't terrorized yet by this brinkmanship there is more to come! Dilish, our driver, had it down to a fine art – too fine for me. He frequently seemed to find the road better on the right – maybe it had not been patched so much and so was less bumpy. That would be fine out in the country when nobody was coming, but he kept going even if a big truck is approaching – straight at it. My blood pressure rose as annihilation seemed imminent. The truck made no effort to move from its centre line. But Dilish was skilled at this sort of driving – he always moved left, just in time.

Overtaking is also a form of brinkmanship. It would be suicidal in some countries but the speed seems a little slower in India. Dilish worried me – he changed gear down, correctly, to gain power but when he was alongside the vehicle he was passing, he felt that he had enough speed to make it and changed to a higher gear – the car slowed slightly during the process and the truck was bearing down in the opposite direction. Would we make it? (We survived the trip, so we always did). Only once in three days did we see an oncoming truck have to stop to prevent a suicidal driver succeeding. Fortunately it was not us, although we had reason to breathe several sighs of relief.

Is it brinkmanship, terror or just another way of driving? Eventually my ears were numbed to the hooting. I was impressed by the narrow margins and small spaces which we managed to pass through. I know that I wouldn't have made it driving myself. We didn't see an accident, although we saw a few piled up trucks and bashed in cars which made me realize that, even with their care and tolerance, accidents can happen.

Having survived, I think it was all worth it. There was so much to see and so much of interest to photograph. Jaipur, with its pink Hawa Mahal dominating the main street, the City Palace with its museums – textiles, carpets and armory, the Albert Museum, palaces and temples, make it a popular place for tourists to visit. Outside the city there is the huge Amber Fort and Palace on the mountainside begun in 1592 by Raja Man Singh. Higher up on the top of the ridge is the Jaigarh Fort, some of which was built as early as 1033. It has some huge water storage wells, an armament museum with guns 400 years old, and the monstrous Jaya Vana cannon which fired 50kg shot (only once on trial). It is claimed that it travelled 32km but I doubt it. There is so much to see that it would need a guide book to cover it all.

There were many sites worth seeing in Rajasthan, but the Jain temple at Ranakpur, which is off the beaten track about 100 km from Udiapur, was fantastic. (C45.3) Built in marble between 1450 and 1499 it covers about 4000 square metres and has 1400 pillars which are all uniquely carved. We saw it in the late afternoon when the low sun shone in among the pillars, appearing to make them glow. It is one of the most beautiful buildings I have seen. The man at the gate, with a deeply wrinkled but tranquil face, told us that his family had been guarding the temple for sixteen generations – since it was built. (C45.4)

Not far away was another gem – the Dilwara temples at Mt. Abu, a hill station with a cooler climate rising from the Thar desert. There are five temples built in the 11 and 12th centuries. Two of them are outstandingly beautiful, carved in marble. Another was built by the masons after work out of scraps as their special monument.

When one is travelling one admires nature's beauty and mans' creations, be they buildings, paintings, sculptures or other contents of museums and palaces. Many of the most beautiful buildings are places of worship, such as the above temples and others, the great cathedrals, churches and mosques. Sainte Chapelle in Paris with its tall, predominantly blue and red Gothic stained glass windows, is a gem of beauty. The inside of the domes in Mohamed Ali Mosque in Cairo (C44.2), the recently cleaned cathedral in Amiens (C44.1), the Golden Temple in Amritsar in the Punjab (C45.1) and the temple of the Emerald Buddah in Bangkok, are a few examples of the wonderful and grandly decorated buildings which I have seen. Others include the almost over-decorated baroque Weiskirsche in Bavaria (C44.3) which contrasts with St. Basils Cathedral on Red Square in Moscow (C44.4), which is formed of small chambers and a series of well known onion domes.

Mediterranean and Middle East

I have mentioned parts of Africa elsewhere but there are some amazing features like the 100m high red sand-dunes in the Namib Desert with their sharp edges highlighted by the intense light and shadows. (C35.3) There are mountains and game reserves, but historically Egypt is hard to beat with its pyramids at Giza and Sachara, tombs and temples going back 4000 or more years. It is awesome to stand amongst them in places like the Karnak Temple in Luxor (C33.4) and contemplate their size, antiquity and amazing construction.

Deserts are dry, barren areas but they can have a stark beauty with dunes, hills and a variety of tones and colours, especially in the soft evening light. And occasionally, almost unexpectedly, a plant or maybe even a flower appears. Such was the case in Petra, Jordan, a hot, dry place with magnificent buildings carved out of the rocks (C34.3&4) While walking up the hill in the intense heat of the midday sun, developing a thirst such as I had never had before, I came across a single, little, pink flower growing out between the rocks.

All around the Mediterranean there are antiquities. Among places I have been are Palmyra (C33.1) and Bosra in Syria (C33.2), Baalbek in Lebanon (C45.5), El Jem (C45.5) and Dougga in Tunisia (C45.6), and Jerrash in Jordan (C34.1), all impressive sites.

Cappadocia in Turkey was a destination I longed to visit after seeing photographs taken by friends in 1960. I eventually visited there. It is a volcanic area with rather soft volcanic ash rock and scattered harder rock which has withstood erosion leaving some amazing pillars. The land is eroded creating some wonderful formations with varying rock colours and natural sculptures. Houses and churches have been excavated in the cliffs by troglodite people. (C34.2) There are several underground cities, descending for six levels where the Hittites hid when invaded, as long as 4000 years ago. It is a spectacular region which also has creative crafts such as pottery, carpet making and onyx carving.

Food

I enjoy food – unfortunately, too much – but I am not an epicure! Being entertained frequently while travelling easily leads to dietary indiscretion. Obviously one encounters a great variety of food. I cannot forget my first satay at a Jalan Campbell street stall in Kuala Lumpur in 1973, a Devonshire tea at Cameron Highlands, a remnant of British culture in Malaysia, baby beef in Buenos Aires (huge, very tender steaks), the tea ceremony at a tea house on the Philosophers Walk in Kyoto, a lunch with about a dozen fish dishes in the woods of Finland, tasty scallops at a restaurant over the sea at Tacloban in the Philippines or the fantastic dinners at Fi and Me's in Launceston, Tasmania in the building where the first anaesthetic for surgery was administered in Australia on 7th June 1847. For presentation it is hard to beat the Japanese – an ice cave like a miniature igloo holding cold shrimp (C26.3) or the hot stone laid on salt on which one cooks small pieces of beef, are examples of originality (C26.4). They are also famous for sushi which we watched being prepared. (C26.5) French cuisine is also well known for its presentation, including desserts. (C26.7) I suppose that if I had been a gourmet or epicure I could have written a book on meals I have had!

In many countries there are roadside stalls where the locals buy food. (C26.2) The hazards of these places to foreign travelers hit me once in the middle of a lecture in Santiago. Fortunately I had just started a video and was able to escape for a few minutes. We had eaten empanadas on the way to the Chilean mountains.

Sometimes meals are memorable because of the setting where they are taken – over the sea at Miraflores in Lima, Peru or beside the sea with breaking waves crashing below at Vina del Mar in Chile or looking out over the mountains at Simla in northern India at the hotel where Oberoi, who eventually owned a great chain of hotels, began his career. At a tea house near Yokohama in Japan I took an exquisite photograph of a rippling rock pool with reflections, not only of the surrounding garden but also of the Venetian blinds and their shadows reflected in the window. (C26.6)

Friends and people

Meeting friends and interesting people is one of the most enjoyable aspects of travel, especially as one grows older. Friends make such a difference, as they usually show you around and often take you to places not usually seen on the usual tourist trips. For example, I have seen an enormous crystal in a cavern in a mine in South America (C35.4), the magnificent hall of the Uruguayan Parliament building, old privately owned homesteads, the funnel-shaped anatomy lecture theatre, and Galileo's lecture stand in Padua in Italy, private art collections not normally open to the public and many other fascinating places. I have been exceptionally privileged to see so many of these things.

27.7. Dr. George Ellis in retirement.

I have mentioned several interesting people that I have met on my travels but one of the most unusual was George Ellis, an anaesthetist, who I met in Brunei.

He was the character on whom Grimsdyke in Richard Gordon's *Doctor in the House* was based. In the book he remained a student for years because he had a grant from a wealthy aunt for as long as he was a student. In fact he came from a well off family and his mother was so pleased when he passed his 1st MB examinations that she paid for him to go on a trip to the continent. He was a student at St. Bartholomew's Hospital in London. He took a liking to the continent and subsequently made many trips there. His progress as a student was slow. He eventually graduated after twelve years having received a telegram while in Greece warning him that he would be thrown out of medical school, if he did not turn up for his examinations. This was unheard of in those days. To many people's surprise he passed. There was a job in anaesthetics which one of the other students wanted, but he failed and so George took up anaesthetics. He had a distinguished career, which included organizing the 4th World Congress of Anaesthesia in London in 1968. When he retired he took a locum in Brunei for six months. He enjoyed it, so he took a 2 year contract. When he applied for his third 2 year contract he was given a 10 year contract – another unique situation. It is unusual to continue practising after 70.

Being well off he could entertain in a grand style. After World War II many Americans came to London and visited Barts, the oldest Hospital in London. If they ran short of money he would lend them some to be repaid in USA. He did this because the British could only take £25 out of the country when they travelled – not enough to do much. When he eventually went to USA the person who looked after his finances there asked if he wanted some money. He suggested $2000. "Was that all?" was the reply. His accumulated money invested was far more.

He drove a Porsche and on the one 70 km road with a lane each way he reached high speeds – over 140kph on at least five occasions. His colleagues were nervous about me travelling with him at 78 years of age. I felt quite safe. He then told me that he liked to drive fast cars fast and so had a grand prix driver teach him how to do it.

When I first met him he told me that we would have dinner together that night and the next night he would have a party where everyone else could meet me. We spent the evening exchanging these and many other stories. He retired from anaesthesia and driving when he turned eighty and moved to Auckland. I last saw him there two years before he died. An unusual, generous and very entertaining man.

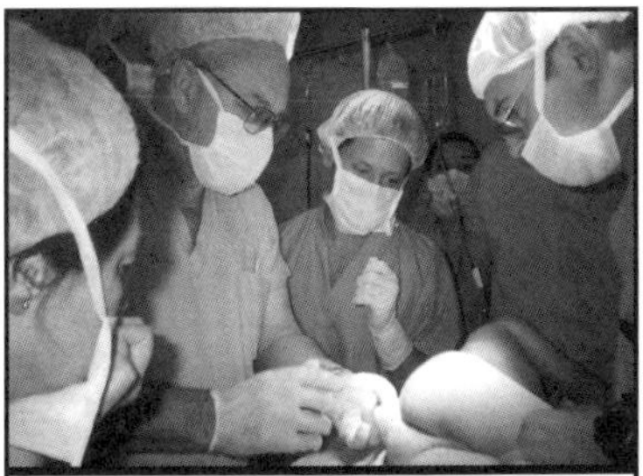

27.8. Teaching regional anaesthesia in Notti Childrens Hospital, Mendoza, Argentina.

I have been very fortunate to combine my pleasure with working and lecturing. In some places I have been able to show anaesthetists practical techniques in the operating theatre, such as how to do nerve blocks or hold a face mask or put a tube in the trachea during anaesthesia. I have had the good fortune to visit Notti Childrens Hospital in Mendoza, Argentina three times. It is easier when one has been before because the people know what you can teach and friendships are developed.

I have only mentioned a sample of the places I have visited in this and other chapters. Travel has certainly provided many scenes for my painting and photography, as well as a fund of knowledge and many happy, interesting and occasionally unexpected experiences. And I have made many friends all over the world.

CHAPTER 28

HOBBIES – REFLECTIONS ON PHOTOGRAPHY AND PAINTING

A balanced life should allow time for the family, activities outside work and the basic requirements of the home. Hobbies, which I was encouraged to have from an early age, provide some of these additional interests. I became a collector of stamps, coins, match box tops, cards from cigarette packets, butterflies and I even had a museum of my own when I was a child. Later, photography and painting became my main interests. I enjoy gardening when I don't have anything more pressing to do.

Stamp collecting was very popular when I was a child. We didn't have so many toys or television as distractions so there was more time for hobbies. It was a great way to learn geography and about other countries. Some people collected sets of stamps of animals, birds, fish, people and various other topics which were enlightening about the places. I also learnt history from them as countries came and went, became amalgamated or changed their names. During my years as Chairman of the WFSA Education Committee, just before fax and email came into common use, I received letters from sixty five countries. I made an exhibit of them in the form of a world map for display at the World Congress of Anaesthesia in Sydney in 1996. Stamp collecting is still interesting, but I think it is a declining hobby as postage is used less and less.

Collecting can result in the accumulation of all sorts of items, some of which eventually become classified as junk! But other items remain interesting and sometimes become valuable.

Photography has been long been an interest in our family. My grandmother was a photographer back in the 1890s and even took such complex subjects as church interiors. Unfortunately, we did not inherit any of her photographs. She passed on her interest to my father, who built his own quarter plate camera with a telephoto lens. He took a magnificent photograph of Mt Kenya, 50km away, from our front verandah.

28.1. Telephoto of Mt Kenya from our house taken with my father's camera.

I remember helping him make contact prints before we had electricity. He used a magnesium flare which gave a short intense flash of light to expose the negative on to the paper.

My brother was also interested in photography and gave me a Baby Brownie Box camera when I was sixteen. It cost 16 shillings – not even one pound! The Brownie cameras were cheap ones produced by Kodak. They took quite good photographs but the lenses were not perfect and sometimes produced slight distortion at the edges. I took this camera to Rhodesia (now Zimbabwe) when I was doing my national service training and photographed that country, and Nyasaland (Malawi) during an Easter weekend visit. Several years later I entered one called "Zambezi refections" in the Canadian Physicians Art Salon, where it was selected as one of 24 pictures for inclusion in the calendar composed of the best entries in the exhibition. (6.7) It is the example that I use to illustrate the point that a good picture is in the eye of the photographer, not in the particular camera that he is using. I find it most irritating when someone sees a good photograph of mine to be asked what sort of camera I used or told "You must have a good camera" as if the camera selected and composed the picture or picked the subject. Of course one needs a good quality camera if one is going to get fine detail clearly in a picture.

I had many pleasant evenings in the darkroom developing photographs during my time in the barracks in Salisbury (now Harare). When I was at university I bought an enlarger with money given to me for my 21st birthday. This enabled me to continue my printing and enlarging, but eventually I no longer had time to do it.

The most challenging photograph that I ever took was the one of my grandmother in Strathpeffer sitting beside the open fire in her kitchen reading the paper with her little dog, Jip, sitting at her feet. It was remarkable not only for the scene but because it was taken on a long exposure with the camera on the table – everything remained perfectly still. The only lighting was the bulb in the ceiling and a window behind me. (11.1)

I took my first colour slides in 1957, when I went with my friend Duncan Forrester to the Outer Hebrides. As I was on a tight budget there was no wastage and some great photographs were obtained – the cliffs of Mingulay with puffins on them, the sandy beach by the ruined village and detail of the things growing in a rock pool. By then I had a Retina Contina 35 mm camera. Some were enlarged and printed in colour 30 years later! (C6&7) Some of my black and white photographs of the trip were used to illustrate an article Duncan wrote about the islands for the Scots magazine.

Time gradually became less available for processing and printing my own black and white films. My son, Fraser, inherited the interest.

Colour slides took over – I have collected thousands from all over the world. Some of these now make a historic record going back for 45 years. Many of my favorite photographs have been printed and enlarged. The quality of prints made from some of these slides 30 to 40 years later has been amazing. There are subjects that are probably not seen any more like Eskimos with tattoos (C48.1) and wearing their sealskin clothes. (C16.2) Many of them are included in this book. My photographs fall into two main categories – records of my travels and experiences and, secondly, my more artistic selection. There are so many things that many people do not even notice which make wonderful pictures.

Some of my trips lent themselves to photography and others to painting. When there are good subjects for both, life can be very busy but very satisfying!

While travel gives one excellent material for interesting photographs, it is how the picture is composed, lit, what angle they are taken from, as well as the topic, which provides interest. My artistic photographs are often of subjects which are around us, but we don't notice or appreciate their potential for a beautiful or dramatic picture. Examples are an old weathered fence post near Broken Hill with several pieces of wire attached (C42.1), or a close up of the minute vegetation in the far north of Canada (C14.2).

My mother taught me to draw. During my early secondary schooling we had art lessons from a very good artist, R McClellan Sim, who painted murals in Nakuru station and designed some of Kenya's stamps. I remember being bored by applying water colour washes and I did not take the lessons very seriously – I usually had C marks. I remember him telling us about having to draw a chair and all the shadows – it sounded very complex but he obviously did it well. That is about all I remember of my art classes. My results certainly did not encourage me to become an artist. I have two or three watercolours painted before 1958 but otherwise I seemed to have made no effort in art until I arrived in Canada.

Victoria Hospital, where I interned, was decorated for Christmas by painting the windows. Someone drew a simple outline and asked me to fill in the colours. I decided that I could do better myself so found a window for myself and painted Santa Claus coming by canoe to a tropical island with palm trees, a sandy beach and blue sea and skies. It was out of context in Canada but reminded me of Africa. I decided then that maybe I could paint. I had used poster paints and they seemed easier to manage than watercolours.

Some time later I bought a set of a dozen small tubes of oil paint. At first my efforts were a bit like paint by numbers as I was not mixing the colours much. Then I found a book on mixing colours and decided that I would paint with only four tubes of paint – the primary colours, red, yellow and blue and also white. I painted with these for two or three years by which time I was thoroughly familiar with the range that could be achieved by mixing the primary colours. I then increased the range of my palette. The great advantage of mixing was that the resulting colours were never exactly the same and thus gave paintings a more realistic appearance.

I did not have formal lessons but gradually learnt tips from artist friends and by looking at paintings in galleries around the world. From one, Frank Emery, I learnt to achieve depth in landscape by painting the distance in paler colours than the foreground. This is most apparent when one is in the mountains and sees range after range fading gradually into the distance as in the Victorian Alps and Snowy mountains of eastern Australia.

I knew that perspective was achieved by convergence of lines as they go away from one. This is a means of making a picture on to a flat surface and giving it a three dimensional feel. While visiting the museum in Taipei, Kenjiro Mori, an anaesthetist friend from Kyoto showed me how the old Chinese paintings used the opposite technique – the lines diverged as they went away. Although it seems strange, this did not look as unusual as I expected. What they seem to have done was to take a three-dimensional view and compress it on to a two-dimensional surface.

My nephew, Ken, is an artist. He taught me how to use blue to create shadows and how to use a fine red line to highlight the joins between buildings and the ground. I found difficulty with greens – there is so much variation and so many shadows in trees and bushes. Greens differ in different countries. In Europe they are much lighter, especially in spring, while in Australia gum trees (eucalyptus) sometimes have some red and often a touch of burnt umber gives them a natural appearance. Terry Dalley (C39.1), my artist friend from schooldays, who has taught at Wimbledon Art College in London most of his life, showed me on a painting trip beside the Thames how he used indigo to enrich the shadows. I have since found this rather intense colour does enrich some paintings considerably. It is also very useful in watercolour painting in the Antarctic where varying shades depict the cold seas and austere mountains well. Donald Cameron, a local artist, suggested adding a little alizarin red to darken the greens and that works too. He also inspired me to use of varying yellows and ochre to produce the gold effect in temples, such as the Golden Temple in Amritsar which is a magnificent, rich subject to paint.

My friend with whom I have done most painting in the country is Rod Read from Beaufort. We visited them on our way home from Hattah Lakes in Northern Victoria where I had been painting. When I showed him my efforts he told me that he had all the gear and asked me to show him how to do it. We went down the paddock and before we finished it was apparent that he had more talent than I had. He then organised a group of his farming friends to have lessons from the, then, young teacher in Beaufort, Sue Jarvis. Rod developed a great style with lots of bright colour,

28.2. Rod Read and the author showing their paintings.

particularly orange. It is certainly a useful colour when painting pictures of central Australia. Twenty-five years later they invited Sue back to Beaufort to run a weekend workshop, which I was invited to attend. Sue taught me some of the fundamentals of portrait painting, something I find difficult. She then painted my portrait as her entry to the Portia Geech Prize – the top portrait prize for women painters in Australia. It did not win but was one of 43 selected from 250 to be hung. It was an interesting painting using the anaesthetic machine and equipment with which I work to frame me. (C39.5) Her greatest work has been a painting of multiculturalism in the city of Dandenong near Melbourne, for the millenium. It includes 146 portraits, each person from a different country.

I have had wonderful opportunities to visit art galleries all over the world. They have been my classroom. Apart from the general enjoyment and appreciation of the picture, one can learn much by careful observation of a painting, such as how the artist produced certain effects, choice of colours, painting technique etc. Visiting exhibitions with a trained artist like my old friend, Terry Dalley can enhance the experience. He showed me how Turner achieved white patches in his watercolours either by scratching back to the white paper with his fingernail or putting some material on the paper to prevent the paint touching the spot. John Constable and Turner have been credited with brightening up painting and giving it a luminosity. When one looks closely at some of Constable's work, such as the *Haywain*, the *Cornfield* or *Dedham Lock*, two versions of which I have seen (one, his Royal Academy entry, and the other one in Melbourne) one can see that he used little spots of white paint to give them a sparkle. It makes the leaves catch the light or the running water look like it is moving.

I had the opportunity once, when I was in Stockholm, to see an exhibition of Turner's water-colours arranged in chronological sequence. It was a very enlightening experience. One could see the evolution from a master draftsman artist to more impressionist pictures with form to bright paintings which were mainly a display of colour, for which he became famous. *The fighting Temeraire*, in the National Gallery in London, still shows the ships in battle but introduces the bright, grand colours. *Vale d 'Aosta* in the National Gallery of Victoria in Melbourne is a stage further when form has been replaced by colour. Many people only see a blaze of colour but I see orange – brown in the left foreground like autumnal bracken on the hillside with white clouds swirling around the valley and mountains. A few blue stokes gives the impression of the valley bottom through the clouds and the hint of the mountains is gained from a few thick white brush strokes sloping down like a glimpse of the snow topped mountains peeking through. I think it is a wonderful painting.

Another example of developing from an accurate, detailed painter towards producing an impression of the same subject and gaining a similar effect when looked at from a distance, is the work of Frans Hals, the famous Dutch portrait painter whom I consider one of the best. His *Laughing Cavalier* in the Wallace Collection in London has the frill the subject is wearing around his neck done in intricate detail. A similar painting of the *Merry Toper*, done later, shows the same item with very little detail but at a distance they look similar. Many painters have gone through this evolution but others, like Vermeer, did not. There are only about 35 of his paintings remaining – did he only do a few in great detail or have many disappeared? His work showed great attention to detail, planning and positioning. I was privileged to see an exhibition of twenty three of his paintings in the Hague in 1996. One thing that struck me about them was that these famous paintings were not large.

Painters often do copies or small preliminary paintings for large ones. I saw an exhibition in Brussels about the workshop of Jan Breughal the younger, which showed how he and his workshop copied his father's famous paintings. He was only four when his father died. Some of the paintings were copied many times, up to seventy in one case. The exhibition showed several copies of a number of the paintings, comparing small differences in detail.

The Impressionists, so unpopular initially in Paris, added wonderful colour to painting. To see their work, particularly Monet's large paintings in New York and Washington, in Paris and in special exhibitons is always a pleasure but one of my favorites is a scene at *Veutreuil* which is in the National Gallery of Victoria in Melbourne. It is not one of his big ones but the pink, red and yellow reflections of the village on the river are exhilarating to see. I have even tried to use this interesting technique on occasion.

I visited the Gauguin museum in Tahiti, expecting to see a few of his works. No such luck. Anything of note has gone elsewhere. Then, as I sat on the beach I saw a lovely scene with fishing nets which I photographed.

28.3. Fishing nets hanging on trees near Gaugin Museum in Tahiti.

I am attracted to paintings of poor people. The *Prodigal Son* by Lionelli Speda in the Louvre is one of my favorites. It shows exquisitely the boy with ragged clothes being welcomed by his father. One of my favorite pictures is *the Soup Kitchen* in the Museo del Belles Artes in Buenos Aires. It is a large masterpiece which I have returned to see each time I have been to Buenos Aires – several figures in a large kitchen with pots on the stove. This gallery is one of the two best I have seen in South America. It has a wonderful collection, not huge but good quality. It includes paintings by the famous Spanish artists, such as El Greco, Ribera, Velasquez, Zubaran, Goya, and others. It is certainly worth a visit. Ribera is one of my favorite portrait painters. Some of his portraits are in El Escorial outside Madrid. That is another treasure trove of art which also has some magnificent El Greco paintings.

The National Gallery of Victoria in Melbourne has a good European collection with many of the well known painters represented, although in small numbers – Constable, Turner, Tiepolo, Rembrandt, Murillo, Monet, van Dyke, Gainsborough and many others. The Tiopolo was bought from the Hermitage during hard times. It is a huge picture of *Cleopatra's feast*. One feature which always fascinates viewers, when it is pointed out, is how the tiles on the floor follow one around as one walks across in front of it. It is created by a geometric trick in the design of the angles. A smaller preliminary version is in the Museum in Stockholm. Another test of observation is a painting which seems to have the wrong foot in an impossible position. I have mentioned the Monet and Turner paintings but there are many, many more treasures, including Goya cartoons.

The Australian paintings are now housed in the spectacular new Australian Art Gallery in Federation Square. It is an unusual building with many awkward angles and projections, but it provides excellent viewing space for the paintings.

The major picture in the Australian collection is a three panel painting called the *Pioneers* by Fred McCubbin. The first panel shows a man and his wife arriving in the bush and setting up a home. The second has the mother with the baby in her arms with their little house behind while the third shows the man kneeling over his wife's grave with the beginnings of Melbourne peeping through the trees. It includes the then newly built dome of the Exhibition Building. The story is that McCubbin was looking for a man to model in the painting when he saw a man walking down Collins Street in Melbourne who had the features he wanted. He went up to him and said "You are the man". The man was somewhat surprised at this strange and unexpected approach but when McCubbin explained himself better the man agreed to sit for him. McCubbin also painted rather sad pictures of lost children which I presume was part of his grieving for the loss of his daughter, Margaret, when she was 4 years old. She fell on the pavement and fractured her skull.

There are many other fine Australian paintings by immigrants such as Louis Buvelot, Eugene von Guerrard and John Glover, who was a well known British painter before he came to Australia, aged 63. The Heidelberg school in Australia, including painters such as Tom Roberts and Arthur Streeton, were a group of painters who painted in the open countryside, stimulated probably by the same forces that inspired the Impressionists to create their colourful paintings, and Tom Thompson and the Group of Seven in Canada about the same time.

There are two other items which I enjoy showing visitors to the National Gallery ofVictoria in Melbourne, especially if they only want to see a few things. One is the magnificent stained glass ceiling in the Great Hall done by Leonard French in his bright glass style. It is huge, maybe the largest stained glass piece made in the 20th century. (C38.3) He also has windows in the National Library in Canberra and a magnificent memorial window to the bush fires which wiped out much of the town of Macedon, about an hours drive north west of Melbourne. It is in the Anglican church. The other item of interest is a minute sculpture of a stag standing on a pedestal under a canopy. The pedestal has a human face carved on it. It is about 3cm high and was done by an unknown prisoner in Pentridge prison.

One of the most intriguing art visits I have made was to Gallen Kallenen's studio in Helsinki. He has been the most outstanding Finnish artist who did some stupendous works. I was walking round his studio and suddenly the scene in the painting before me was very, very familiar – it was Mt Kenya done from about 20km. from where I grew up. I found out that he had spent a year there in 1909 which was in the very early years of European settlement. There were only a handful of whites in Nyeri district then. On my next visit to Helsinki I was taken there again because at that time there was a special exhibition of all his Kenya paintings. What a thrill for me. His paintings stand out in their national collection in the Ateneum

Paintings are to be found all over the world. Out at Svolvaer in the Lofoten islands, off the west coast of Norway, there just happened to be a special exhibition of paintings by Gunnar Berg when we visited, celebrating the centenary of his birth. They were mainly seascapes and portraits but the strong colour and bold rendering made them unforgettable. He died when he was only thirty but he had already produced some magnificent paintings. The main collection of his work is in Tromso.

Tuberculosis was rampant in the nineteenth century and a number of painters died when only thirty or so. Paul Peel, a Canadian working in Paris, did some sensitive paintings, which hang in the Toronto Art gallery. One is of a mother sitting beside her baby in the cot with a cat beside her and the other was two nude children standing warming themselves in front of an open fire. I was intrigued to find a print of the latter in a house in the Folk Museum in Moe, a town in Gippsland, east of Melbourne.

Canada had its equivalent of Australia's Heidelberg school. They were referred to as the Group of Seven. Tom Thomson (1877-1917), a brilliant colourist, painted with them but drowned during a trip to his favorite Algonquin Park, before they formed the group in 1920. The group exhibited until 1932. It consisted of A.Y.Jackson (1882-1974) who even painted in Yellowknife, the North West Territories and Yukon and is said to have travelled Canada more extensively than anyone else; J.E.H.Macdonald (1873-1932); Lauren Harris (1885-1970) who later developed a distinctive linear style; Arthur Lismer (1885-1969); Frank Varley (1881-1969); F. Carmichael (1890-1945) and Frank Johnston (1888-1949), who was replaced in 1926 by a younger man, A.J.Casson. It is notable how long some of these men lived. Others followed and even current painters such as Bruno Cote in Quebec produce similar bold, rich paintings that appeal greatly to me. They usually painted small boards out in the countryside and then painted larger ones at home. The McMichael collection at Kleinberg, 45km out of Toronto, is the amazing home to many of their standard (about 12x10") outdoor paintings. It is a meandering series of buildings joined at angles so that at the ends of each there are large windows looking out on to the bush through panoramic windows. The scenes change with the seasons but resemble many of the paintings. Conceptually, it is an amazing gallery. Their larger paintings are to be seen in Ottawa and Toronto Galleries. In addition there is an excellent collection of their work and that of other Canadian artists in the Thompson collection which has been housed on the eighth floor of the Hudson Bay building in Toronto. They form another stunning collection.

One of my favorite galleries, which has a collection with paintings by most of the most well known European and British painters presented in beautiful rooms, is the Scottish National Gallery in Edinburgh.. Its other advantage is that one can view it in an hour or two, something that is impossible in the great galleries like the Louvre or the Prado in Madrid. The latter took me three hours to do a quick walk around to gain a feel of what was there followed by another visit to see some things in more detail. Obviously it has a great Spanish collection. One, *Las Meninas*, can be viewed in a mirror as that is how it was painted. It has about six layers of people and dogs and the painter, Velaquez is standing in the middle ground. About twenty years ago the

Illustrated London News ran a survey with thirty leading art critics and gallery directors, in which they were asked to select their ten favorite paintings. *Las Meninas* received fourteen votes; the next most popular, Vermeer's *view of Delft*, received eight. So while *Mona Lisa* is often quoted as the most famous painting with its incredible smile it did not rate highly in this survey. I personally think it is beautiful but overated.

One occasionally has an unexpected surprise. Such was the case in finding the Ohara Gallery in an old Japanese town in the middle of Kurushiki, near Okayama. This was established by a wealthy cotton manufacturer, Ohara, who had a painter friend working in Europe when the Impressionists and people like Picasso were active. He was commissioned to buy the paintings so one finds this amazing collection with two large Rodin sculptures beside the entrance and paintings such as a Monet "water lilies" inside. It probably has the best European collection in Japan.

Galleries devoted to individual artists are really interesting as one can follow the evolution of their painting. Examples are van Gogh in Amsterdam, Picasso in Paris, Munch in Oslo. His painting did not appeal much to me. The Rubens collection of twenty-one huge paintings of "the life of Marie de Medici" in the Louvre in Paris and Tinteretto's enormous paintings in Scuola Grande di San Rocco in Venice, 56 in all, are amazing in the magnitude of the work. There were many enormous works produced. Among the most famous that I have had the privilege of seeing are Michaelangelo's painting in the Sistine Chapel in the Vatican, which took four years to execute, and Giotto's [1305-6] decoration of Capella Arena in Padua. After I visited the latter with my daughter, Catherine, we sat outside and I did a painting of the chapel as a reminder of the occasion.

In 1981 I went with one of my sons to a school weekend camp in the country. I found a paint box and pad for watercolours and thought that I would take them and try watercolour painting again. To my amazement I did three paintings in 15 to 20 minutes each. They were just quick sketches but caught the scene. I had made an important discovery – I could do watercolours and furthermore I could obtain a good representation in a short time and the equipment was not much to carry. I have never traveled without them since and have accumulated a collection of pictures from all over the world. I have even painted under an umbrella in the soft Irish rain. I have also had the water on my box freeze in the Antarctic, bringing my painting to a halt! While I stood in dismay at my plight I witnessed an aggressive skua attack and take a baby penguin from its mother. I thought that was the end of the affair but the penguin struck back and rescued the fluffy ball that was its chick. Skuas are constantly on the lookout for sickly or weak birds. The penguins reduce their risk by breaking skua eggs before they hatch, thereby keeping their predators' numbers down.

Watercolours are different from oils – one has to work from light to gradually darken the colour with additional paint while with oils, strong colours can be laid down first and the lighter ones applied later. I find watercolours easier to create atmosphere in mountain landscapes and skies. They were wonderful to produce the delicate hues of the Antarctic with its soft light.

Gouache is another medium which some people use, particularly the white, to enhance the picture or for lines. Paul Sandby, who was one of England's early leading water-colourists around 1800 used it to put in rods and lines in fishing scenes. He painted around Windsor and so the major collection of his work is in the Queen's collection. There are several in Nottingham but, interestingly, a major collection of his work was found in the attic of a farmhouse in the Western District of Victoria, Australia. It was purchased and is now housed in a special room in the Hamilton Art Gallery in western Victoria. This is one of the very good small galleries found in country Victoria, others being in Ballarat, Bendigo, Benalla and Mildura.

I have also used acrylics but they tend to dry quickly, especially on hot days, so one has to work very quickly. I took them to the Antarctic instead of oils as the latter would have been difficult to carry, especially with turpentine being flammable. I thought acrylics would be good because it is cold. I did not realize that it was a very dry cold so that they dried very quickly in that climate. So again, I had to work quickly – 20 minutes. One day I went on deck to paint Mt. Terror as we returned from cruising along the Ross Ice Shelf. I had forgotten my brushes but had a palette knife. I completed the painting in less than twenty minutes because acrylic paints dry very quickly in the cold dry Antarctic atmosphere. (C39.6)

Painting can be a great foil for the stresses of routine work, especially when one has had as busy a life as I had. An hour or two painting can be completely absorbing and free one's mind of all other troubles. I have recommended it as a hobby to many colleagues and those who have taken it up have found the same relaxation in it.

28.4. Cape Valentine, Elephant Island, Antarctica.

I have painted in water colours, oils and acrylics as well as sketching especially when travelling. When we were sailing by I sketched the length of Elephant Island, where Shackleton left most of his men when he went to South Georgia for help, on seven sequential pages. The last part shows the island disappearing into fog.

I have used some of these and watercolours done while travelling, supplemented by photographs to construct composite collage paintings of some trips such as my climb of Mt Kilimanjaro, (C3.1) travelling in northern Chile (C32.3) or my trip to the Nahanni Valley in Canada. These incorporate various views in such a way that one can travel through the picture as if on the journey.

I sometimes paint other subjects, such as flowers, which are challenging, combining realism with impression. I have painted *Reflections on a London canal* (C40.2) which is realistic but received commendation in a show as abstract art!

I acquired a movie camera while I was in Yellowknife which I used mainly to film birds. It was an important nesting area for many birds, such as loons, grebes and ducks. I read that birds cannot count and that if two people go into a hide and one leaves the bird thinks it is all clear. The person remaining can then film. I had great pleasure doing this with a red throated grebe. (C15.5) Memories of times like that are ones to cherish.

Unfortunately I found movies and still photography together became rather expensive so the movie work had to be put aside, especially when I returned to low-paid training jobs. I was able to revive my interest when I became established at the Royal Childrens

Hospital. I made several teaching films there. The first was filmed by a wonderful photographer called Joe Szpanski who had emigrated from Poland. He was meticulous but sometimes a little slow. Filming medical teaching films which show clinical activity requires a clear idea of what has to be taken and the ability to take the shots immediately when asked. Where appropriate, a little humour keeps the audience attentive. I like to make them practical showing exactly how to perform techniques.

My fourth film, "*Lives can be saved*", was on the Laerdal resuscitation bag – a dry subject one could say. I thought it would be more relevant if it was shown in use in real situations before describing it in detail. It opens with a little girl walking into a swimming pool area where the protective gate has been wedged open. She sits down by the pool, takes off her shoes and then there is a splash! The next shot shows her being resuscitated. This is followed by someone leaving another pool and carefully closing the gate. Then my son, Ken, who was nine at the time and used to playing war games in the street where the children often fell dead, rode his bicycle down the sidewalk. My daughter, Catherine, backed our Kombi out of the drive and stopped. Ken was about twenty centimetres away from it when he fell off his bike on to the grass verge as if he had been hit. It was the first take. Suddenly our Director of Intensive Care, Alan Duncan, appeared in his big red Mercedes. He stopped and produced his Laerdal resuscitator from the boot. The film goes on with demonstrations on resuscitation, taking the equipment to pieces, sterilizing it and concludes with another action situation. I was jogging round the park and collapsed. Two people (son and daughter) passing by came to help. One went to the road and waved down a car for help – the big red Mercedes again! As the commentator says "the outlook is bad if resuscitation is not started early", the camera is zooming in on the tombstones in the cemetery next door! Much of the film was taken outdoors with trees and gardens around so I selected the bird songs recorded at 5 am in November, when this is a cacophony of beautiful sound, to provide appropriate background music. I contributed more to the production of this film than any other as I wrote the script, directed the filming and did all the cutting and splicing – a slow tedious job compared to the ease with which videos can now be made with computer editing. That was my last film before going into video production of my teaching material.

The clarity of 16mm film was much better than video, but they are heavy to carry and are being used less and less. Video suffers from the vagaries of the player. Imagine my dismay when showing a new video for the first time overseas – its Premiere – when it came out in black and white only showing 2/3 of the picture and the sound failed as well. It was even more frustrating when the following video played normally. Colour is often distorted. On one occasion *Lives can be saved* was so off colour and had a grey hue that someone asked me afterwards where I got the cadaver to use in the film. It was my living son!

Sculpture is another art form. I did not realise how much we can derive from our sense of touch until I visited an exhibition of small Henry Moore pieces where one could put gloves on and feel them. Suddenly sculpture had a new dimension. One can feel things that may not be noticed when looking.

There are some amazing collections of an individual sculptor's work in several places – Rodin in Paris, Carl Milles in Stockhlom and probably the greatest being Vigeland's work in Frogner Park, Oslo. It covers a huge area with 192 statues culminating in the intricately carved 17 metre high Wheel of Life. All these are worth seeing if one has the chance. For a surprise, the Art Gallery of Sao Paulo in Brazil is another – it has a large collection of about 70 of Degas' ballet dancer sculptures as well as some excellent paintings, including about ten Renoirs.

One of my favorite sculptures is in the sculpture house in the Ballarat Gardens, 120 km west of Melbourne. It has several, but one in particular, called Modesty, is of a girl shrouded in a veil. The amazing thing is that one can see her face and other features through the veil and yet it is made of marble. (C38.5)

I enjoy flowers and have photographed and even painted some – hydrangeas, delphiniums, irises and others. I enjoy gardening when I do not have other more pressing things to do. I can understand how keen gardeners do not become depressed because they work with growing plants which are colourful and often beautiful. My old Maths teacher, Jim Duff, gave me some orchids years ago and they grew in profusion. Monstera deliciosa with its huge split leaves is interesting because it produces a fruit which is edible. It grows well in our garden (C42.2).

Creative activities have given me great pleasure. Photography and painting have made my travels more worthwhile as well as providing me with wonderful memories. The pictures are my diaries. Hobbies are a diversion from work, a form of relaxation which can be rejuvenating. They can provide important occupation in retirement when one has more time.

Chapter 29

Concluding Comments

I have told many tales which were about events that interested me and often involved me. They have been the stories I have told people in conversation. It is amazing how many interconnections there are. For example the 1919 influenza epidemic and effects it had in India and Labrador, Baden Powell's friendship with Nansen and our family and how I was able to help Monty with finding information for his books, in Italy and Australia. There are many coincidences in life if one takes an interest in people and leads conversations in the right direction or provides a key clue, often by chance. My father also had the gift of finding connections through his interest in the people he met.

My full time work finished at the end of 2000. I passed on my final administrative responsibility, being Director of Anaesthesia, three months earlier to Dr Rob Eyres. It was the conclusion of 26 years in the position. He asked me to stay on in some part time capacity so that I could continue teaching. I appreciated this as it would have been hard to suddenly give up all my work. In addition, I had become President of the World Federation of Societies of Anaesthesiologists so I wanted to retain a clinical involvement while I was doing this. I accepted to work on three consecutive days each fortnight and to run tutorials about once per month. I still enjoy the thrill of seeing someone learn something useful that they did not know or fully understand, whether he/she is a student or a trainee anaesthetist. I was glad of extra time to devote to my presidential role which also included travel. I visited thirty societies during my term, to teach and lecture at their congresses.

Retirement brings new challenges. Advancing years is associated with reduced physical capacity for work. The rate that this happens varies and some people continue very actively for many years. For those who have no outside interests, hobbies, garden or sporting activity, life can be rather dull and often such people fade away rapidly. I have plenty of interests such as painting, writing, photography, gardening and tennis. Keen sportsmen often become depressed when they cannot play. Keen gardeners, on the other hand, rarely become depressed. I had an old uncle who lived to 23 days short of a century who regressed mentally when his wife died and he had to leave his beloved garden. Later, when he moved to an old folks home with a large garden where he could work, his mental acuity improved considerably and remained so until the end of his life – an interesting observation.

Healthy children and a happy family is something I am very grateful to have had. One of the pleasures of retirement is having more time to watch grandchildren growing. They differ in their progress but each week new words and skills develop. It is fun to be able to do more and more with them as they grow older.

I appreciate that I have had a nice home and lived in relatively stable and peaceful countries, something millions of the world's people never experience. So many have suffered, and sometimes lost everything, in floods, drought, fire, earthquakes and other natural disasters, and worse, man led conflict, suppression, ethnic cleansing and extermination. Probably the worst event, which I have mentioned twice in this book, was the 1919 influenza pandemic which killed over twenty million people and left many shattered families, in only a few months. How can one help? I have tried to help by training and teaching their anaesthetists, so that their patients receive better medical care. I have trained people from many countries and visited many to lecture and teach. This has given me great pleasure and satisfaction although in the overall scheme of things it is a miniscule contribution. The consolation is that every little bit helps.

Leprosy was a disease that for centuries led the sufferers to be ostracized and cast out of their homes. At Tumutumu hospital, which my father ran for thirty years, we had a colony of twenty lepers. My first direct association with medicine, which therefore became significant in my later life, was going with my mother to supervise their treatment and check their haemoglobin levels, when the first effective anti-leprosy drugs became available about 1949. Dapsone and Solapsone changed the lives of these people. The disease could be cured but the structural damage could not be reversed. One patient was blind and another had lost almost all his fingers. Some were hideously deformed with skin nodules. Some had less serious skin manifestations of the disease. There were twenty patients in the leper colony which occupied about half an acre, much of it a vegetable garden which they cultivated so that they could grow some of their own food.

There is a Biblical story (Luke 17) about the ten lepers who came to Jesus asking to be cured. After he had given them instructions they left and presumably recovered, but only one came back to thank Him. How often in life things are taken for granted and yet the benefits of showing appreciation are unbounded. Once I was asked by an earnest young anaesthetist, "If you were to give me one piece of advice, what would it be?" I was taken aback by the question and did not know what to say, but after some thought I said, "Don't forget to thank those who help you, no matter what their station in life is." People work and function better when appreciation of their efforts is expressed.

Who or what motivated me. Obviously my father engendered an interest in medicine and passed on some of his interests. My mother imparted to me an appreciation of nature – animals, birds, and flowers. She instilled the importance of careful observation. She taught me until I went to school aged nine and then continued to encourage me to study my weaker subjects during the holidays. I always felt I was a plodder at university but I must have shown some enthusiasm and had an enquiring mind. Why else would my professor of Anatomy, after I had failed my term exam yet again, call me in to his office and tell me that he thought I had been working too hard and that I should go fishing in the Highlands! It was an amazing comment.

Probably the most useful comment I heard in a lecture as a student was not to believe all that books (and I mumbled "and professors") say. My neighbours laughed. Professor Tulloch asked what the joke was ? He agreed emphatically when he heard what I had said. We should assess information to see if it sounds logical before accepting it.

Duncan Forrester introduced me to grouse beating and exploring the Highlands and islands of Scotland which gave me immense enjoyment. He stimulated an interest in bird watching, enhanced later by Sandy Middleton, and although I never really became a serious ornithologist, I had many enjoyable times observing birds in various parts of the world.

I had many good teachers during my training but Al Cox, with whom I learnt much about research, also inspired my interest in teaching. It was in this area that I was able to help establish teaching programmes and train people. To inspire people to do the same gave me great satisfaction. My teaching also resulted in travel. Nearly all my trips overseas were associated with teaching or lecturing.

I have also been lucky to have many wonderful colleagues with whom to work and do research. The story of these people and my medical work is detailed in my other, medical memoirs – *Catalyst*

(Brolga Publishing). It tells about my life, mainly as an anaesthetist, at the Royal Childrens Hospital in Melbourne, the interesting medical developments with which I was involved and all the other aspects of my work. This second volume is the other part of my memoirs which shows that there is more to life than just work, although many parts of this story are associated with my work and what I did before I became a paediatric anaesthetist. I was fortunate to have so many interesting experiences.

The opportunity to help others, especially those less fortunate; to teach and inspire people, especially the young; and to show appreciation to others; to help people see the other person's point of view when there was conflict, with resulting conciliation, all helped to make a satisfying life.

I hope the tales and pictures of places, people, events, and things now past and gone forever, have provided you, my reader, with pleasure, interest and some amusement.

Bibliography

Chapter 1

H.E.Scott. A saint in Kenya – the life of Marion Scott Stevenson. Hodder and Staughton, London 1936.

V de Watteville. Speak to the Earth. Methuen, London 1935.

Chapter 2

Monty Brown: Where Giants Trod.

Chapter 3

Jim Corbett: Maneating Leopard of Rudraprayag. Oxford University Press 1948

Jim Corbett: Maneaters of Kumaon. Oxford University Press 1944

Monty Brown: One January afternoon – in Women in Kenya.

V.Newland; Unpublished Journals owned by L.Matheson

Fridtjof Nansen: Farthest North. George Newnes, London 1898 (2 volumes).

Chapter 9

Clarence Finlayson; The Strath – The biography of Strathpeffer. The St. Andrew Press, Edinburgh 1979.

R.G.Cant: University of St Andrews. Oliver and Boyd 1946

Chapter 13

J. Lennox Kerr: Wilfred Grenfell : His life and work . Harrap 1959

W.T.Grenfell: Labrador Doctor – an autobiography. Hodder and Staughton c. 1921

Them Days, Labrador. March 1986

Them Days, Labrador. Winter 1998.

? : Alluring Labrador. Robinson & Blackman, Grand Falls Newfoundland

W.A. Paddon: Labrador Doctor. James Lorimer & Co., Toronto.

Chapters 16 & 19

C.W.Jefferys: Dramatic episodes in Canada's story . Star Printing,

Toronto,1930.

Bruce Hutchinson: The Incredible Canadian.

Pierre Berton: The Mysterious North. Alfred A. Knopf, New York. 1959

W.R.Salt & A.L.Wilk: The Birds of Alberta. Hamly Press, Edmonton . 1958

Ronald Syme: Trail to the North. Hodder & Stoughton 1959. (Samuel Hearne).

Chapter 21

Ken McGoogan. "Fatal Passage". 2001, Harper Collins Publishers, Canada.

Chapter 25

Kester Brown: Catalyst: medical memoirs of a world anaesthetist. Brolga Publishing, Australia 2004.

Chapter 26

V. Serventy. Australia's National Parks . Rigby1978.

Chapter 27

Bruce Chatwin: In Patagonia, Picador (1972)

Edward Evans: British Polar Explorers. William Collins, London 1943

Scott's Last Expedition, Volume 2. Smith, Elder and Co, London 1913.

Worsley F.A. Endurance: An epic of polar adventure. 1931. Philip Allen and Co, London.

Caroline Alexander: The Endurance – Shackleton's legendary Antarctic expedition – with photographs by Frank Hurley. Bloomsbury Publishing, London 1998.

Janet Crawford: That first Antarctic winter. The story of the Southern Cross expedition of 1898–1900 as told in the diaries of Louis Charles Bernacchi. South Latitude Research Ltd, Christchurch 1998.

Ann Savours : The voyages of the Discovery. Chatham Publishing 2001.

Richard McElree and David Harrowfield: Polar Castaways – The Ross Sea Party (1914-17) of Sir Ernest Shackleton. University Press, Christchurch 2004.

Order your copy of:

FREE SPIRIT

			Qty
ISBN 1920785 53 1	RRP	AU$35.00	.....
	Postage within Aust.	AU$9.75	.....
	Postage overseas	AU$19.00	.....

	TOTAL*	$________	

* All prices include GST

Also available:

CATALYST

The companion volume detailing the author's professional life in medicine and anaesthesia.

ISBN 1920785 38 8		Qty
RRP	AU$30.00	.....
Postage within Aust.	AU$9.75	.....
Postage overseas	AU$19.00	.....

TOTAL*	$________	

* All prices include GST

Double Deal:

			Qty
BOTH "Free Spirit" + "Catalyst"		AU$60.00	.....
	Postage within Aust.	AU$13.00	.....
	Postage overseas	AU$33.00	.....
	TOTAL*	$________	

* All prices include GST

ORDER FORM

Name: ____

Address: ____

____

____

Phone: ____

Email Address: ______________________________________

Method of Payment:

❑ Money Order ❑ Cheque ❑ Bankcard ❑ MasterCard ❑ Visa

Cardholders Name: ________________________________

Credit Card Number: ______________________________

Signature: ______________________ Expiry Date: __________

Allow 21 days for delivery.

Payment to:

Better Bookshop (ABN 14 067 257 390)
PO Box 12544
A'Beckett Street, Melbourne, 8006
Victoria, Australia
Fax: +61 3 9671 4741
Email: betterbookshop@brolgapublishing.com.au